SCENE OF THE CRIME

A Little Piece of Goodnight

Ed Brubaker Writer / **Michael Lark** Penciller

Sean Phillips / **Michael Lark** Inkers

James Sinclair Colorist / **John Costanza** Letterer

SCENE OF THE CRIME created by Ed Brubaker and Michael Lark

SCENE OF THE CRIME: A LITTLE PIECE OF GOODNIGHT

Published by DC Comics.
Cover and compilation copyright © 2000 DC Comics.
All Rights Reserved.

Originally published in single magazine form
as SCENE OF THE CRIME 1-4 and Vertigo: Winter's Edge 2.
Copyright © 1998, 1999 Ed Brubaker and Michael Lark.
All Rights Reserved. All characters, their distinctive
likenesses and related indicia featured in this
publication are trademarks of DC Comics.
The stories, characters, and incidents featured in
this publication are entirely fictional.

DC Comics, 1700 Broadway, New York, NY 10019
A division of Warner Bros. -
A Time Warner Entertainment Company
Printed in Canada. First Printing.
ISBN: 1-56389-670-2

Cover illustration by Michael Lark.
Cover color by Addie Blaustein.

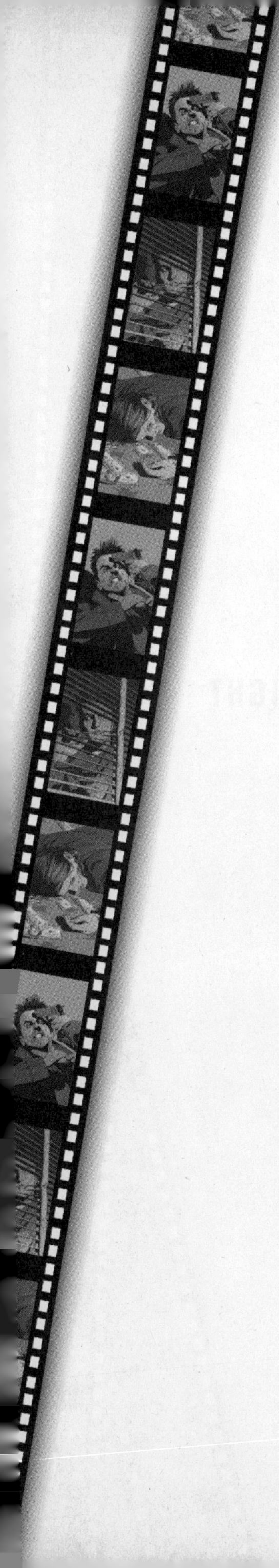

ED BRUBAKER:

To my father,

William F. Brubaker,

to give him something

he can enjoy for once;

to Melanie, for more

obvious reasons;

and to the memory of

Kenneth Millar, a.k.a.

Ross Macdonald, who left

big footsteps to walk in.

MICHAEL LARK:

To Carl, who is teaching me

to accept life's mysteries.

And, of course, to Debra.

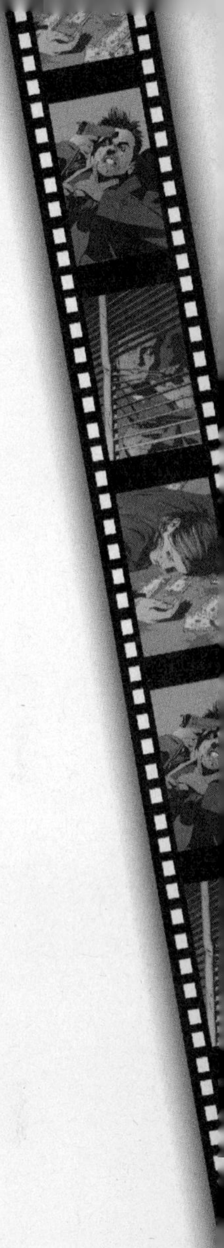

A LITTLE PIECE OF GOODNIGHT

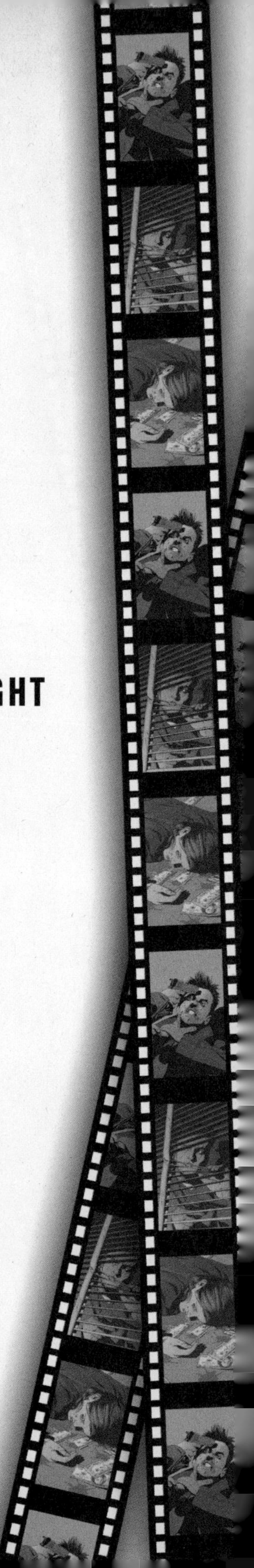

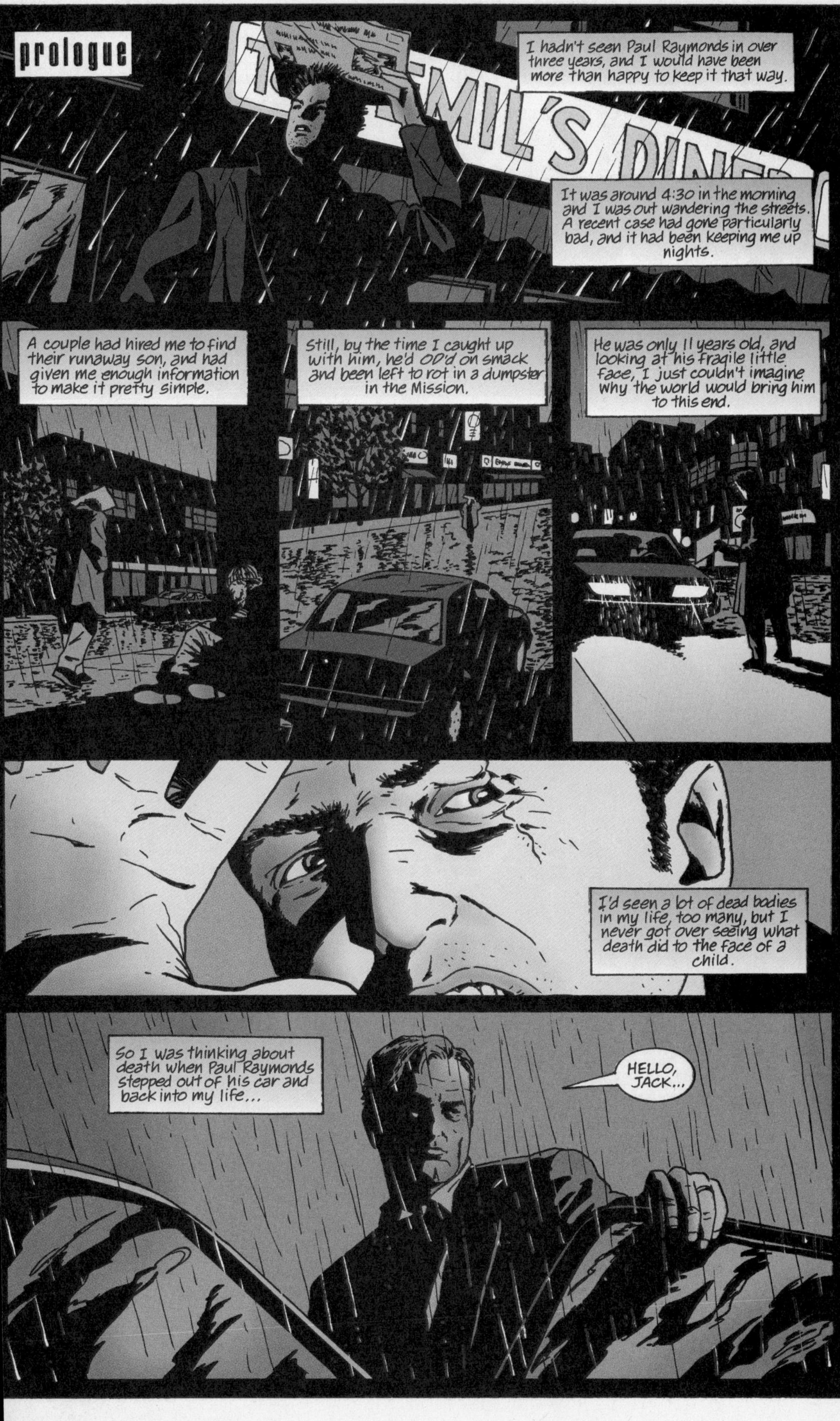
prologue
EMIL'S DINER
I hadn't seen Paul Raymonds in over three years, and I would have been more than happy to keep it that way.
It was around 4:30 in the morning and I was out wandering the streets. A recent case had gone particularly bad, and it had been keeping me up nights.
A couple had hired me to find their runaway son, and had given me enough information to make it pretty simple.
Still, by the time I caught up with him, he'd OD'd on smack and been left to rot in a dumpster in the Mission.
He was only 11 years old, and looking at his fragile little face, I just couldn't imagine why the world would bring him to this end.
I'd seen a lot of dead bodies in my life, too many, but I never got over seeing what death did to the face of a child.
So I was thinking about death when Paul Raymonds stepped out of his car and back into my life...
HELLO, JACK...

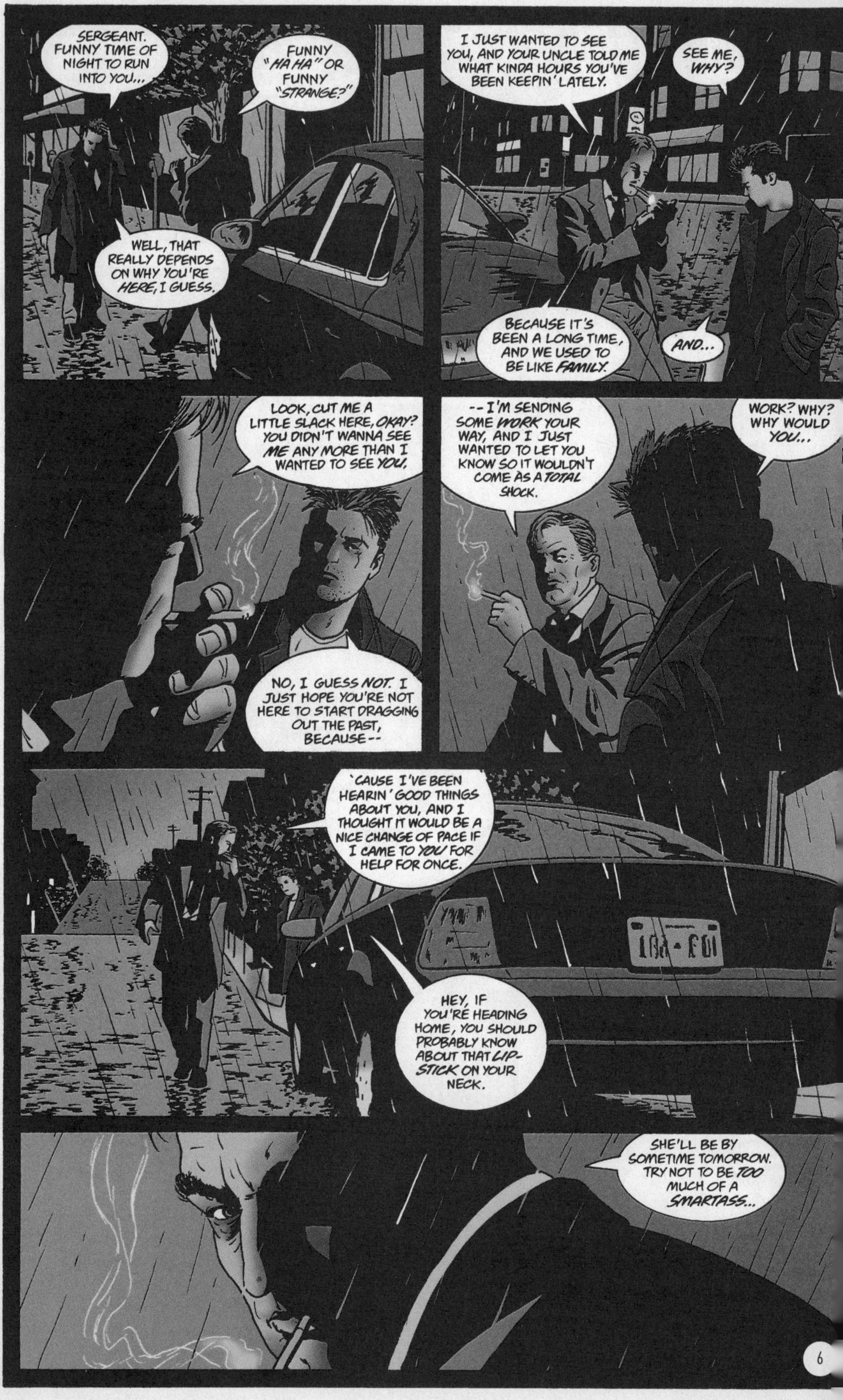
SERGEANT. FUNNY TIME OF NIGHT TO RUN INTO YOU...
FUNNY "HA HA" OR FUNNY "STRANGE?"
WELL, THAT REALLY DEPENDS ON WHY YOU'RE HERE, I GUESS.
I JUST WANTED TO SEE YOU, AND YOUR UNCLE TOLD ME WHAT KINDA HOURS YOU'VE BEEN KEEPIN' LATELY.
SEE ME, WHY?
BECAUSE IT'S BEEN A LONG TIME, AND WE USED TO BE LIKE FAMILY.
AND...
LOOK, CUT ME A LITTLE SLACK HERE, OKAY? YOU DIDN'T WANNA SEE ME ANY MORE THAN I WANTED TO SEE YOU.
NO, I GUESS NOT. I JUST HOPE YOU'RE NOT HERE TO START DRAGGING OUT THE PAST, BECAUSE--
--I'M SENDING SOME WORK YOUR WAY, AND I JUST WANTED TO LET YOU KNOW SO IT WOULDN'T COME AS A TOTAL SHOCK.
WORK? WHY? WHY WOULD YOU...
'CAUSE I'VE BEEN HEARIN' GOOD THINGS ABOUT YOU, AND I THOUGHT IT WOULD BE A NICE CHANGE OF PACE IF I CAME TO YOU FOR HELP FOR ONCE.
HEY, IF YOU'RE HEADING HOME, YOU SHOULD PROBABLY KNOW ABOUT THAT LIP-STICK ON YOUR NECK.
SHE'LL BE BY SOMETIME TOMORROW. TRY NOT TO BE TOO MUCH OF A SMARTASS...

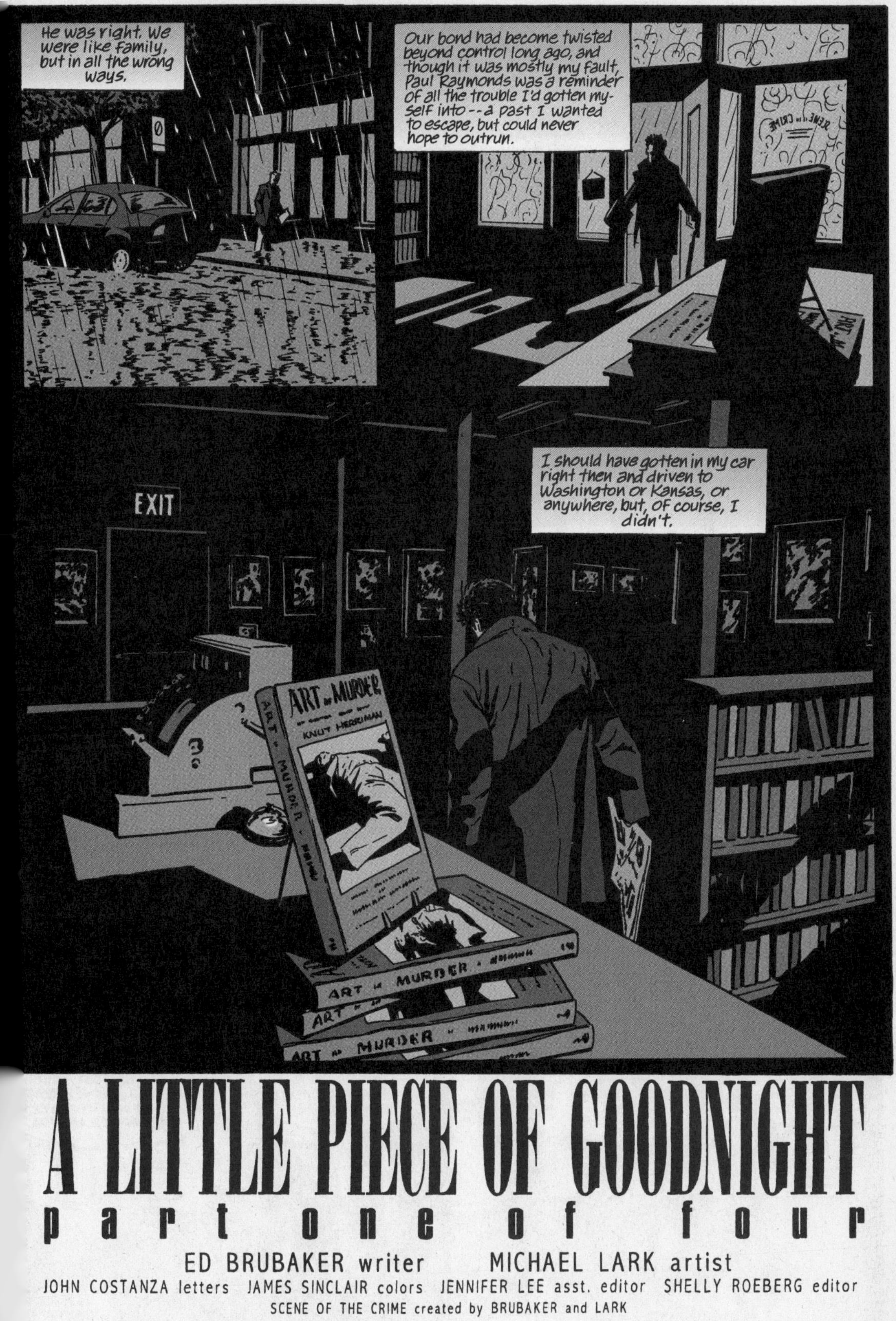
He was right. We were like family, but in all the wrong ways.
Our bond had become twisted beyond control long ago, and though it was mostly my fault, Paul Raymonds was a reminder of all the trouble I'd gotten myself into -- a past I wanted to escape, but could never hope to outrun.
SCENE OF THE CRIME
EXIT
I should have gotten in my car right then and driven to Washington or Kansas, or anywhere, but, of course, I didn't.
ART of MURDER
KNUT HERRMAN
ART of MURDER
ART of MURDER

A LITTLE PIECE OF GOODNIGHT

part one of four

ED BRUBAKER writer   MICHAEL LARK artist

JOHN COSTANZA letters JAMES SINCLAIR colors JENNIFER LEE asst. editor SHELLY ROEBERG editor

SCENE OF THE CRIME created by BRUBAKER and LARK

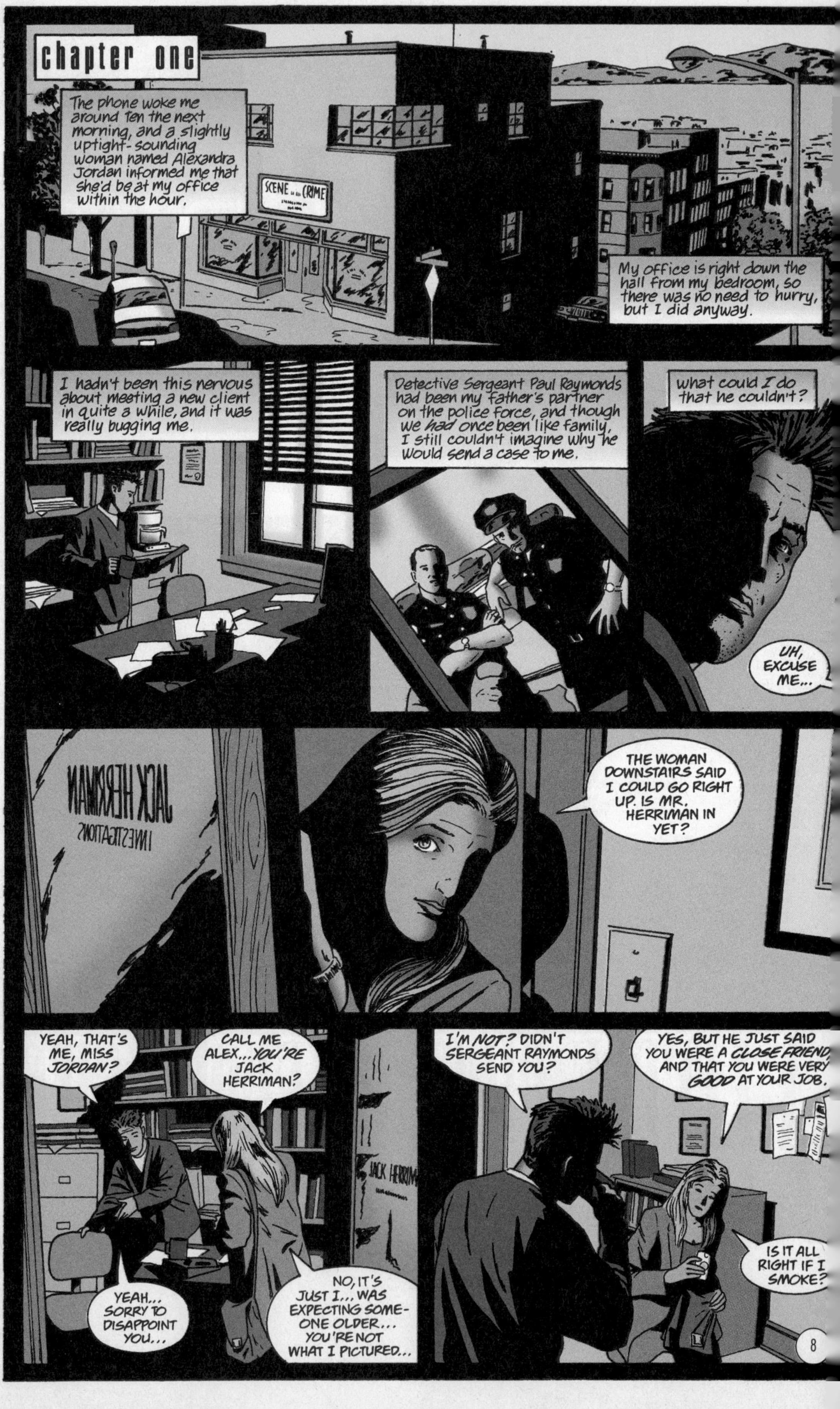

chapter one
The phone woke me around ten the next morning, and a slightly uptight-sounding woman named Alexandra Jordan informed me that she'd be at my office within the hour.
SCENE of the CRIME
My office is right down the hall from my bedroom, so there was no need to hurry, but I did anyway.
I hadn't been this nervous about meeting a new client in quite a while, and it was really bugging me.
Detective Sergeant Paul Raymonds had been my father's partner on the police force, and though we *had* once been like family, I still couldn't imagine why he would send a case to me.
What could *I* do that he couldn't?
UH, EXCUSE ME...
JACK HERRIMAN
INVESTIGATIONS
THE WOMAN DOWNSTAIRS SAID I COULD GO RIGHT UP. IS MR. HERRIMAN IN YET?
YEAH, THAT'S ME, MISS JORDAN?
CALL ME ALEX... *YOU'RE* JACK HERRIMAN?
YEAH... SORRY TO DISAPPOINT YOU...
NO, IT'S JUST I... WAS EXPECTING SOME-ONE OLDER... YOU'RE NOT WHAT I PICTURED...
I'M *NOT*? DIDN'T SERGEANT RAYMONDS SEND YOU?
YES, BUT HE JUST SAID YOU WERE A *CLOSE FRIEND*, AND THAT YOU WERE VERY *GOOD* AT YOUR JOB.
IS IT ALL RIGHT IF I SMOKE?

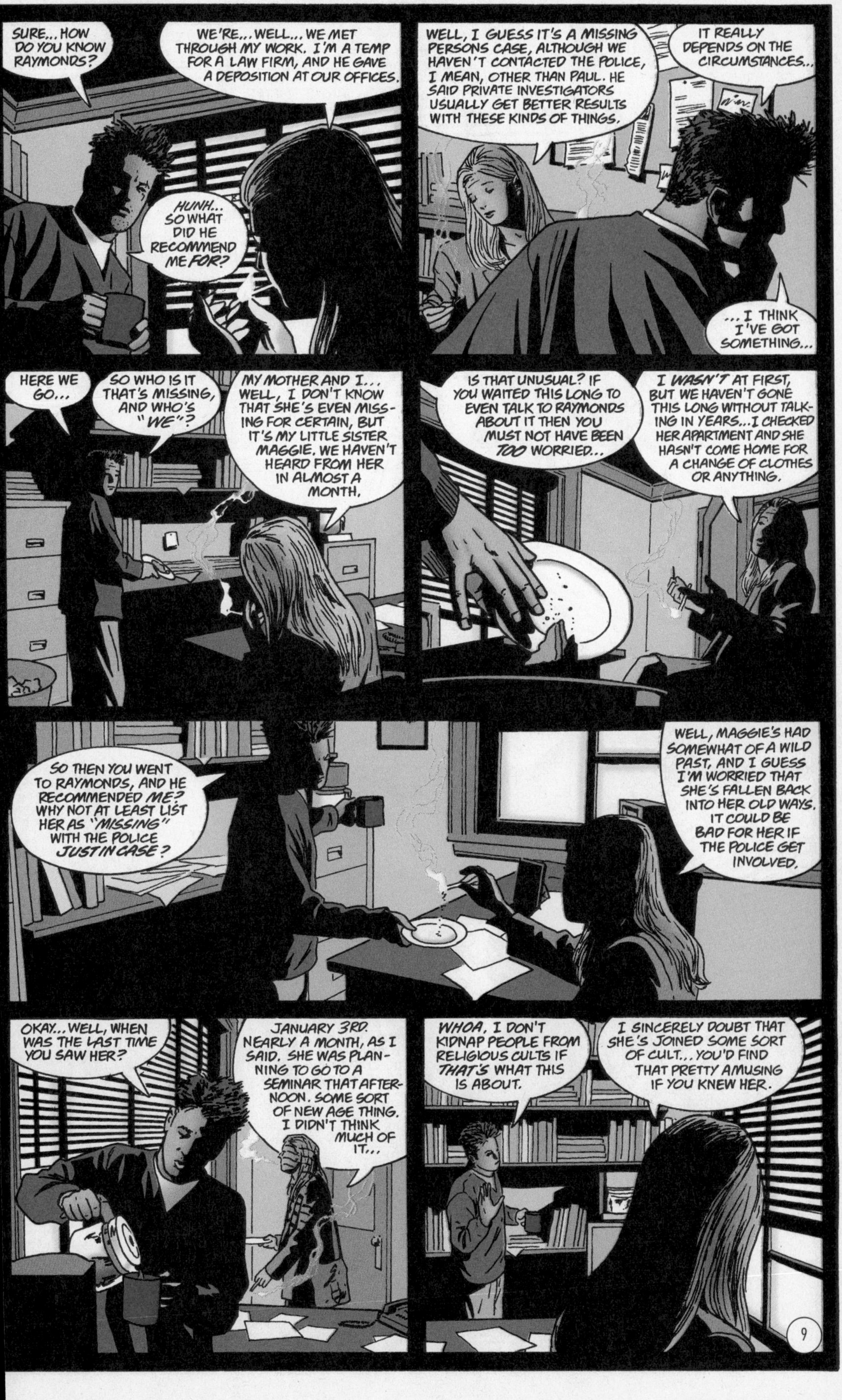
SURE... HOW DO YOU KNOW RAYMONDS?
WE'RE... WELL... WE MET THROUGH MY WORK. I'M A TEMP FOR A LAW FIRM, AND HE GAVE A DEPOSITION AT OUR OFFICES.
HUNH... SO WHAT DID HE RECOMMEND ME FOR?
WELL, I GUESS IT'S A MISSING PERSONS CASE, ALTHOUGH WE HAVEN'T CONTACTED THE POLICE, I MEAN, OTHER THAN PAUL. HE SAID PRIVATE INVESTIGATORS USUALLY GET BETTER RESULTS WITH THESE KINDS OF THINGS.
IT REALLY DEPENDS ON THE CIRCUMSTANCES...
...I THINK I'VE GOT SOMETHING...
HERE WE GO...
SO WHO IS IT THAT'S MISSING, AND WHO'S "WE"?
MY MOTHER AND I... WELL, I DON'T KNOW THAT SHE'S EVEN MISSING FOR CERTAIN, BUT IT'S MY LITTLE SISTER MAGGIE. WE HAVEN'T HEARD FROM HER IN ALMOST A MONTH.
IS THAT UNUSUAL? IF YOU WAITED THIS LONG TO EVEN TALK TO RAYMONDS ABOUT IT THEN YOU MUST NOT HAVE BEEN TOO WORRIED...
I WASN'T AT FIRST, BUT WE HAVEN'T GONE THIS LONG WITHOUT TALKING IN YEARS...I CHECKED HER APARTMENT AND SHE HASN'T COME HOME FOR A CHANGE OF CLOTHES OR ANYTHING.
SO THEN YOU WENT TO RAYMONDS, AND HE RECOMMENDED ME? WHY NOT AT LEAST LIST HER AS "MISSING" WITH THE POLICE JUST IN CASE?
WELL, MAGGIE'S HAD SOMEWHAT OF A WILD PAST, AND I GUESS I'M WORRIED THAT SHE'S FALLEN BACK INTO HER OLD WAYS. IT COULD BE BAD FOR HER IF THE POLICE GET INVOLVED.
OKAY... WELL, WHEN WAS THE LAST TIME YOU SAW HER?
JANUARY 3RD. NEARLY A MONTH, AS I SAID. SHE WAS PLANNING TO GO TO A SEMINAR THAT AFTERNOON. SOME SORT OF NEW AGE THING. I DIDN'T THINK MUCH OF IT...
WHOA, I DON'T KIDNAP PEOPLE FROM RELIGIOUS CULTS IF THAT'S WHAT THIS IS ABOUT.
I SINCERELY DOUBT THAT SHE'S JOINED SOME SORT OF CULT... YOU'D FIND THAT PRETTY AMUSING IF YOU KNEW HER.
9

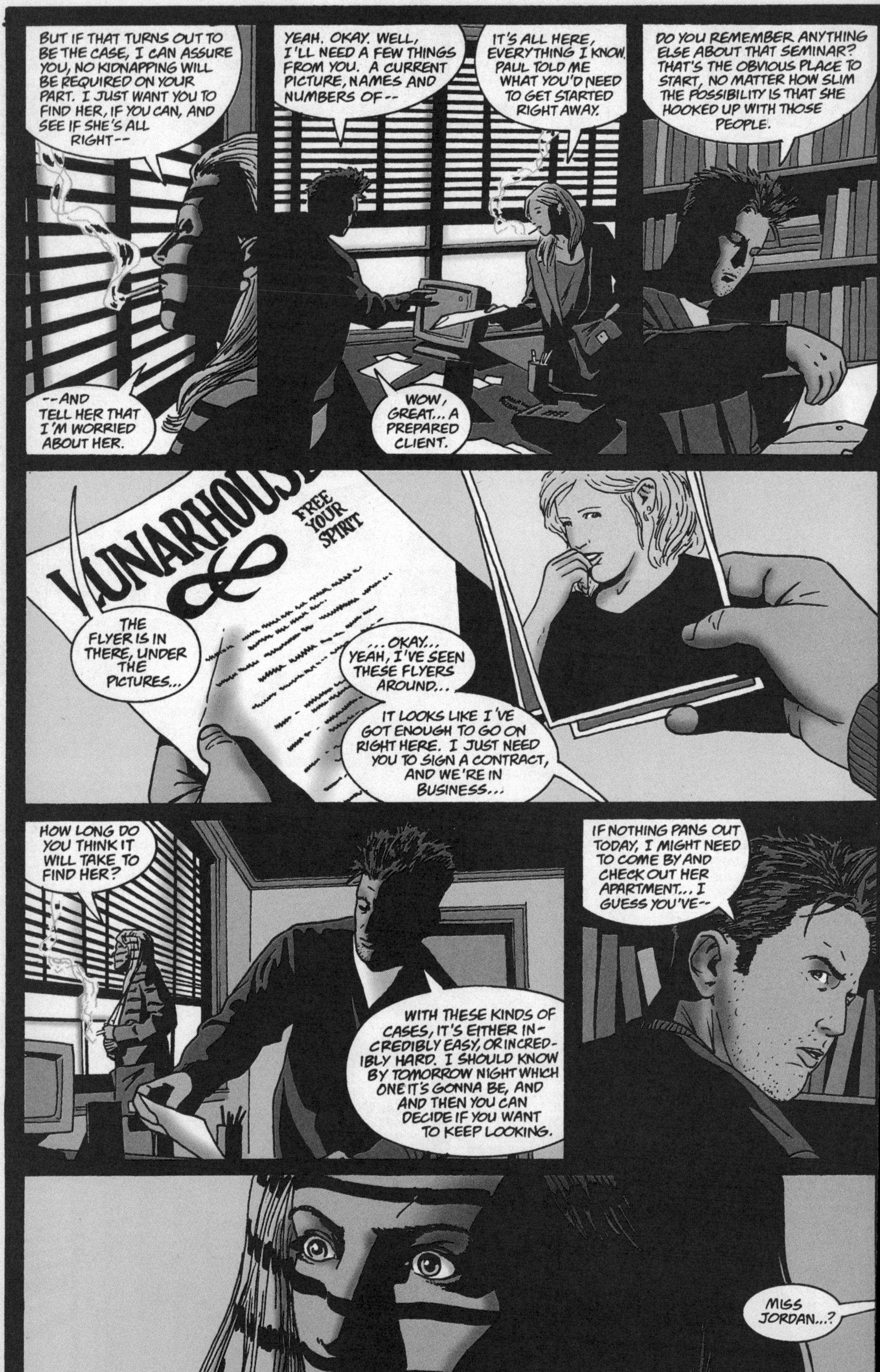

BUT IF THAT TURNS OUT TO BE THE CASE, I CAN ASSURE YOU, NO KIDNAPPING WILL BE REQUIRED ON YOUR PART. I JUST WANT YOU TO FIND HER, IF YOU CAN, AND SEE IF SHE'S ALL RIGHT--
--AND TELL HER THAT I'M WORRIED ABOUT HER.
YEAH. OKAY. WELL, I'LL NEED A FEW THINGS FROM YOU. A CURRENT PICTURE, NAMES AND NUMBERS OF--
IT'S ALL HERE, EVERYTHING I KNOW. PAUL TOLD ME WHAT YOU'D NEED TO GET STARTED RIGHT AWAY.
WOW, GREAT... A PREPARED CLIENT.
DO YOU REMEMBER ANYTHING ELSE ABOUT THAT SEMINAR? THAT'S THE OBVIOUS PLACE TO START, NO MATTER HOW SLIM THE POSSIBILITY IS THAT SHE HOOKED UP WITH THOSE PEOPLE.
LUNARHOUSE
FREE YOUR SPIRIT
THE FLYER IS IN THERE, UNDER THE PICTURES...
...OKAY... YEAH, I'VE SEEN THESE FLYERS AROUND...
IT LOOKS LIKE I'VE GOT ENOUGH TO GO ON RIGHT HERE. I JUST NEED YOU TO SIGN A CONTRACT, AND WE'RE IN BUSINESS...
HOW LONG DO YOU THINK IT WILL TAKE TO FIND HER?
WITH THESE KINDS OF CASES, IT'S EITHER INCREDIBLY EASY, OR INCREDIBLY HARD. I SHOULD KNOW BY TOMORROW NIGHT WHICH ONE IT'S GONNA BE, AND AND THEN YOU CAN DECIDE IF YOU WANT TO KEEP LOOKING.
IF NOTHING PANS OUT TODAY, I MIGHT NEED TO COME BY AND CHECK OUT HER APARTMENT... I GUESS YOU'VE--
MISS JORDAN...?

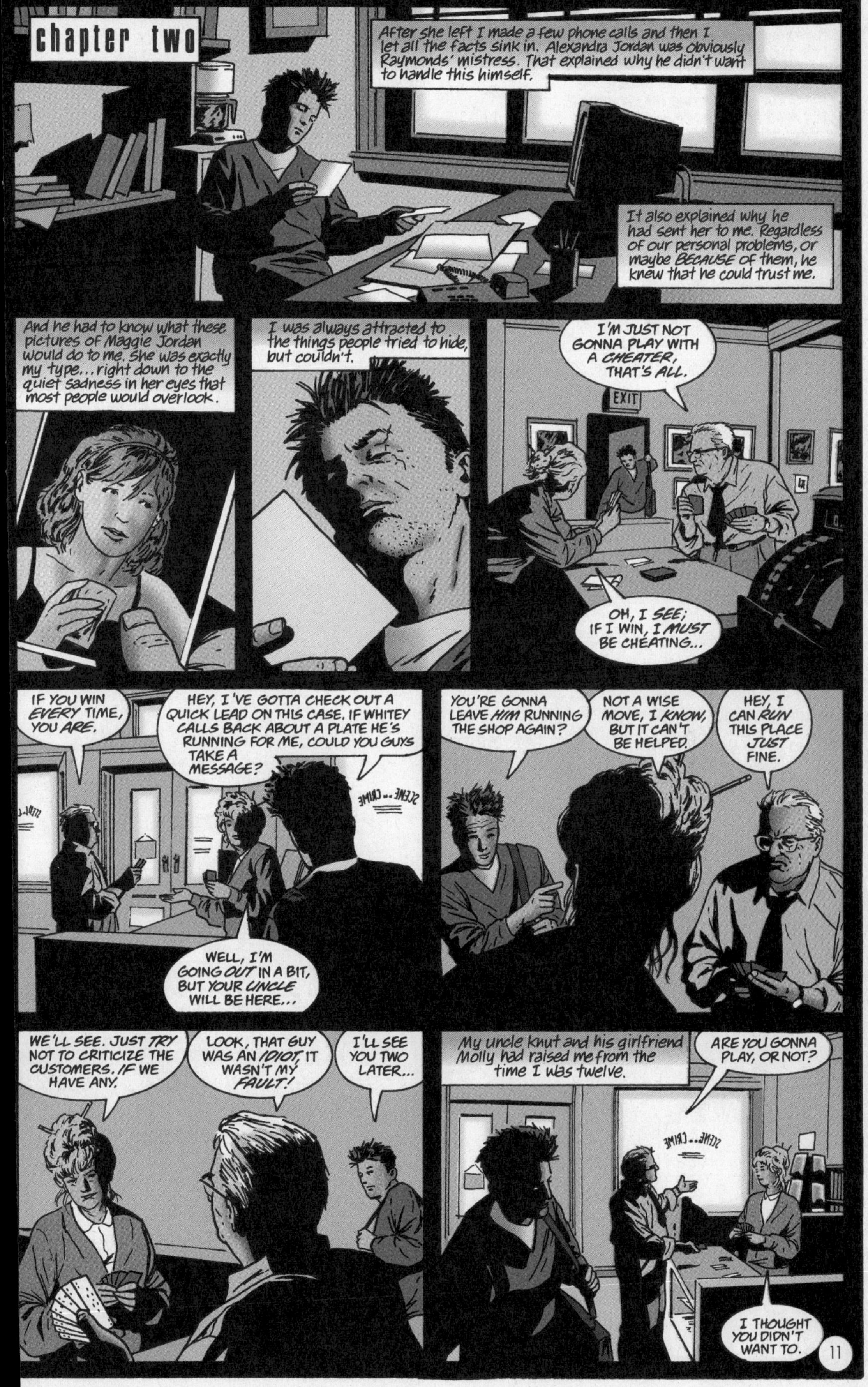
chapter two
After she left I made a few phone calls and then I let all the facts sink in. Alexandra Jordan was obviously Raymonds' mistress. That explained why he didn't want to handle this himself.
It also explained why he had sent her to me. Regardless of our personal problems, or maybe BECAUSE of them, he knew that he could trust me.
And he had to know what these pictures of Maggie Jordan would do to me. She was exactly my type... right down to the quiet sadness in her eyes that most people would overlook.
I was always attracted to the things people tried to hide, but couldn't.
I'M JUST NOT GONNA PLAY WITH A CHEATER, THAT'S ALL.
EXIT
OH, I SEE; IF I WIN, I MUST BE CHEATING...
IF YOU WIN EVERY TIME, YOU ARE.
HEY, I'VE GOTTA CHECK OUT A QUICK LEAD ON THIS CASE. IF WHITEY CALLS BACK ABOUT A PLATE HE'S RUNNING FOR ME, COULD YOU GUYS TAKE A MESSAGE?
WELL, I'M GOING OUT IN A BIT, BUT YOUR UNCLE WILL BE HERE...
YOU'RE GONNA LEAVE HIM RUNNING THE SHOP AGAIN?
NOT A WISE MOVE, I KNOW, BUT IT CAN'T BE HELPED.
HEY, I CAN RUN THIS PLACE JUST FINE.
WE'LL SEE. JUST TRY NOT TO CRITICIZE THE CUSTOMERS. IF WE HAVE ANY.
LOOK, THAT GUY WAS AN IDIOT, IT WASN'T MY FAULT!
I'LL SEE YOU TWO LATER...
My uncle Knut and his girlfriend Molly had raised me from the time I was twelve.
ARE YOU GONNA PLAY, OR NOT?
I THOUGHT YOU DIDN'T WANT TO.

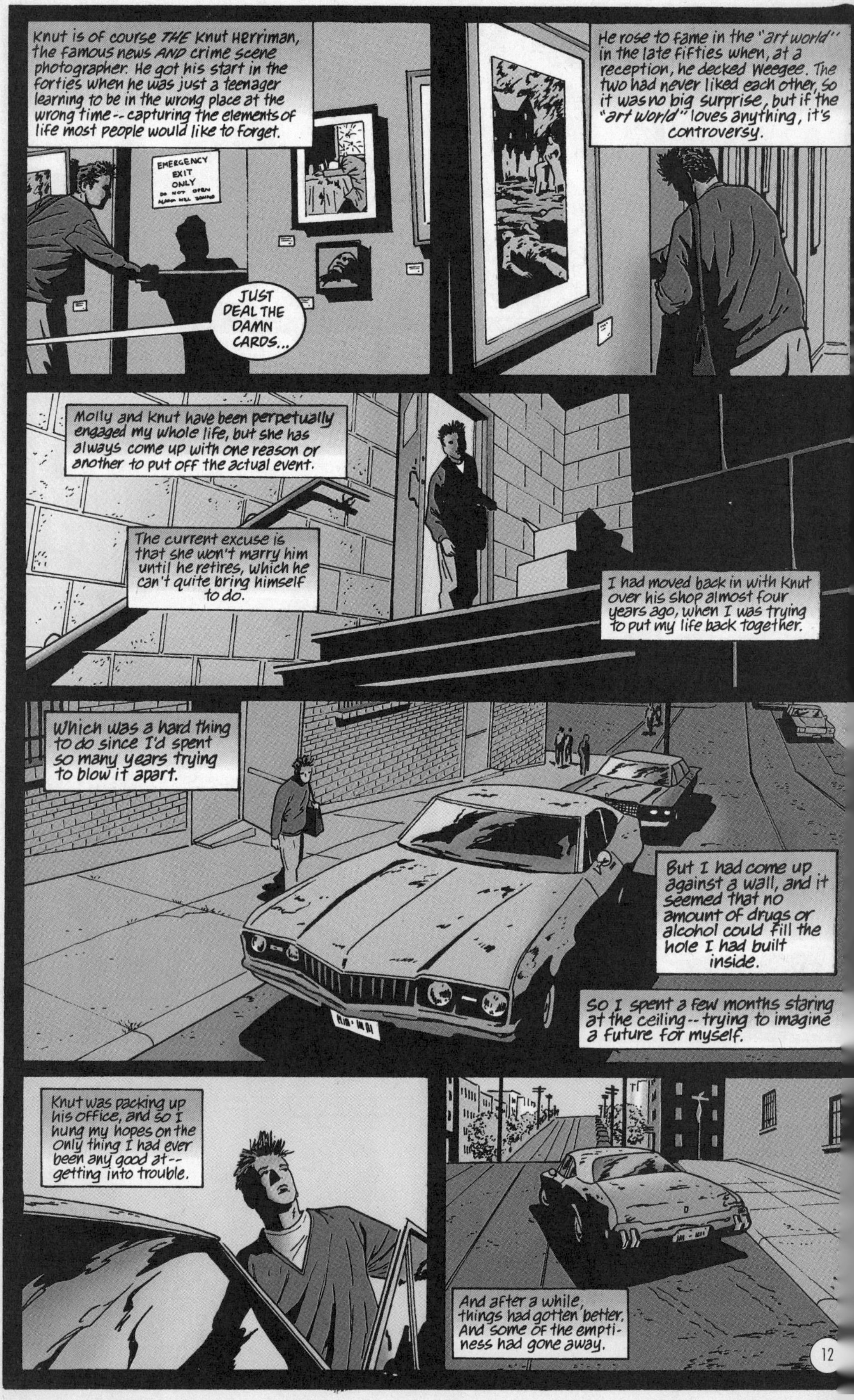

Knut is of course THE Knut Herriman, the famous news AND crime scene photographer. He got his start in the forties when he was just a teenager learning to be in the wrong place at the wrong time -- capturing the elements of life most people would like to forget.
EMERGENCY EXIT ONLY
JUST DEAL THE DAMN CARDS...
He rose to fame in the "art world" in the late fifties when, at a reception, he decked Weegee. The two had never liked each other, so it was no big surprise, but if the "art world" loves anything, it's controversy.
Molly and Knut have been perpetually engaged my whole life, but she has always come up with one reason or another to put off the actual event.
The current excuse is that she won't marry him until he retires, which he can't quite bring himself to do.
I had moved back in with Knut over his shop almost four years ago, when I was trying to put my life back together.
Which was a hard thing to do since I'd spent so many years trying to blow it apart.
But I had come up against a wall, and it seemed that no amount of drugs or alcohol could fill the hole I had built inside.
So I spent a few months staring at the ceiling -- trying to imagine a future for myself.
Knut was packing up his office, and so I hung my hopes on the only thing I had ever been any good at -- getting into trouble.
And after a while, things had gotten better. And some of the emptiness had gone away.

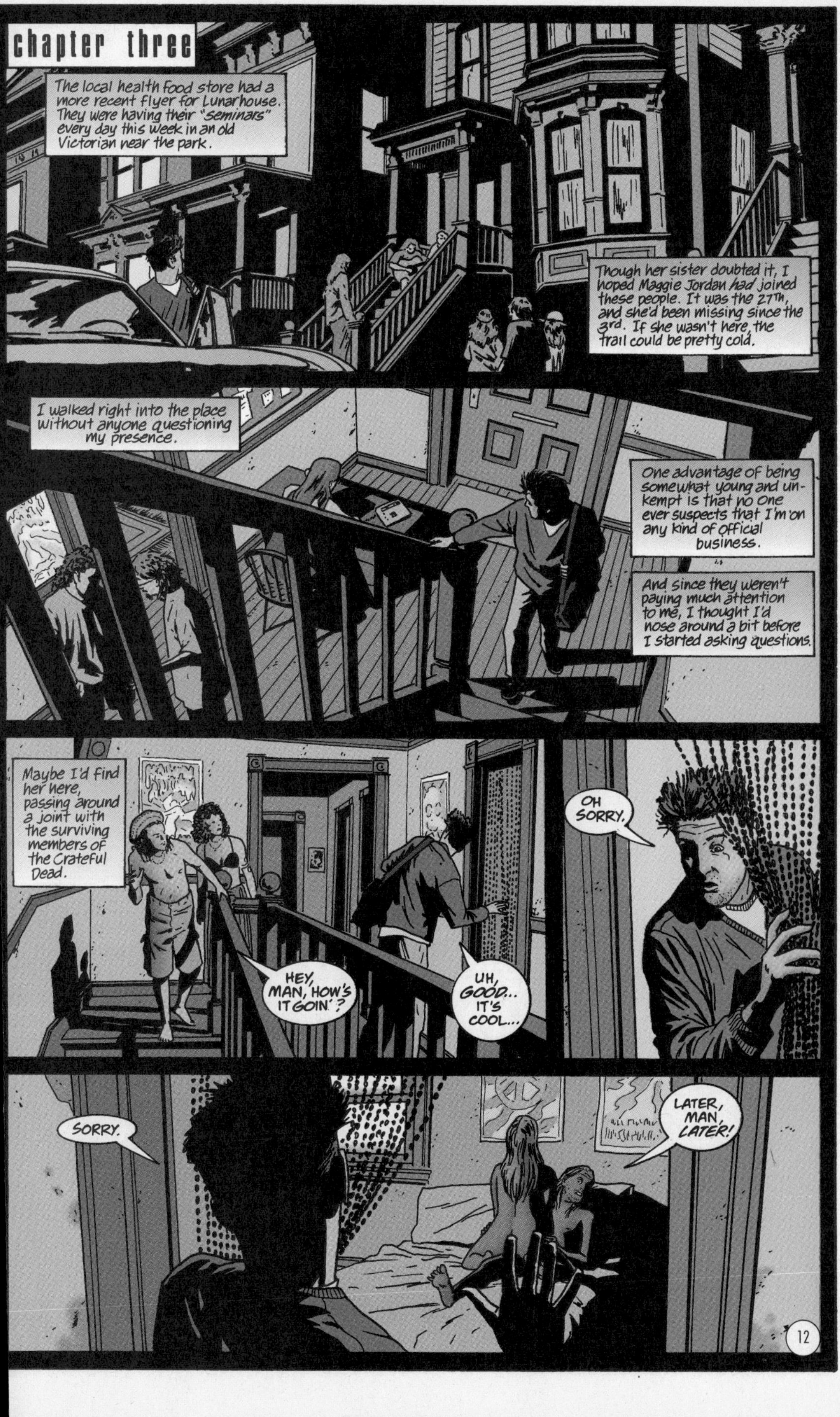
chapter three
The local health food store had a more recent flyer for Lunarhouse. They were having their "seminars" every day this week in an old Victorian near the park.
Though her sister doubted it, I hoped Maggie Jordan had joined these people. It was the 27th, and she'd been missing since the 3rd. If she wasn't here, the trail could be pretty cold.
I walked right into the place without anyone questioning my presence.
One advantage of being somewhat young and unkempt is that no one ever suspects that I'm on any kind of official business.
And since they weren't paying much attention to me, I thought I'd nose around a bit before I started asking questions.
Maybe I'd find her here, passing around a joint with the surviving members of the Grateful Dead.
HEY, MAN, HOW'S IT GOIN'?
UH, GOOD... IT'S COOL...
OH SORRY.
SORRY.
LATER, MAN, LATER!

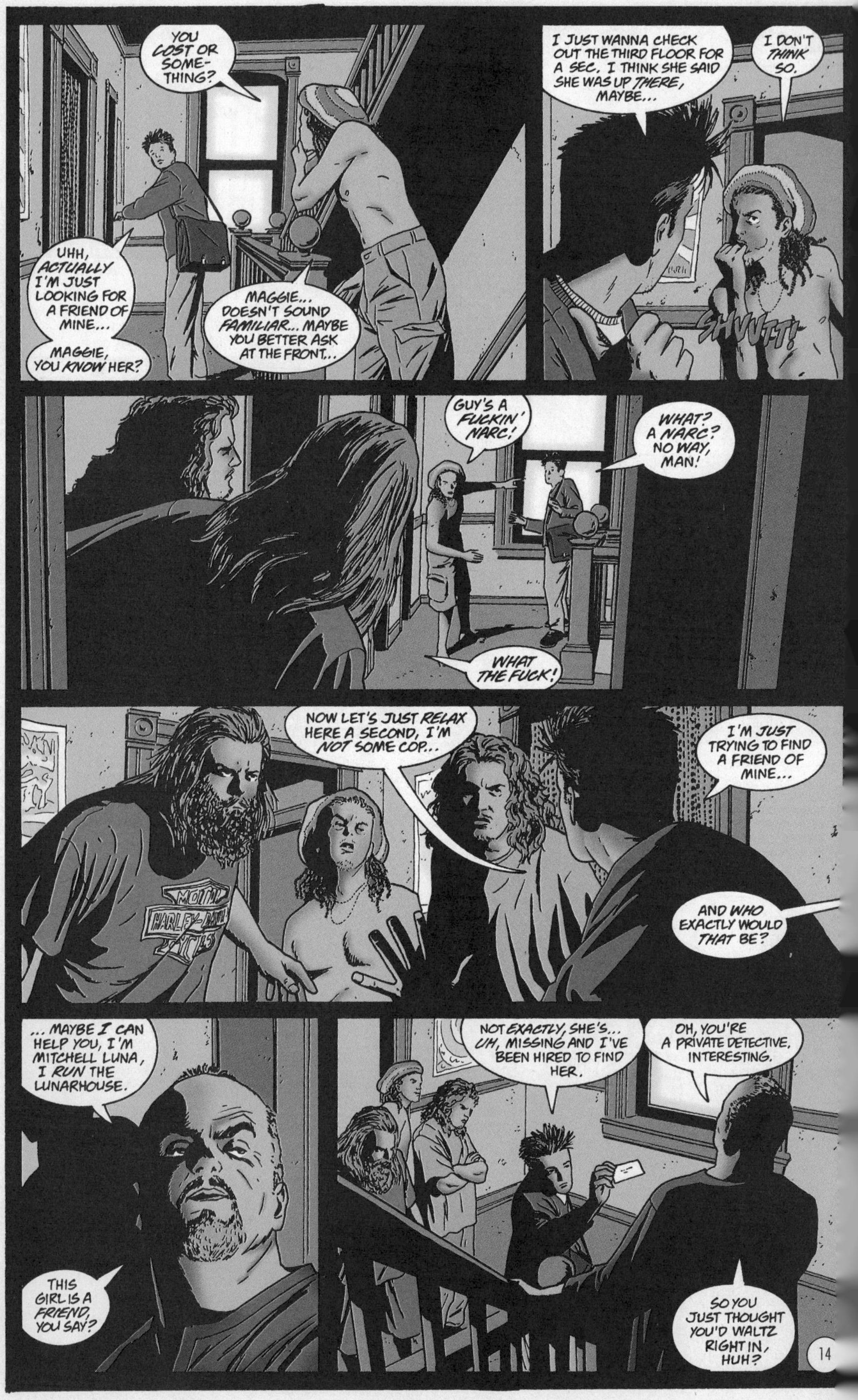

YOU LOST OR SOME-THING?
UHH, ACTUALLY I'M JUST LOOKING FOR A FRIEND OF MINE...
MAGGIE, YOU KNOW HER?
MAGGIE... DOESN'T SOUND FAMILIAR... MAYBE YOU BETTER ASK AT THE FRONT...
I JUST WANNA CHECK OUT THE THIRD FLOOR FOR A SEC. I THINK SHE SAID SHE WAS UP THERE, MAYBE...
I DON'T THINK SO.
SHVVTT!
GUY'S A FUCKIN' NARC!
WHAT? A NARC? NO WAY, MAN!
WHAT THE FUCK!
NOW LET'S JUST RELAX HERE A SECOND, I'M NOT SOME COP...
I'M JUST TRYING TO FIND A FRIEND OF MINE...
AND WHO EXACTLY WOULD THAT BE?
... MAYBE I CAN HELP YOU, I'M MITCHELL LUNA, I RUN THE LUNARHOUSE.
THIS GIRL IS A FRIEND, YOU SAY?
NOT EXACTLY, SHE'S... UH, MISSING AND I'VE BEEN HIRED TO FIND HER.
OH, YOU'RE A PRIVATE DETECTIVE. INTERESTING.
SO YOU JUST THOUGHT YOU'D WALTZ RIGHT IN, HUH?

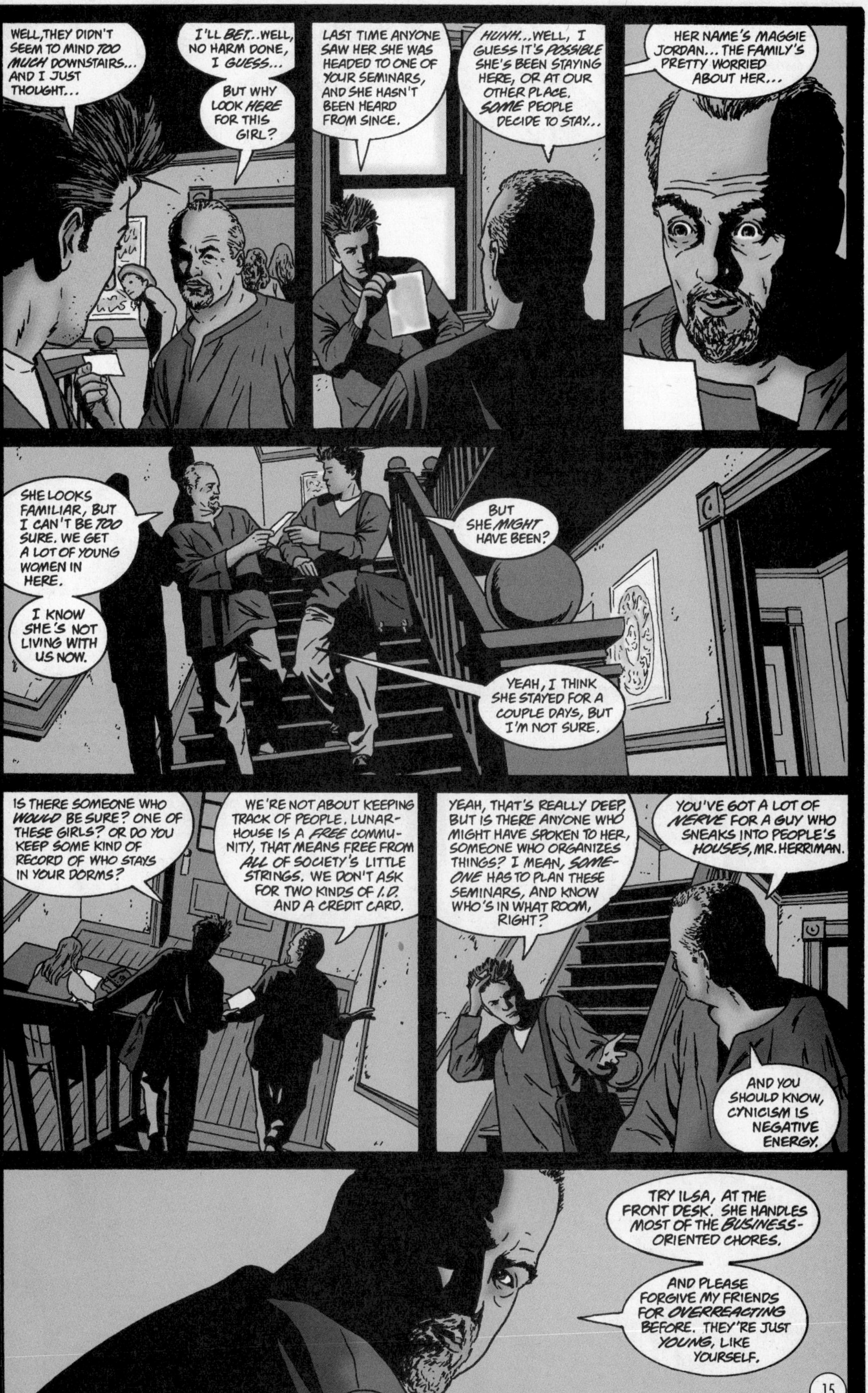

WELL, THEY DIDN'T SEEM TO MIND TOO MUCH DOWNSTAIRS... AND I JUST THOUGHT...
I'LL BET...WELL, NO HARM DONE, I GUESS...
BUT WHY LOOK HERE FOR THIS GIRL?
LAST TIME ANYONE SAW HER SHE WAS HEADED TO ONE OF YOUR SEMINARS, AND SHE HASN'T BEEN HEARD FROM SINCE.
HUNH...WELL, I GUESS IT'S POSSIBLE SHE'S BEEN STAYING HERE, OR AT OUR OTHER PLACE. SOME PEOPLE DECIDE TO STAY...
HER NAME'S MAGGIE JORDAN... THE FAMILY'S PRETTY WORRIED ABOUT HER...
SHE LOOKS FAMILIAR, BUT I CAN'T BE TOO SURE. WE GET A LOT OF YOUNG WOMEN IN HERE.
I KNOW SHE'S NOT LIVING WITH US NOW.
BUT SHE MIGHT HAVE BEEN?
YEAH, I THINK SHE STAYED FOR A COUPLE DAYS, BUT I'M NOT SURE.
IS THERE SOMEONE WHO WOULD BE SURE? ONE OF THESE GIRLS? OR DO YOU KEEP SOME KIND OF RECORD OF WHO STAYS IN YOUR DORMS?
WE'RE NOT ABOUT KEEPING TRACK OF PEOPLE. LUNARHOUSE IS A FREE COMMUNITY, THAT MEANS FREE FROM ALL OF SOCIETY'S LITTLE STRINGS. WE DON'T ASK FOR TWO KINDS OF I.D. AND A CREDIT CARD.
YEAH, THAT'S REALLY DEEP, BUT IS THERE ANYONE WHO MIGHT HAVE SPOKEN TO HER, SOMEONE WHO ORGANIZES THINGS? I MEAN, SOMEONE HAS TO PLAN THESE SEMINARS, AND KNOW WHO'S IN WHAT ROOM, RIGHT?
YOU'VE GOT A LOT OF NERVE FOR A GUY WHO SNEAKS INTO PEOPLE'S HOUSES, MR. HERRIMAN.
AND YOU SHOULD KNOW, CYNICISM IS NEGATIVE ENERGY.
TRY ILSA, AT THE FRONT DESK. SHE HANDLES MOST OF THE BUSINESS-ORIENTED CHORES.
AND PLEASE FORGIVE MY FRIENDS FOR OVERREACTING BEFORE. THEY'RE JUST YOUNG, LIKE YOURSELF.

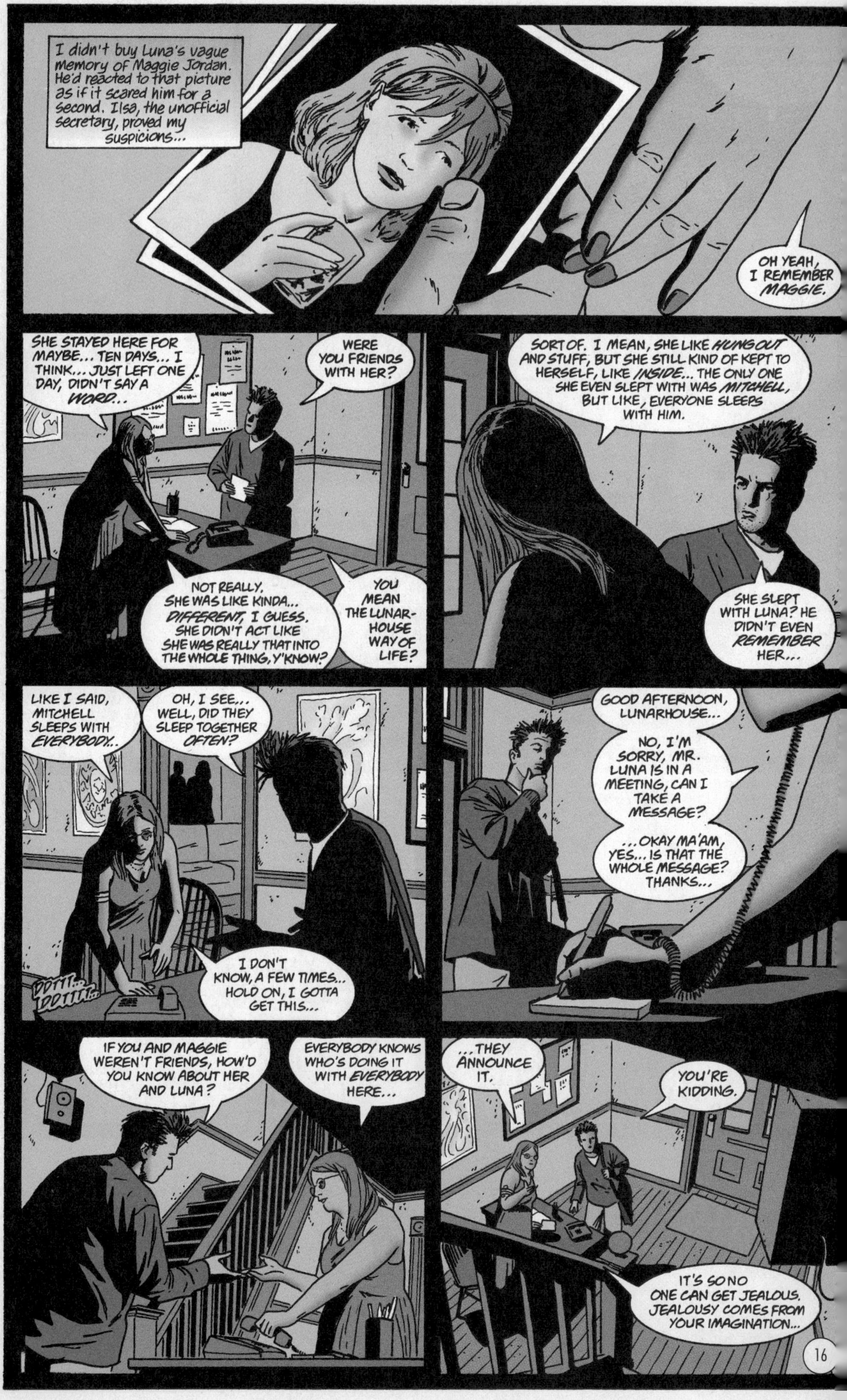
I didn't buy Luna's vague memory of Maggie Jordan. He'd reacted to that picture as if it scared him for a second. Ilsa, the unofficial secretary, proved my suspicions...
OH YEAH, I REMEMBER MAGGIE.
SHE STAYED HERE FOR MAYBE... TEN DAYS... I THINK... JUST LEFT ONE DAY, DIDN'T SAY A WORD...
WERE YOU FRIENDS WITH HER?
NOT REALLY. SHE WAS LIKE KINDA... DIFFERENT, I GUESS. SHE DIDN'T ACT LIKE SHE WAS REALLY THAT INTO THE WHOLE THING, Y'KNOW?
YOU MEAN THE LUNAR-HOUSE WAY OF LIFE?
SORT OF. I MEAN, SHE LIKE HUNG OUT AND STUFF, BUT SHE STILL KIND OF KEPT TO HERSELF, LIKE INSIDE... THE ONLY ONE SHE EVEN SLEPT WITH WAS MITCHELL, BUT LIKE, EVERYONE SLEEPS WITH HIM.
SHE SLEPT WITH LUNA? HE DIDN'T EVEN REMEMBER HER...
LIKE I SAID, MITCHELL SLEEPS WITH EVERYBODY...
OH, I SEE... WELL, DID THEY SLEEP TOGETHER OFTEN?
DDTTT... DDTTT...
I DON'T KNOW, A FEW TIMES... HOLD ON, I GOTTA GET THIS...
GOOD AFTERNOON, LUNARHOUSE...
NO, I'M SORRY, MR. LUNA IS IN A MEETING, CAN I TAKE A MESSAGE?
...OKAY MA'AM, YES... IS THAT THE WHOLE MESSAGE? THANKS...
IF YOU AND MAGGIE WEREN'T FRIENDS, HOW'D YOU KNOW ABOUT HER AND LUNA?
EVERYBODY KNOWS WHO'S DOING IT WITH EVERYBODY HERE...
...THEY ANNOUNCE IT.
YOU'RE KIDDING.
IT'S SO NO ONE CAN GET JEALOUS. JEALOUSY COMES FROM YOUR IMAGINATION...

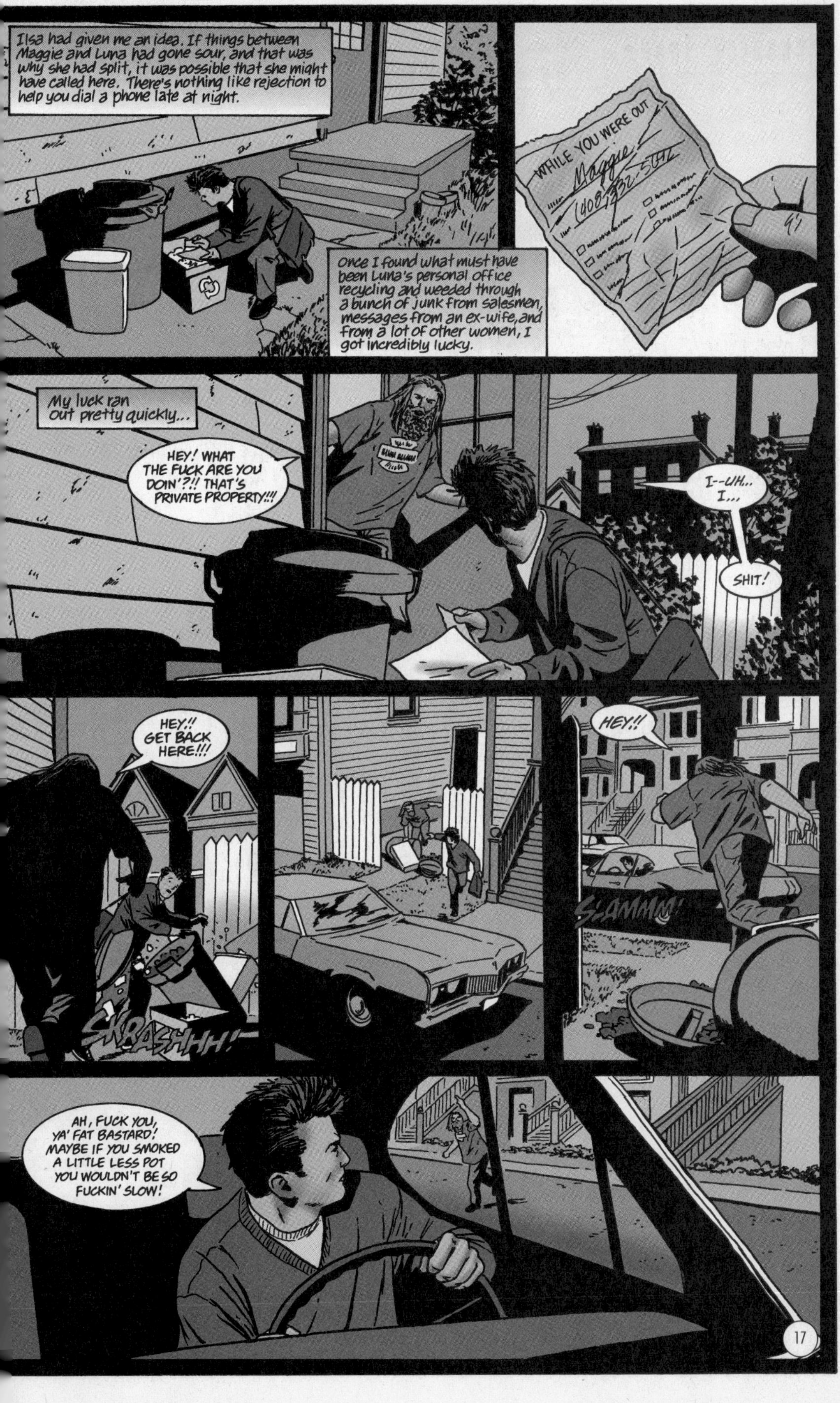

Ilsa had given me an idea. If things between Maggie and Luna had gone sour, and that was why she had split, it was possible that she might have called here. There's nothing like rejection to help you dial a phone late at night.
WHILE YOU WERE OUT
Maggie
Once I found what must have been Luna's personal office recycling and weeded through a bunch of junk from salesmen, messages from an ex-wife, and from a lot of other women, I got incredibly lucky.
My luck ran out pretty quickly...
HEY! WHAT THE FUCK ARE YOU DOIN'?!! THAT'S PRIVATE PROPERTY!!!
I--UH... I...
SHIT!
HEY!! GET BACK HERE!!!
SKRASHHH!
HEY!!
S-LAMMM!
AH, FUCK YOU, YA' FAT BASTARD! MAYBE IF YOU SMOKED A LITTLE LESS POT YOU WOULDN'T BE SO FUCKIN' SLOW!

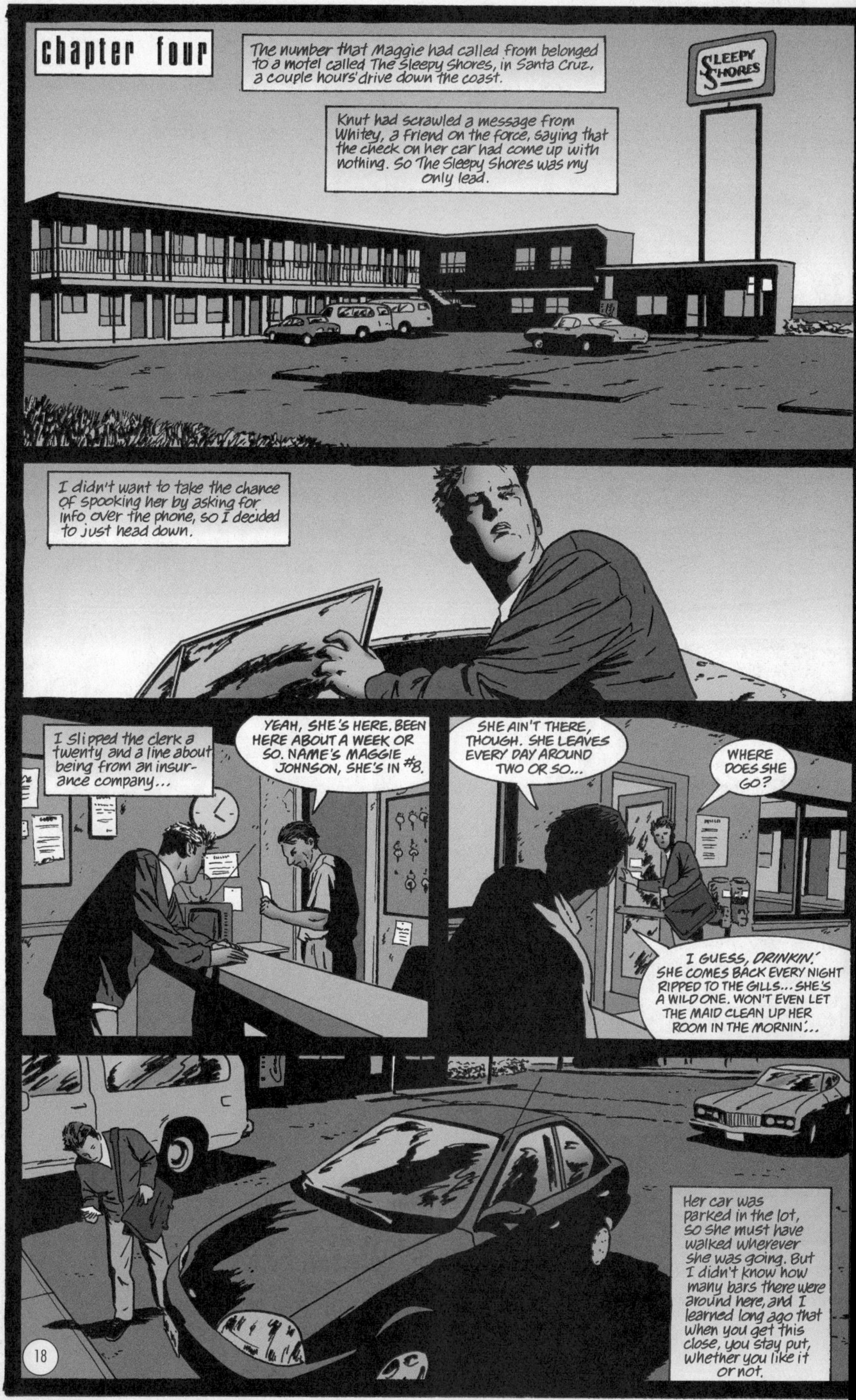
chapter four
The number that Maggie had called from belonged to a motel called The Sleepy Shores, in Santa Cruz, a couple hours' drive down the coast.
SLEEPY SHORES
Knut had scrawled a message from Whitey, a friend on the force, saying that the check on her car had come up with nothing. So The Sleepy Shores was my only lead.
I didn't want to take the chance of spooking her by asking for info over the phone, so I decided to just head down.
I slipped the clerk a twenty and a line about being from an insurance company...
YEAH, SHE'S HERE. BEEN HERE ABOUT A WEEK OR SO. NAME'S MAGGIE JOHNSON, SHE'S IN #8.
SHE AIN'T THERE, THOUGH. SHE LEAVES EVERY DAY AROUND TWO OR SO...
WHERE DOES SHE GO?
I GUESS, DRINKIN'. SHE COMES BACK EVERY NIGHT RIPPED TO THE GILLS... SHE'S A WILD ONE. WON'T EVEN LET THE MAID CLEAN UP HER ROOM IN THE MORNIN'...
Her car was parked in the lot, so she must have walked wherever she was going. But I didn't know how many bars there were around here, and I learned long ago that when you get this close, you stay put, whether you like it or not.

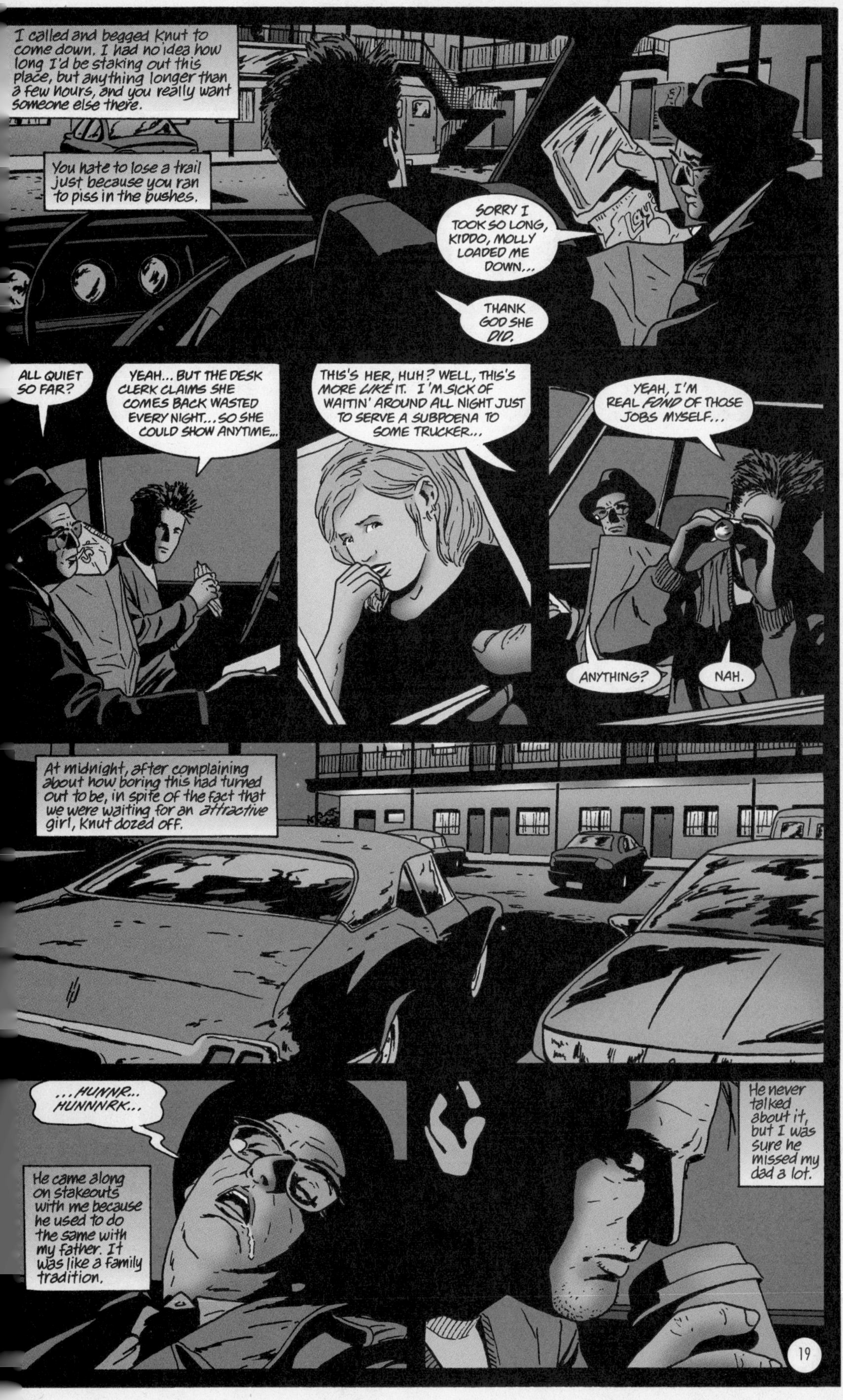

I called and begged Knut to come down. I had no idea how long I'd be staking out this place, but anything longer than a few hours, and you really want someone else there.
You hate to lose a trail just because you ran to piss in the bushes.
SORRY I TOOK SO LONG, KIDDO, MOLLY LOADED ME DOWN...
THANK GOD SHE DID.
ALL QUIET SO FAR?
YEAH... BUT THE DESK CLERK CLAIMS SHE COMES BACK WASTED EVERY NIGHT... SO SHE COULD SHOW ANYTIME...
THIS'S HER, HUH? WELL, THIS'S MORE LIKE IT. I'M SICK OF WAITIN' AROUND ALL NIGHT JUST TO SERVE A SUBPOENA TO SOME TRUCKER...
YEAH, I'M REAL FOND OF THOSE JOBS MYSELF...
ANYTHING?
NAH.
At midnight, after complaining about how boring this had turned out to be, in spite of the fact that we were waiting for an attractive girl, Knut dozed off.
...HUNNR... HUNNNRK...
He came along on stakeouts with me because he used to do the same with my father. It was like a family tradition.
He never talked about it, but I was sure he missed my dad a lot.

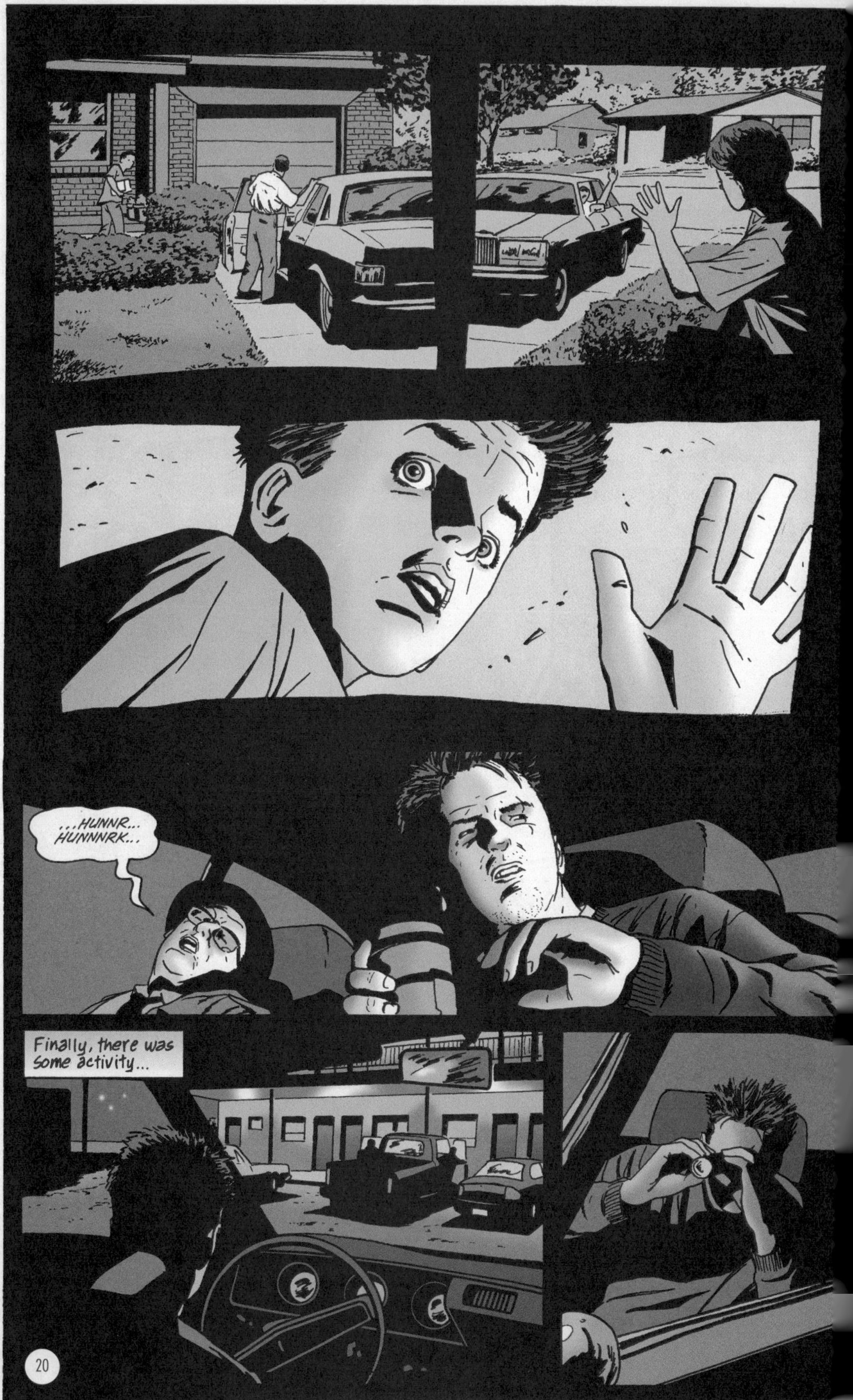
...HUNNR...
HUNNNRK...
Finally, there was some activity...

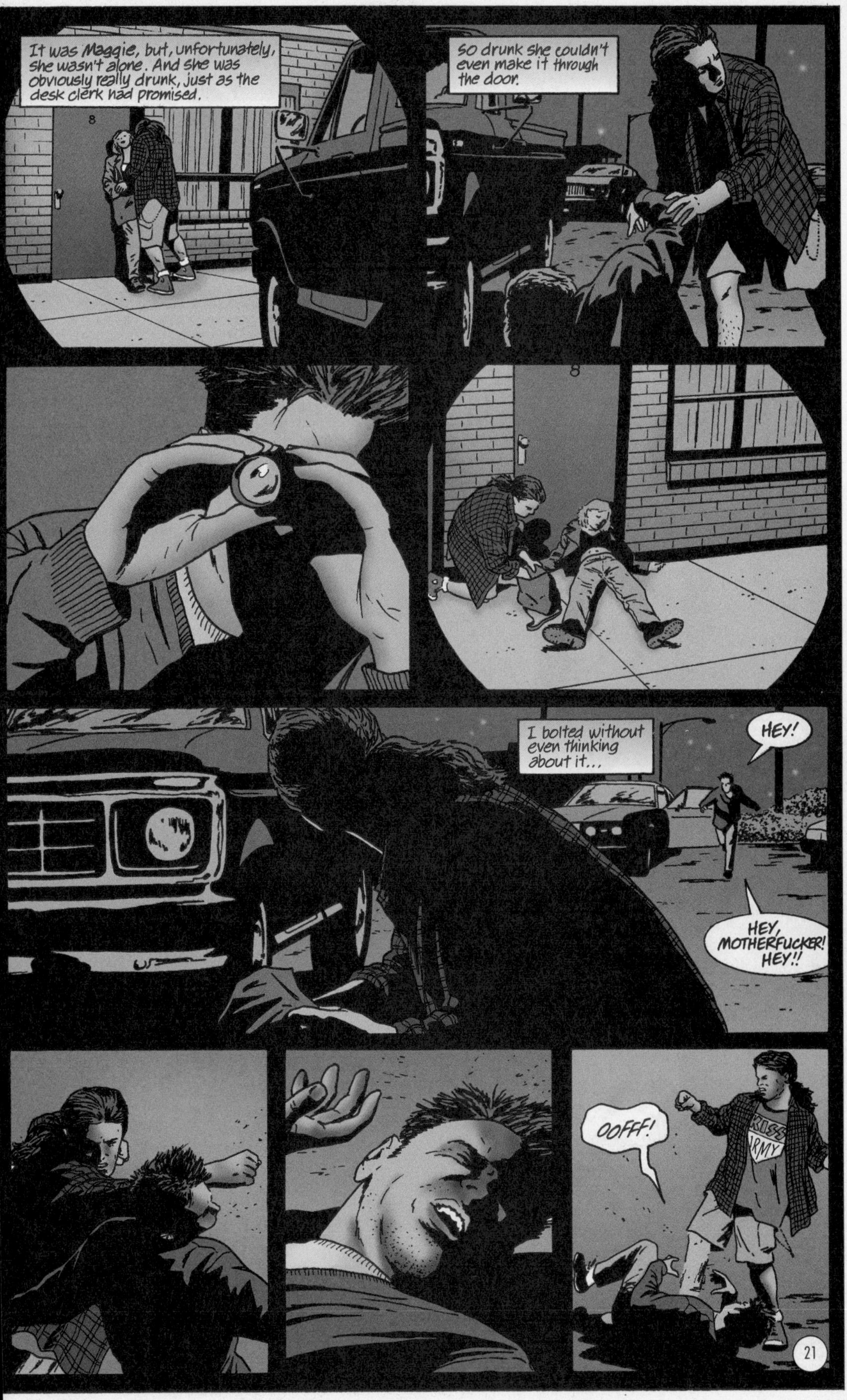
It was Maggie, but, unfortunately, she wasn't alone. And she was obviously really drunk, just as the desk clerk had promised.
So drunk she couldn't even make it through the door.
I bolted without even thinking about it...
HEY!
HEY, MOTHERFUCKER! HEY!!
OOFFF!
KISS ARMY

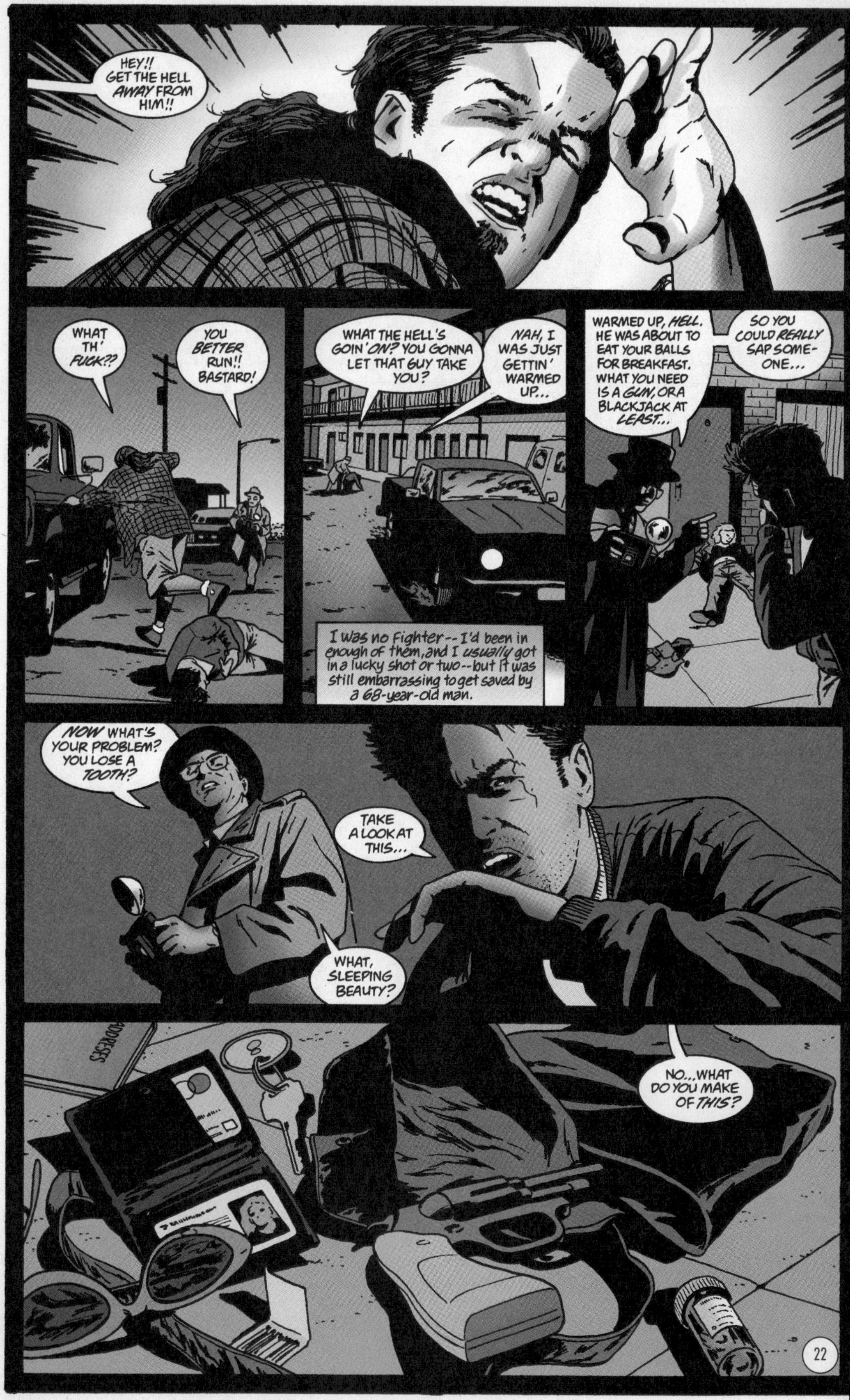

HEY!! GET THE HELL AWAY FROM HIM!!
WHAT TH' FUCK??
YOU BETTER RUN!! BASTARD!
WHAT THE HELL'S GOIN' ON? YOU GONNA LET THAT GUY TAKE YOU?
NAH, I WAS JUST GETTIN' WARMED UP...
I was no fighter -- I'd been in enough of them, and I usually got in a lucky shot or two -- but it was still embarrassing to get saved by a 68-year-old man.
WARMED UP, HELL. HE WAS ABOUT TO EAT YOUR BALLS FOR BREAKFAST. WHAT YOU NEED IS A GUN, OR A BLACKJACK AT LEAST...
SO YOU COULD REALLY SAP SOMEONE...
NOW WHAT'S YOUR PROBLEM? YOU LOSE A TOOTH?
TAKE A LOOK AT THIS...
WHAT, SLEEPING BEAUTY?
NO... WHAT DO YOU MAKE OF THIS?

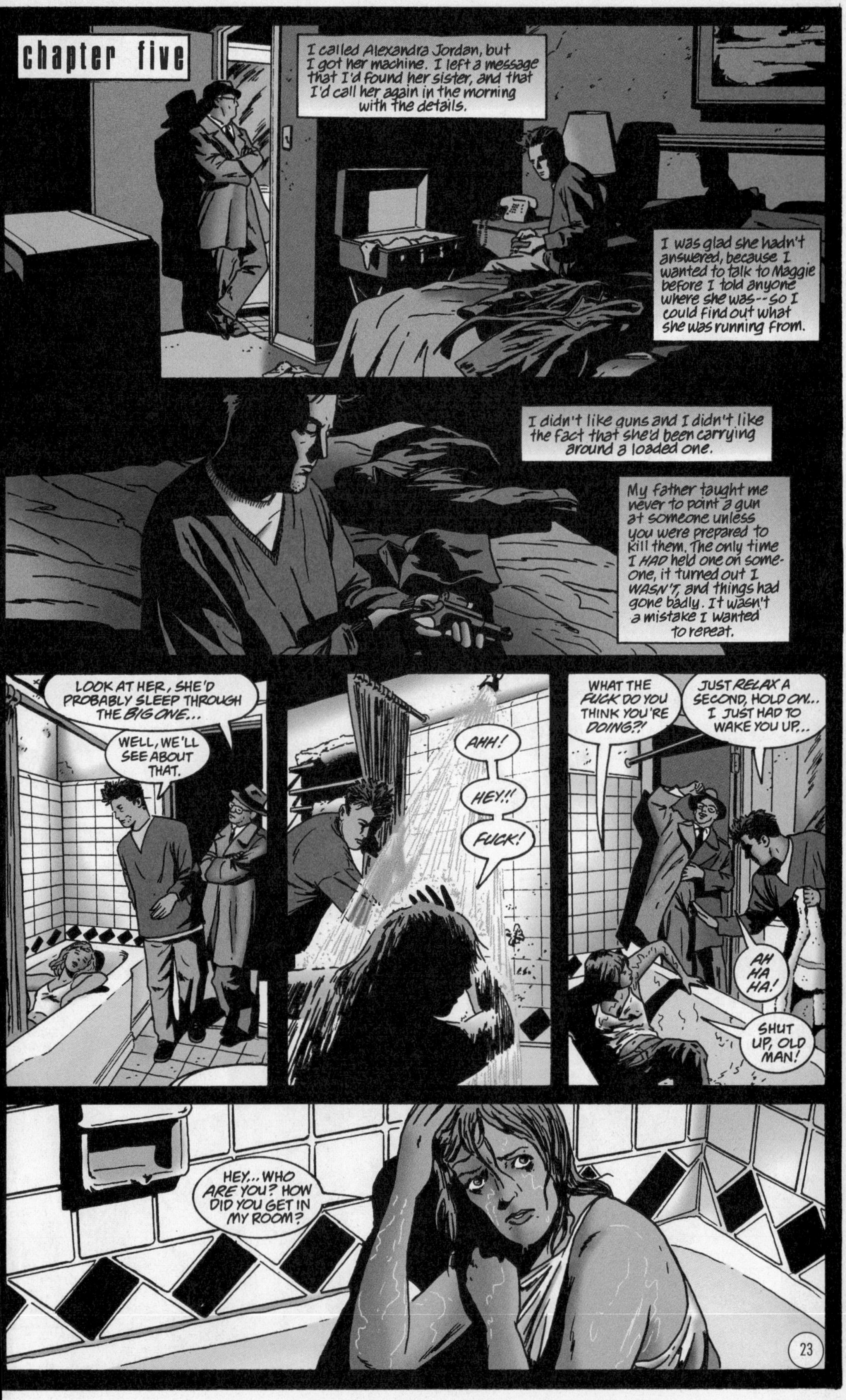
chapter five
I called Alexandra Jordan, but I got her machine. I left a message that I'd found her sister, and that I'd call her again in the morning with the details.
I was glad she hadn't answered, because I wanted to talk to Maggie before I told anyone where she was--so I could find out what she was running from.
I didn't like guns and I didn't like the fact that she'd been carrying around a loaded one.
My father taught me never to point a gun at someone unless you were prepared to kill them. The only time I HAD held one on some-one, it turned out I WASN'T, and things had gone badly. It wasn't a mistake I wanted to repeat.
LOOK AT HER, SHE'D PROBABLY SLEEP THROUGH THE BIG ONE...
WELL, WE'LL SEE ABOUT THAT.
AHH!
HEY!!
FUCK!
WHAT THE FUCK DO YOU THINK YOU'RE DOING?!
JUST RELAX A SECOND, HOLD ON... I JUST HAD TO WAKE YOU UP...
AH HA HA!
SHUT UP, OLD MAN!
HEY... WHO ARE YOU? HOW DID YOU GET IN MY ROOM?

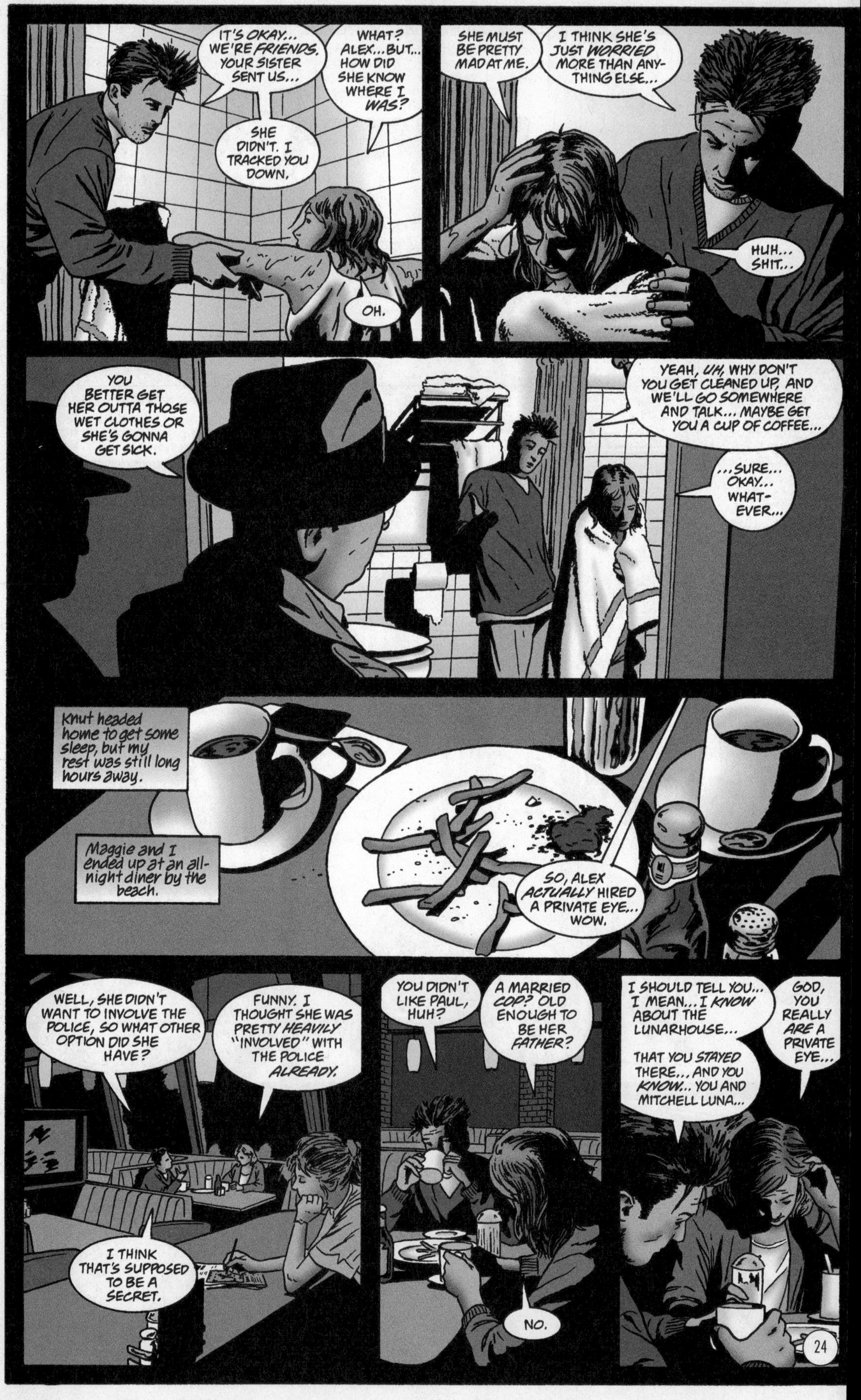
IT'S OKAY... WE'RE FRIENDS. YOUR SISTER SENT US...
WHAT? ALEX... BUT... HOW DID SHE KNOW WHERE I WAS?
SHE DIDN'T. I TRACKED YOU DOWN.
OH.
SHE MUST BE PRETTY MAD AT ME.
I THINK SHE'S JUST WORRIED MORE THAN ANYTHING ELSE...
HUH... SHIT...
YOU BETTER GET HER OUTTA THOSE WET CLOTHES OR SHE'S GONNA GET SICK.
YEAH, UH, WHY DON'T YOU GET CLEANED UP, AND WE'LL GO SOMEWHERE AND TALK... MAYBE GET YOU A CUP OF COFFEE...
...SURE... OKAY... WHATEVER...
Knut headed home to get some sleep, but my rest was still long hours away.
Maggie and I ended up at an all-night diner by the beach.
SO, ALEX ACTUALLY HIRED A PRIVATE EYE... WOW.
WELL, SHE DIDN'T WANT TO INVOLVE THE POLICE, SO WHAT OTHER OPTION DID SHE HAVE?
FUNNY. I THOUGHT SHE WAS PRETTY HEAVILY "INVOLVED" WITH THE POLICE ALREADY.
I THINK THAT'S SUPPOSED TO BE A SECRET.
YOU DIDN'T LIKE PAUL, HUH?
A MARRIED COP? OLD ENOUGH TO BE HER FATHER?
NO.
I SHOULD TELL YOU... I MEAN... I KNOW ABOUT THE LUNARHOUSE...
THAT YOU STAYED THERE... AND YOU KNOW... YOU AND MITCHELL LUNA...
GOD, YOU REALLY ARE A PRIVATE EYE...

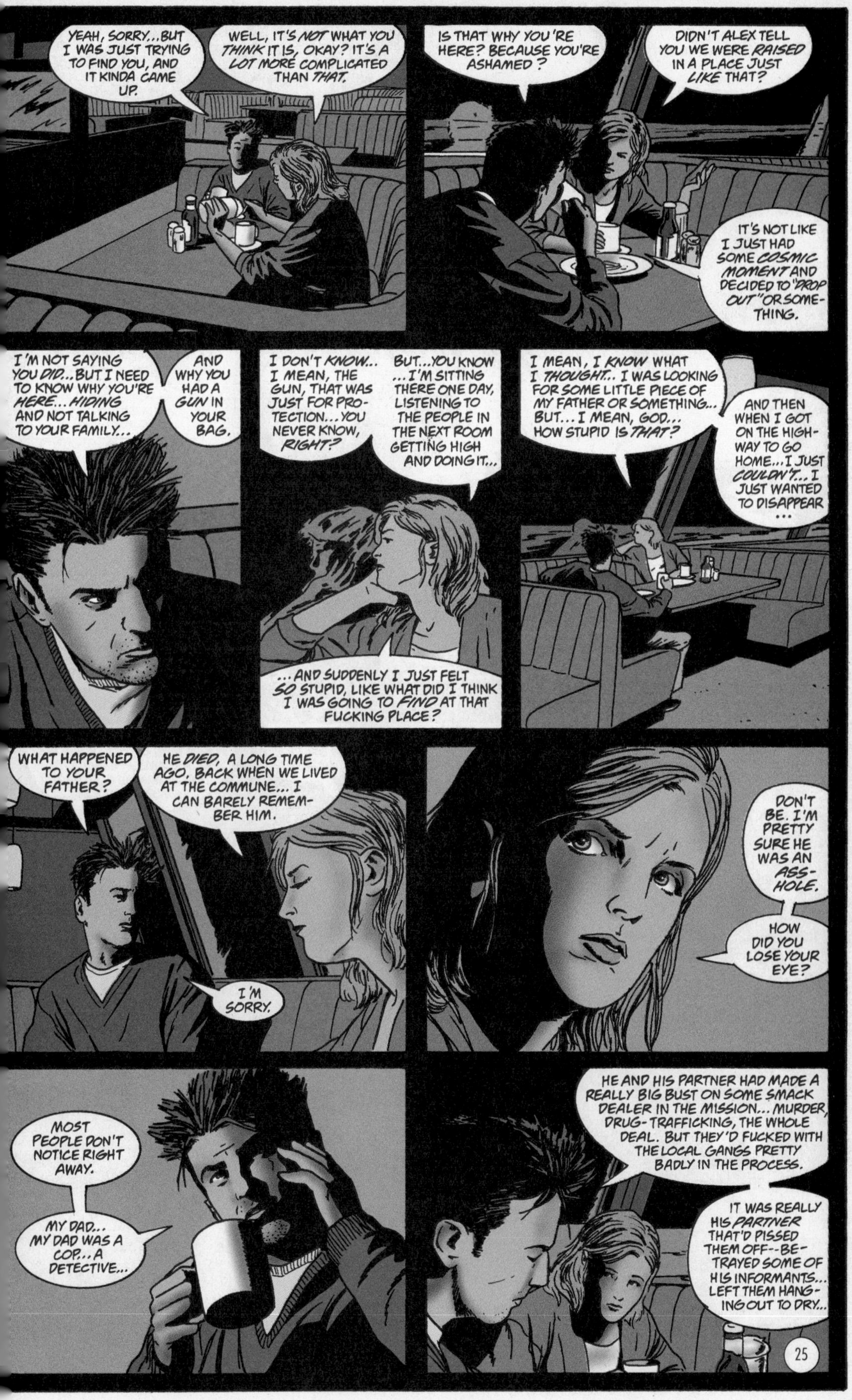

YEAH, SORRY...BUT I WAS JUST TRYING TO FIND YOU, AND IT KINDA CAME UP.
WELL, IT'S NOT WHAT YOU THINK IT IS, OKAY? IT'S A LOT MORE COMPLICATED THAN THAT.
IS THAT WHY YOU'RE HERE? BECAUSE YOU'RE ASHAMED?
DIDN'T ALEX TELL YOU WE WERE RAISED IN A PLACE JUST LIKE THAT?
IT'S NOT LIKE I JUST HAD SOME COSMIC MOMENT AND DECIDED TO "DROP OUT" OR SOME-THING.
I'M NOT SAYING YOU DID...BUT I NEED TO KNOW WHY YOU'RE HERE... HIDING AND NOT TALKING TO YOUR FAMILY...
AND WHY YOU HAD A GUN IN YOUR BAG.
I DON'T KNOW... I MEAN, THE GUN, THAT WAS JUST FOR PRO-TECTION... YOU NEVER KNOW, RIGHT?
BUT...YOU KNOW ...I'M SITTING THERE ONE DAY, LISTENING TO THE PEOPLE IN THE NEXT ROOM GETTING HIGH AND DOING IT...
...AND SUDDENLY I JUST FELT SO STUPID, LIKE WHAT DID I THINK I WAS GOING TO FIND AT THAT FUCKING PLACE?
I MEAN, I KNOW WHAT I THOUGHT... I WAS LOOKING FOR SOME LITTLE PIECE OF MY FATHER OR SOMETHING... BUT... I MEAN, GOD... HOW STUPID IS THAT?
AND THEN WHEN I GOT ON THE HIGH-WAY TO GO HOME...I JUST COULDN'T... I JUST WANTED TO DISAPPEAR...
WHAT HAPPENED TO YOUR FATHER?
HE DIED, A LONG TIME AGO, BACK WHEN WE LIVED AT THE COMMUNE... I CAN BARELY REMEM-BER HIM.
I'M SORRY.
DON'T BE. I'M PRETTY SURE HE WAS AN ASS-HOLE.
HOW DID YOU LOSE YOUR EYE?
MOST PEOPLE DON'T NOTICE RIGHT AWAY.
MY DAD... MY DAD WAS A COP... A DETECTIVE...
HE AND HIS PARTNER HAD MADE A REALLY BIG BUST ON SOME SMACK DEALER IN THE MISSION... MURDER, DRUG-TRAFFICKING, THE WHOLE DEAL. BUT THEY'D FUCKED WITH THE LOCAL GANGS PRETTY BADLY IN THE PROCESS.
IT WAS REALLY HIS PARTNER THAT'D PISSED THEM OFF--BE-TRAYED SOME OF HIS INFORMANTS... LEFT THEM HANG-ING OUT TO DRY...

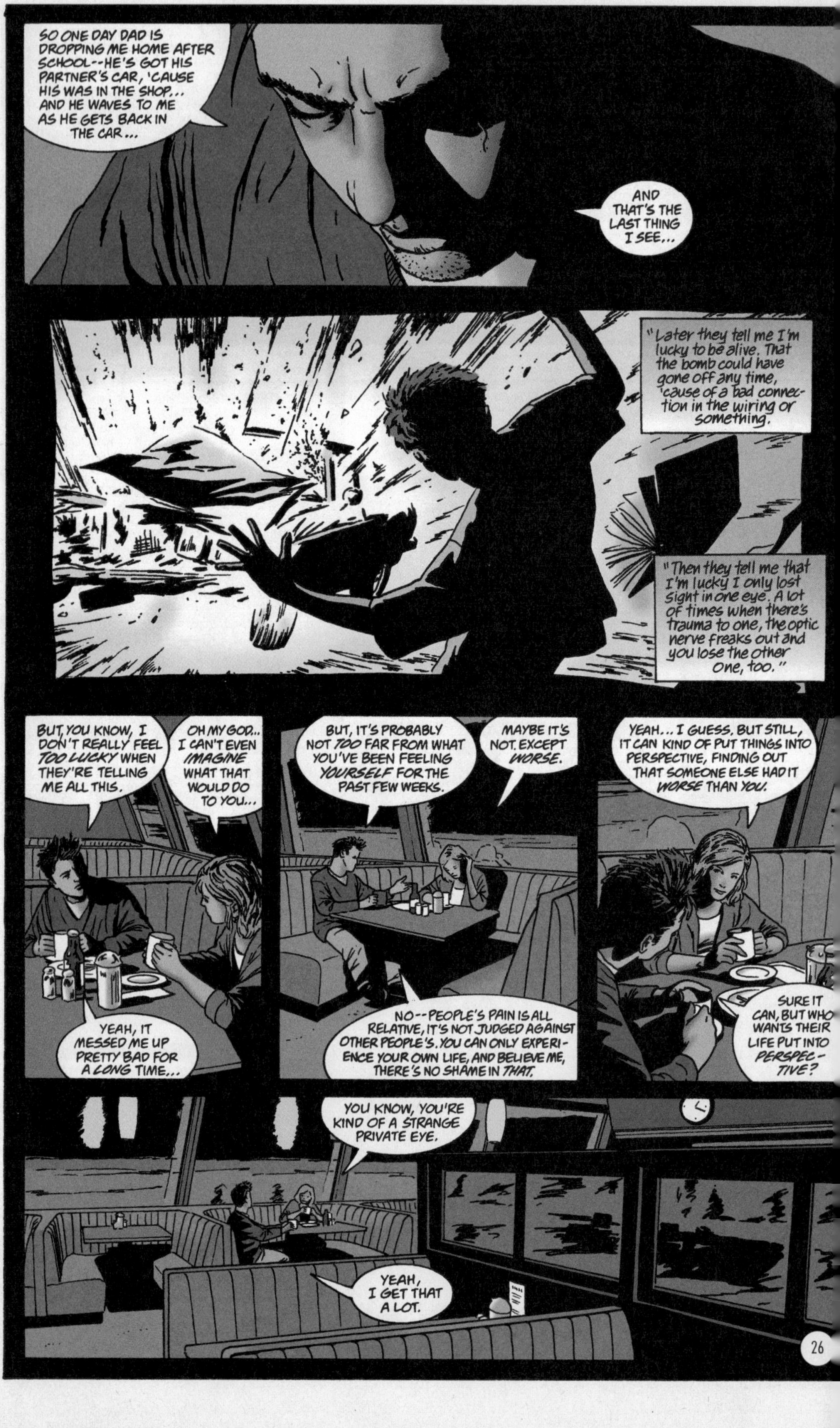

SO ONE DAY DAD IS DROPPING ME HOME AFTER SCHOOL--HE'S GOT HIS PARTNER'S CAR, 'CAUSE HIS WAS IN THE SHOP... AND HE WAVES TO ME AS HE GETS BACK IN THE CAR...
AND THAT'S THE LAST THING I SEE...
"Later they tell me I'm lucky to be alive. That the bomb could have gone off any time, 'cause of a bad connection in the wiring or something.
"Then they tell me that I'm lucky I only lost sight in one eye. A lot of times when there's trauma to one, the optic nerve freaks out and you lose the other one, too."
BUT, YOU KNOW, I DON'T REALLY FEEL TOO LUCKY WHEN THEY'RE TELLING ME ALL THIS.
OH MY GOD... I CAN'T EVEN IMAGINE WHAT THAT WOULD DO TO YOU...
YEAH, IT MESSED ME UP PRETTY BAD FOR A LONG TIME...
BUT, IT'S PROBABLY NOT TOO FAR FROM WHAT YOU'VE BEEN FEELING YOURSELF FOR THE PAST FEW WEEKS.
MAYBE IT'S NOT. EXCEPT WORSE.
NO--PEOPLE'S PAIN IS ALL RELATIVE, IT'S NOT JUDGED AGAINST OTHER PEOPLE'S. YOU CAN ONLY EXPERIENCE YOUR OWN LIFE, AND BELIEVE ME, THERE'S NO SHAME IN THAT.
YEAH... I GUESS. BUT STILL, IT CAN KIND OF PUT THINGS INTO PERSPECTIVE, FINDING OUT THAT SOMEONE ELSE HAD IT WORSE THAN YOU.
SURE IT CAN, BUT WHO WANTS THEIR LIFE PUT INTO PERSPECTIVE?
YOU KNOW, YOU'RE KIND OF A STRANGE PRIVATE EYE.
YEAH, I GET THAT A LOT.

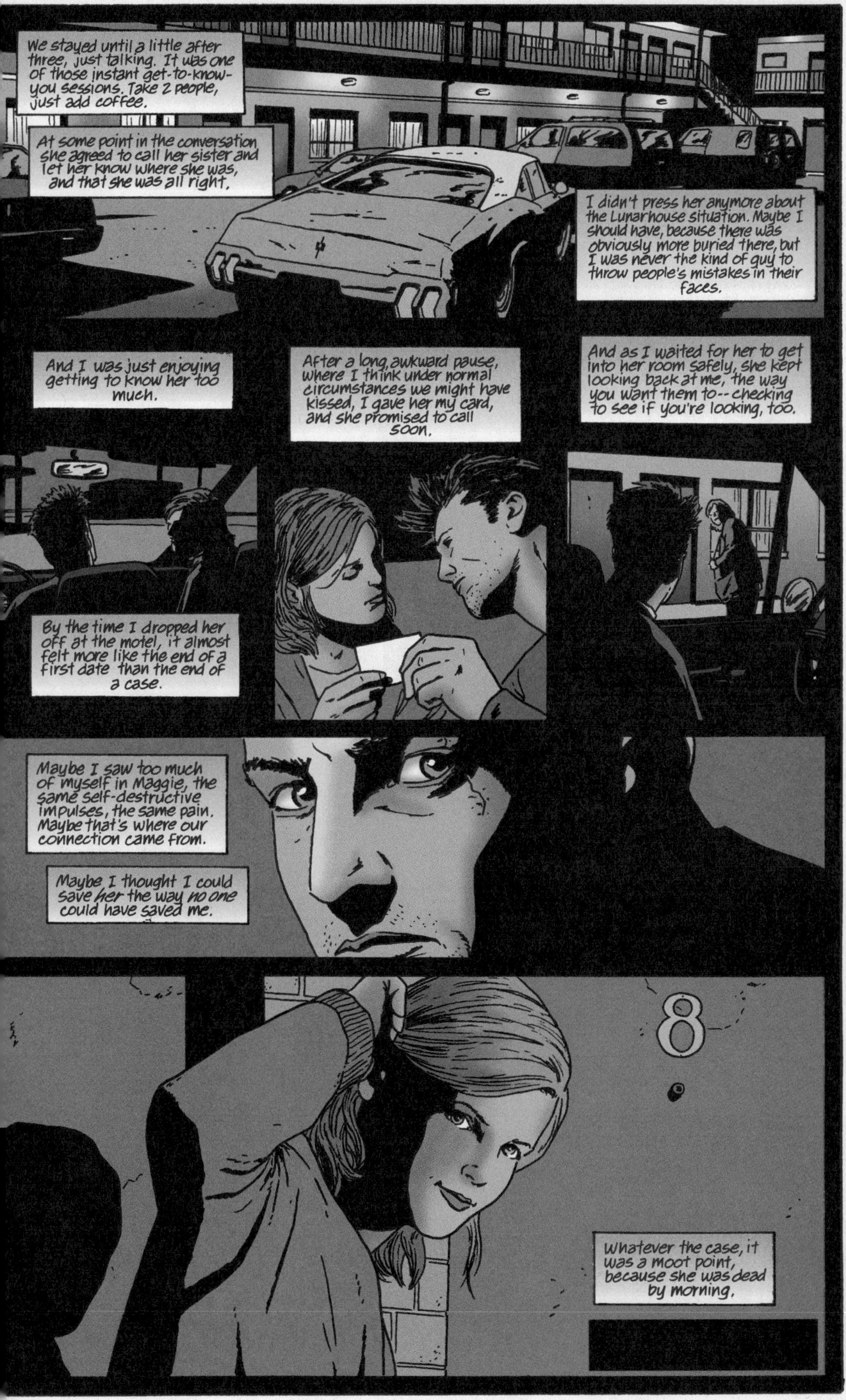
We stayed until a little after three, just talking. It was one of those instant get-to-know-you sessions. Take 2 people, just add coffee.
At some point in the conversation she agreed to call her sister and let her know where she was, and that she was all right.
I didn't press her anymore about the Lunarhouse situation. Maybe I should have, because there was obviously more buried there, but I was never the kind of guy to throw people's mistakes in their faces.
And I was just enjoying getting to know her too much.
By the time I dropped her off at the motel, it almost felt more like the end of a first date than the end of a case.
After a long, awkward pause, where I think under normal circumstances we might have kissed, I gave her my card, and she promised to call soon.
And as I waited for her to get into her room safely, she kept looking back at me, the way you want them to--checking to see if you're looking, too.
Maybe I saw too much of myself in Maggie, the same self-destructive impulses, the same pain. Maybe that's where our connection came from.
Maybe I thought I could save *her* the way *no one* could have saved me.
8
Whatever the case, it was a moot point, because she was dead by morning.

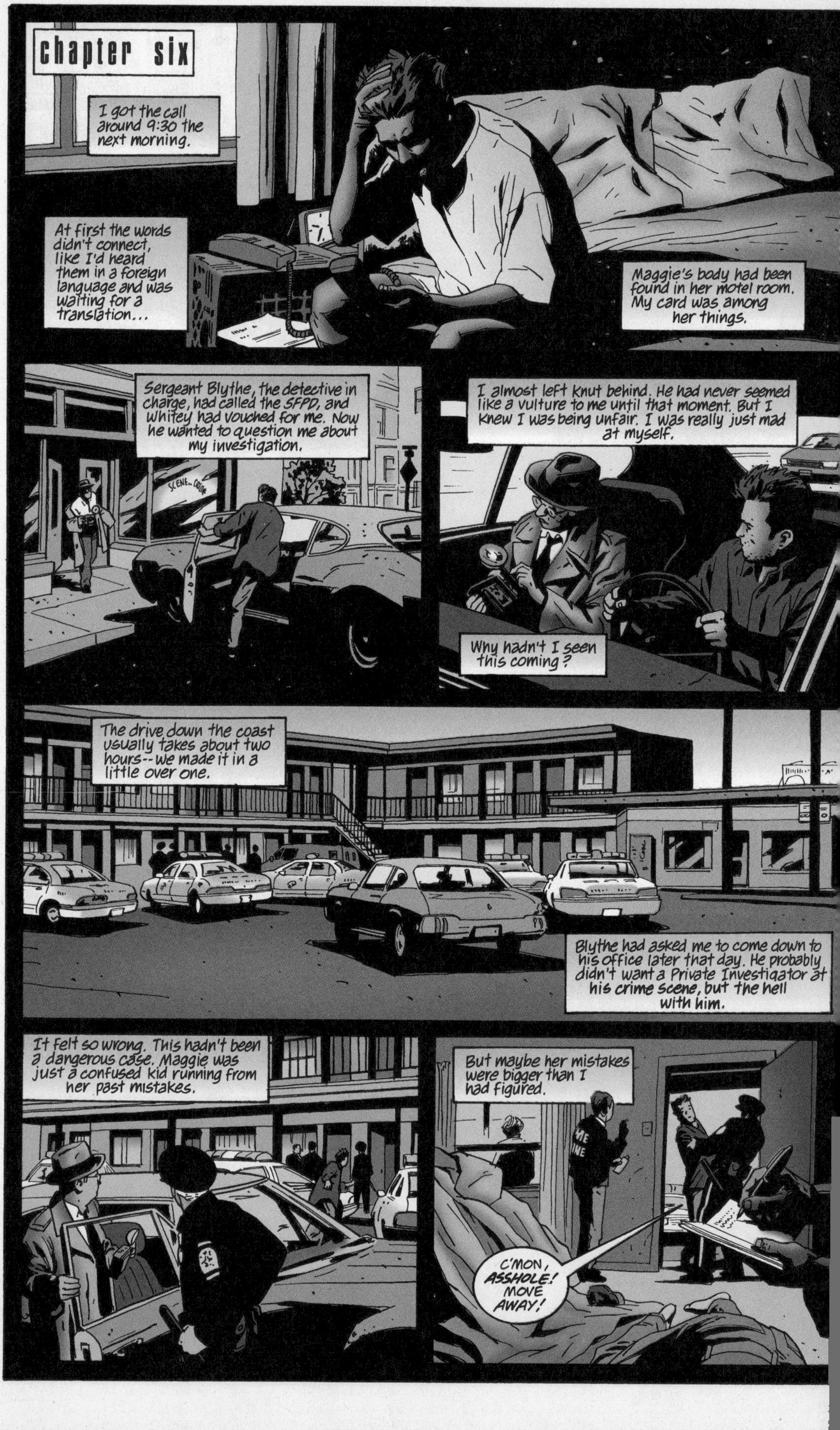
chapter six
I got the call around 9:30 the next morning.
At first the words didn't connect, like I'd heard them in a foreign language and was waiting for a translation...
Maggie's body had been found in her motel room. My card was among her things.
Sergeant Blythe, the detective in charge, had called the SFPD, and Whitey had vouched for me. Now he wanted to question me about my investigation.
I almost left Knut behind. He had never seemed like a vulture to me until that moment. But I knew I was being unfair. I was really just mad at myself.
Why hadn't I seen this coming?
The drive down the coast usually takes about two hours--we made it in a little over one.
Blythe had asked me to come down to his office later that day. He probably didn't want a Private Investigator at his crime scene, but the hell with him.
It felt so wrong. This hadn't been a dangerous case. Maggie was just a confused kid running from her past mistakes.
But maybe her mistakes were bigger than I had figured.
C'MON, ASSHOLE! MOVE AWAY!

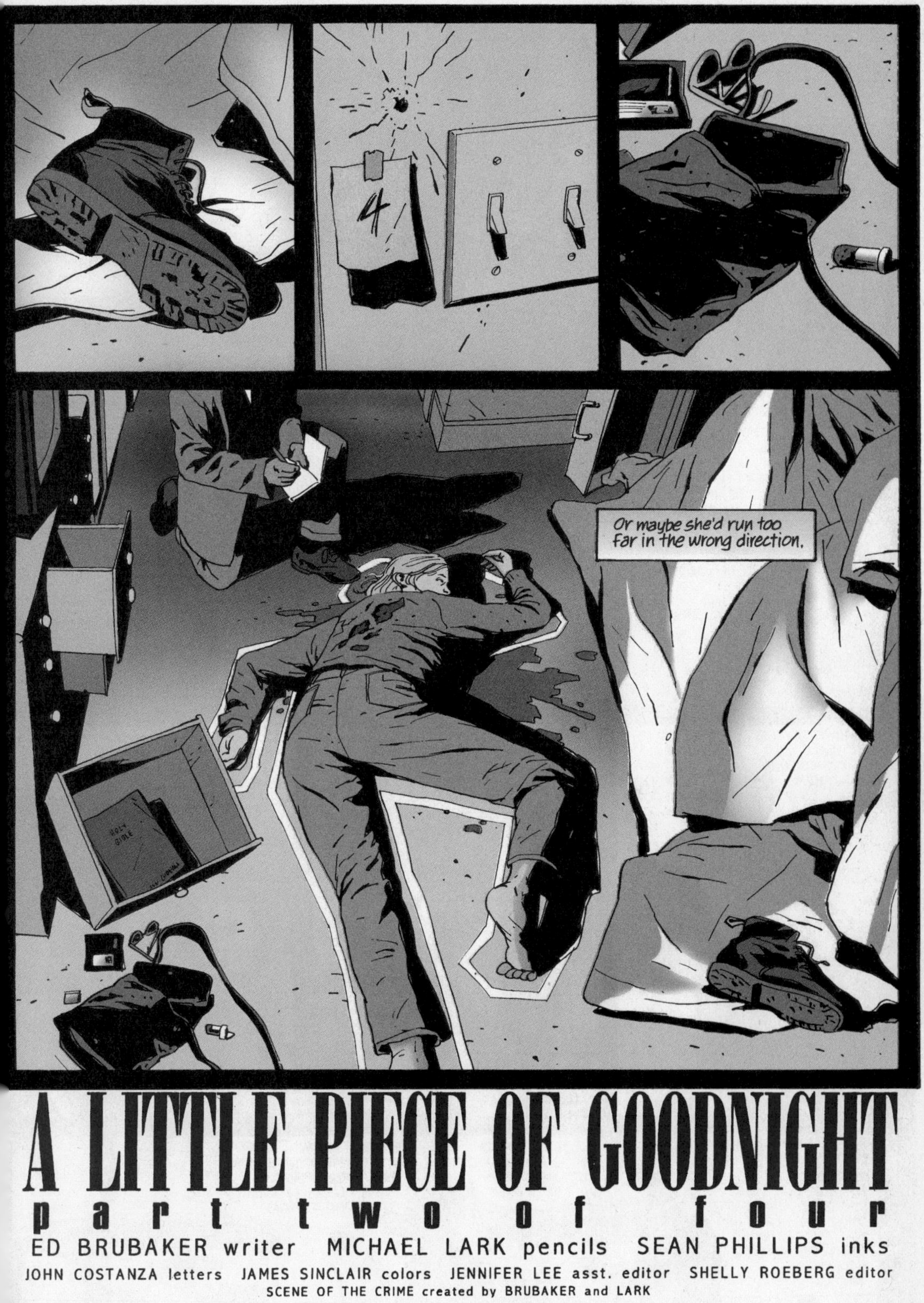
4
Or maybe she'd run too far in the wrong direction.

A LITTLE PIECE OF GOODNIGHT

part two of four

ED BRUBAKER writer MICHAEL LARK pencils SEAN PHILLIPS inks
JOHN COSTANZA letters JAMES SINCLAIR colors JENNIFER LEE asst. editor SHELLY ROEBERG editor
SCENE OF THE CRIME created by BRUBAKER and LARK

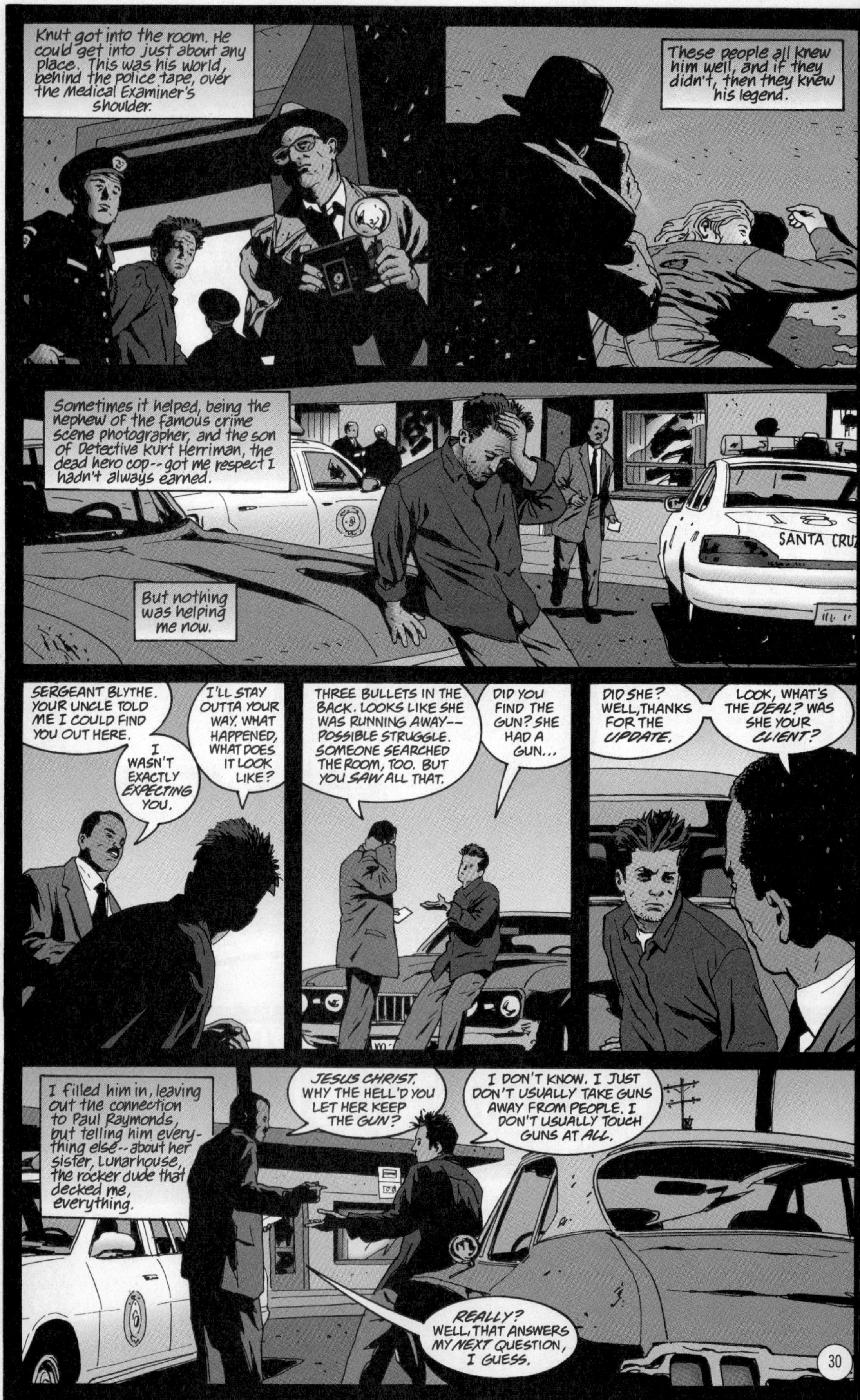

Knut got into the room. He could get into just about any place. This was his world, behind the police tape, over the Medical Examiner's shoulder.
These people all knew him well, and if they didn't, then they knew his legend.
Sometimes it helped, being the nephew of the famous crime scene photographer, and the son of Detective Kurt Herriman, the dead hero cop--got me respect I hadn't always earned.
SANTA CRUZ
But nothing was helping me now.
SERGEANT BLYTHE. YOUR UNCLE TOLD ME I COULD FIND YOU OUT HERE.
I WASN'T EXACTLY EXPECTING YOU.
I'LL STAY OUTTA YOUR WAY. WHAT HAPPENED, WHAT DOES IT LOOK LIKE?
THREE BULLETS IN THE BACK. LOOKS LIKE SHE WAS RUNNING AWAY-- POSSIBLE STRUGGLE. SOMEONE SEARCHED THE ROOM, TOO. BUT YOU SAW ALL THAT.
DID YOU FIND THE GUN? SHE HAD A GUN...
DID SHE? WELL, THANKS FOR THE UPDATE.
LOOK, WHAT'S THE DEAL? WAS SHE YOUR CLIENT?
I filled him in, leaving out the connection to Paul Raymonds, but telling him everything else--about her sister, Lunarhouse, the rocker dude that decked me, everything.
JESUS CHRIST, WHY THE HELL'D YOU LET HER KEEP THE GUN?
I DON'T KNOW. I JUST DON'T USUALLY TAKE GUNS AWAY FROM PEOPLE. I DON'T USUALLY TOUCH GUNS AT ALL.
REALLY? WELL, THAT ANSWERS MY NEXT QUESTION, I GUESS.

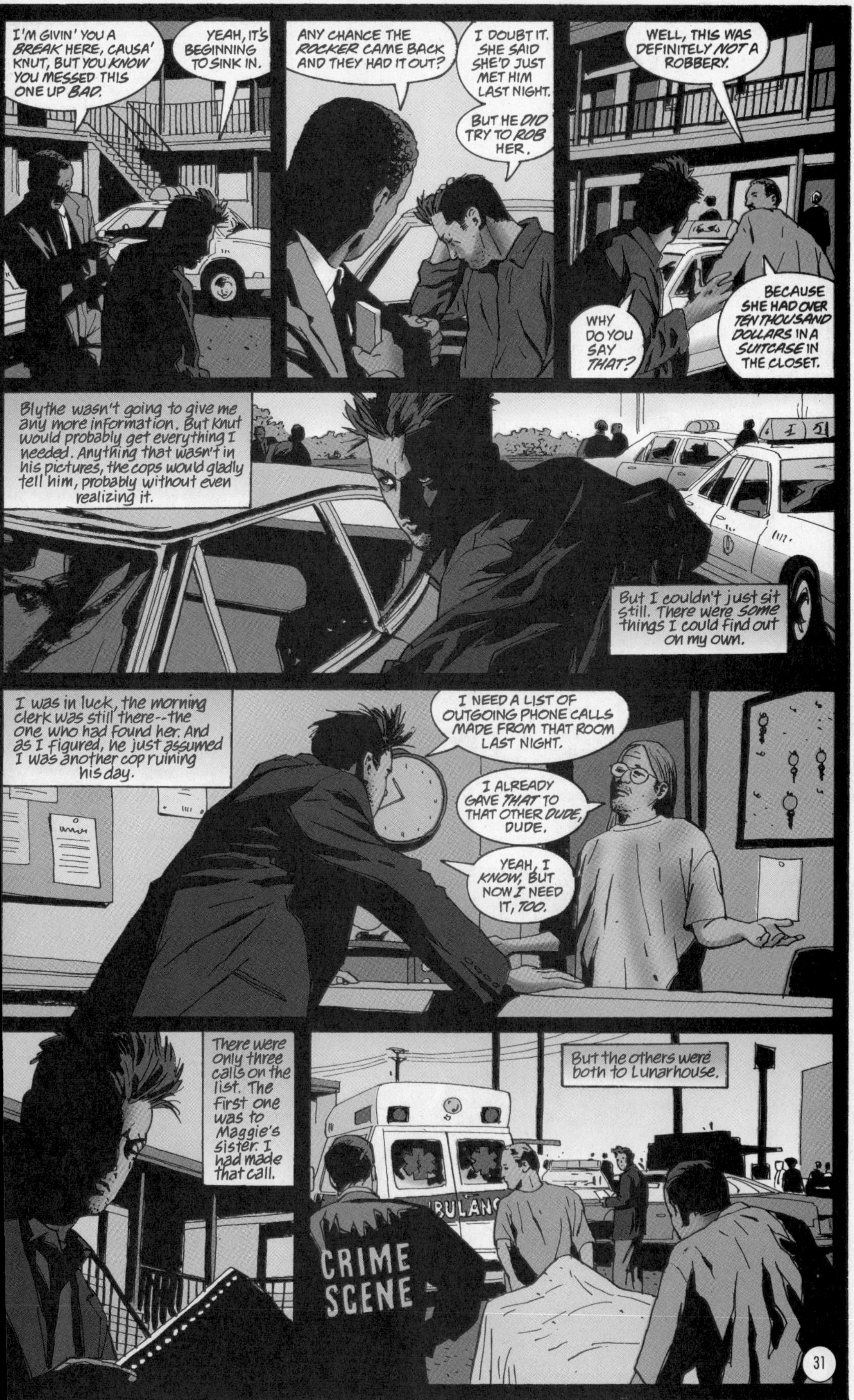
I'M GIVIN' YOU A BREAK HERE, CAUSA' KNUT, BUT YOU KNOW YOU MESSED THIS ONE UP BAD.
YEAH, IT'S BEGINNING TO SINK IN.
ANY CHANCE THE ROCKER CAME BACK AND THEY HAD IT OUT?
I DOUBT IT. SHE SAID SHE'D JUST MET HIM LAST NIGHT.
BUT HE DID TRY TO ROB HER.
WELL, THIS WAS DEFINITELY NOT A ROBBERY.
WHY DO YOU SAY THAT?
BECAUSE SHE HAD OVER TEN THOUSAND DOLLARS IN A SUITCASE IN THE CLOSET.
Blythe wasn't going to give me any more information. But Knut would probably get everything I needed. Anything that wasn't in his pictures, the cops would gladly tell him, probably without even realizing it.
But I couldn't just sit still. There were some things I could find out on my own.
I was in luck, the morning clerk was still there--the one who had found her. And as I figured, he just assumed I was another cop ruining his day.
I NEED A LIST OF OUTGOING PHONE CALLS MADE FROM THAT ROOM LAST NIGHT.
I ALREADY GAVE THAT TO THAT OTHER DUDE, DUDE.
YEAH, I KNOW, BUT NOW I NEED IT, TOO.
There were only three calls on the list. The first one was to Maggie's sister. I had made that call.
But the others were both to Lunarhouse.
CRIME SCENE

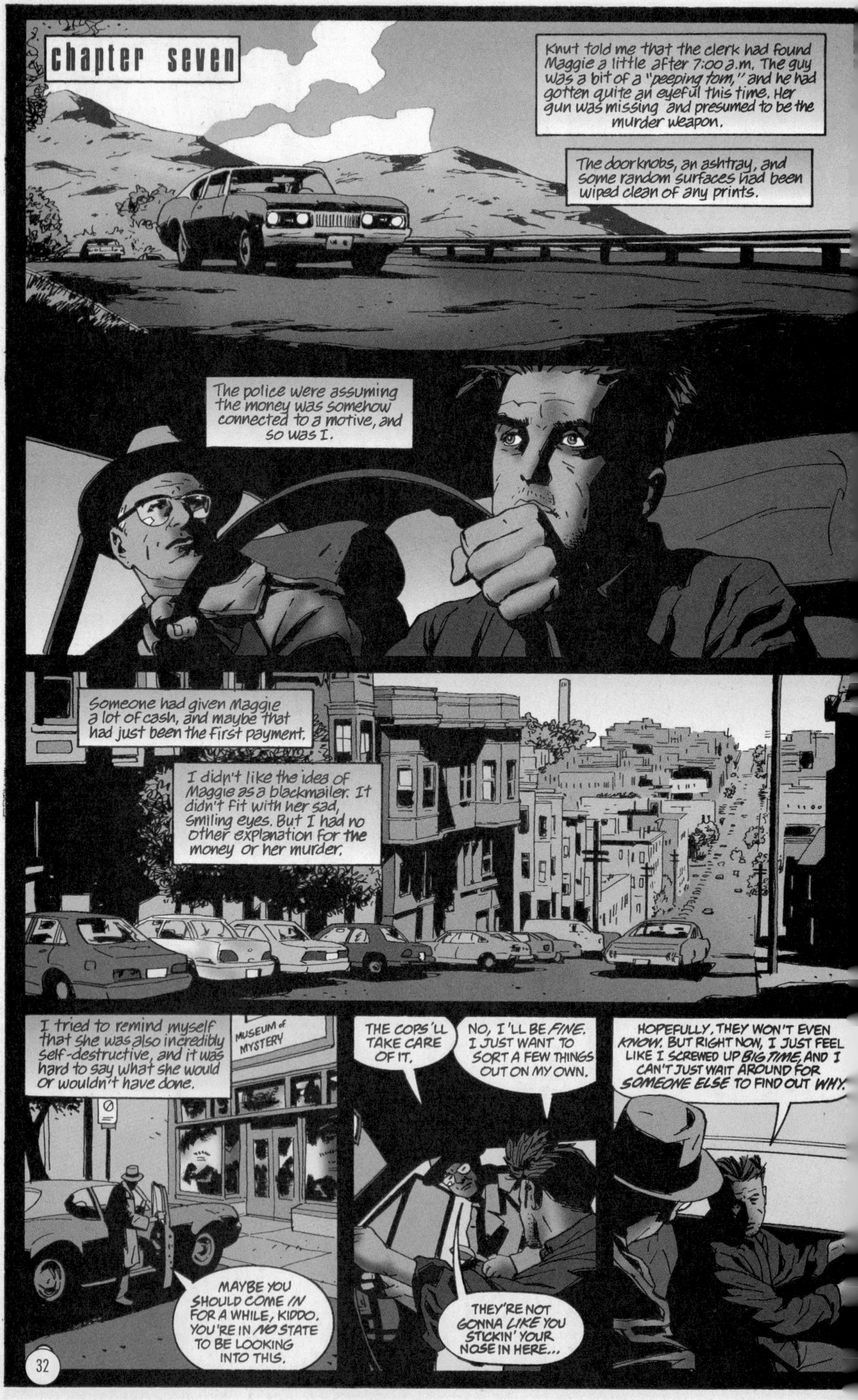
chapter seven
Knut told me that the clerk had found Maggie a little after 7:00 a.m. The guy was a bit of a "peeping tom," and he had gotten quite an eyeful this time. Her gun was missing and presumed to be the murder weapon.
The doorknobs, an ashtray, and some random surfaces had been wiped clean of any prints.
The police were assuming the money was somehow connected to a motive, and so was I.
Someone had given Maggie a lot of cash, and maybe that had just been the first payment.
I didn't like the idea of Maggie as a blackmailer. It didn't fit with her sad, smiling eyes. But I had no other explanation for the money or her murder.
I tried to remind myself that she was also incredibly self-destructive, and it was hard to say what she would or wouldn't have done.
MUSEUM of MYSTERY
MAYBE YOU SHOULD COME IN FOR A WHILE, KIDDO. YOU'RE IN NO STATE TO BE LOOKING INTO THIS.
THE COPS'LL TAKE CARE OF IT.
NO, I'LL BE FINE. I JUST WANT TO SORT A FEW THINGS OUT ON MY OWN.
THEY'RE NOT GONNA LIKE YOU STICKIN' YOUR NOSE IN HERE...
HOPEFULLY, THEY WON'T EVEN KNOW. BUT RIGHT NOW, I JUST FEEL LIKE I SCREWED UP BIG TIME, AND I CAN'T JUST WAIT AROUND FOR SOMEONE ELSE TO FIND OUT WHY.

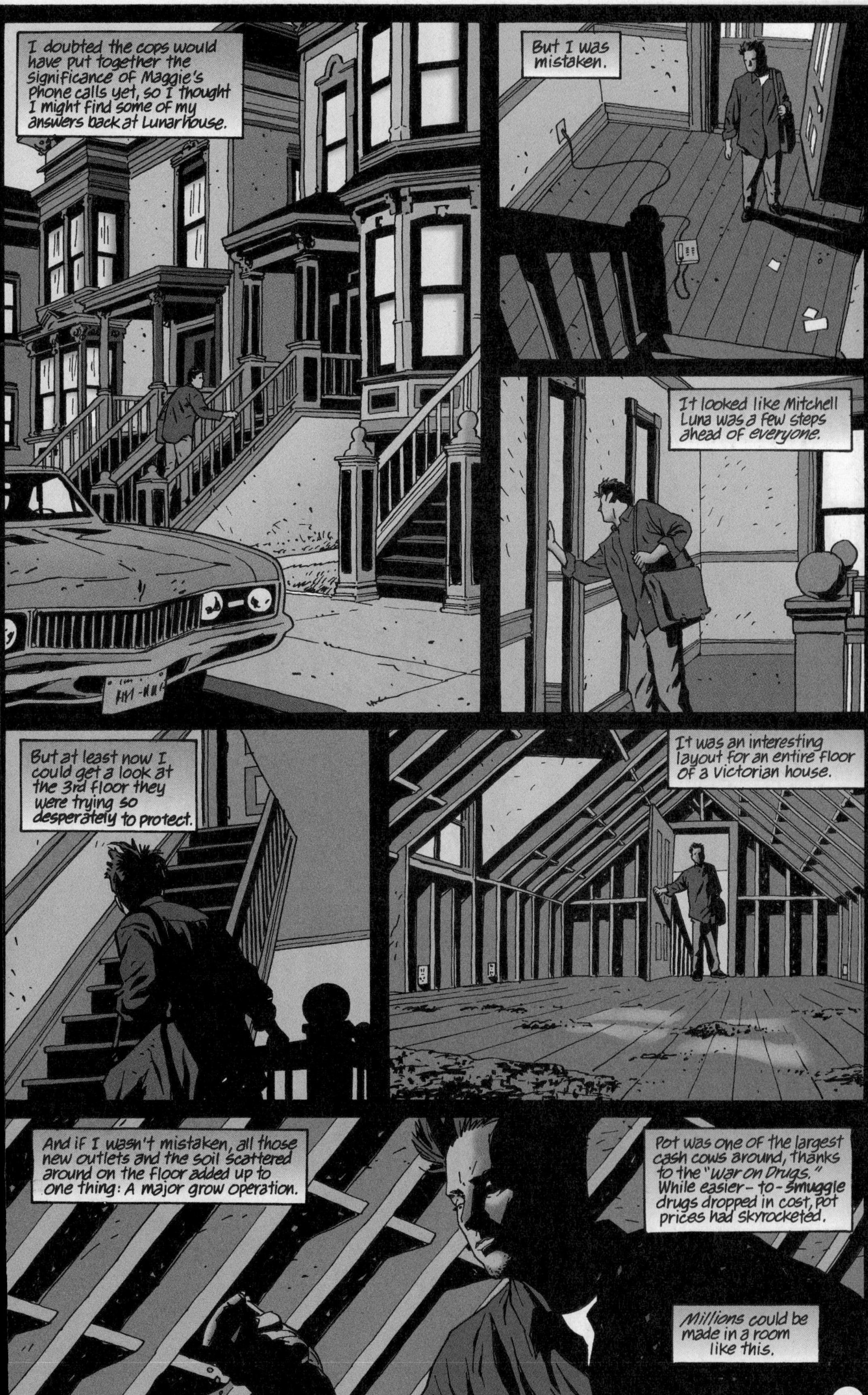
I doubted the cops would have put together the significance of Maggie's phone calls yet, so I thought I might find some of my answers back at Lunarhouse.
But I was mistaken.
It looked like Mitchell Luna was a few steps ahead of everyone.
But at least now I could get a look at the 3rd floor they were trying so desperately to protect.
It was an interesting layout for an entire floor of a Victorian house.
And if I wasn't mistaken, all those new outlets and the soil scattered around on the floor added up to one thing: A major grow operation.
Pot was one of the largest cash cows around, thanks to the "War on Drugs." While easier-to-smuggle drugs dropped in cost, pot prices had skyrocketed.
Millions could be made in a room like this.

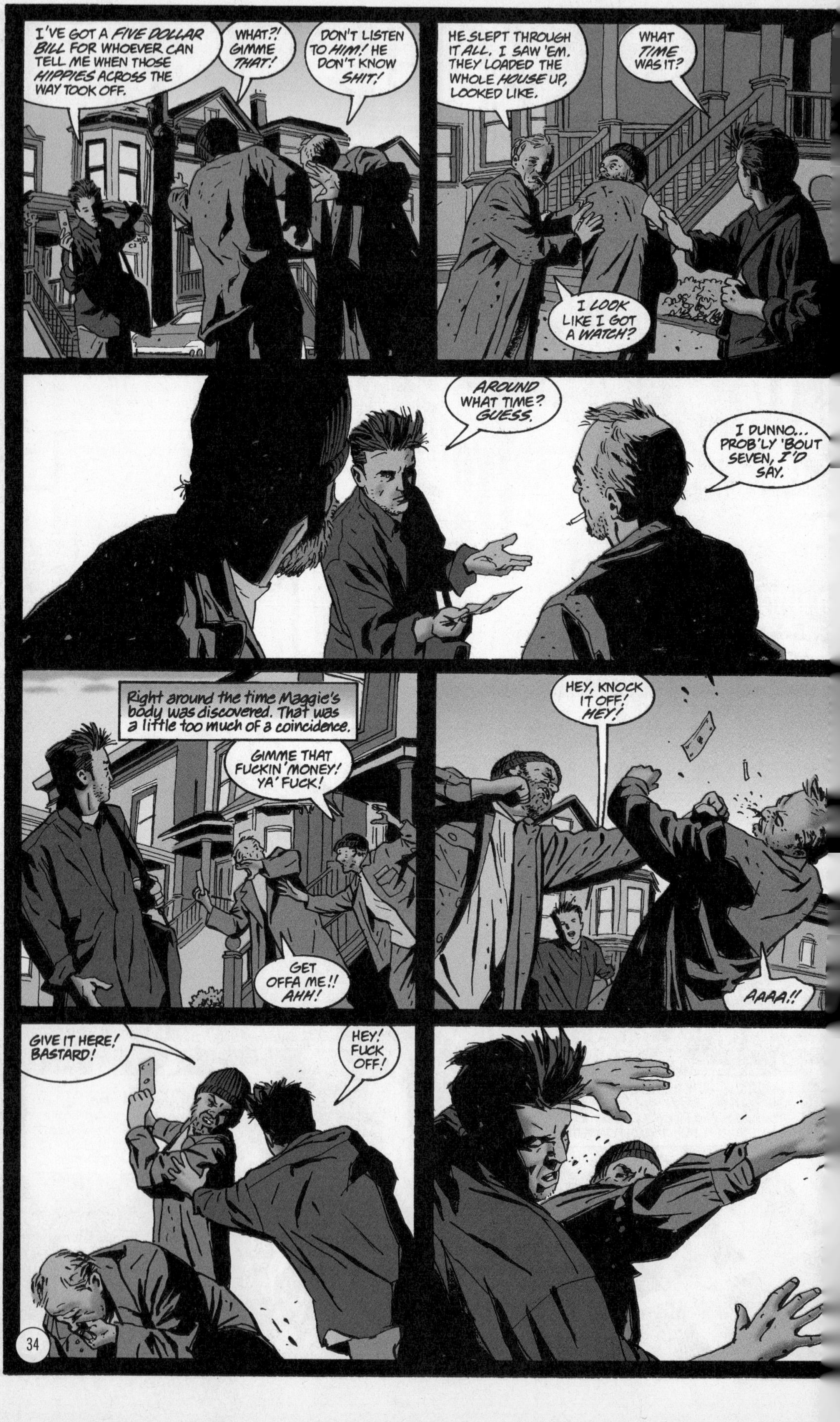

I'VE GOT A FIVE DOLLAR BILL FOR WHOEVER CAN TELL ME WHEN THOSE HIPPIES ACROSS THE WAY TOOK OFF.
WHAT?! GIMME THAT!
DON'T LISTEN TO HIM! HE DON'T KNOW SHIT!
HE SLEPT THROUGH IT ALL. I SAW 'EM. THEY LOADED THE WHOLE HOUSE UP, LOOKED LIKE.
WHAT TIME WAS IT?
I LOOK LIKE I GOT A WATCH?
AROUND WHAT TIME? GUESS.
I DUNNO... PROB'LY 'BOUT SEVEN, I'D SAY.
Right around the time Maggie's body was discovered. That was a little too much of a coincidence.
GIMME THAT FUCKIN' MONEY! YA' FUCK!
GET OFFA ME!! AHH!
HEY, KNOCK IT OFF! HEY!
AAAA!!
GIVE IT HERE! BASTARD!
HEY! FUCK OFF!

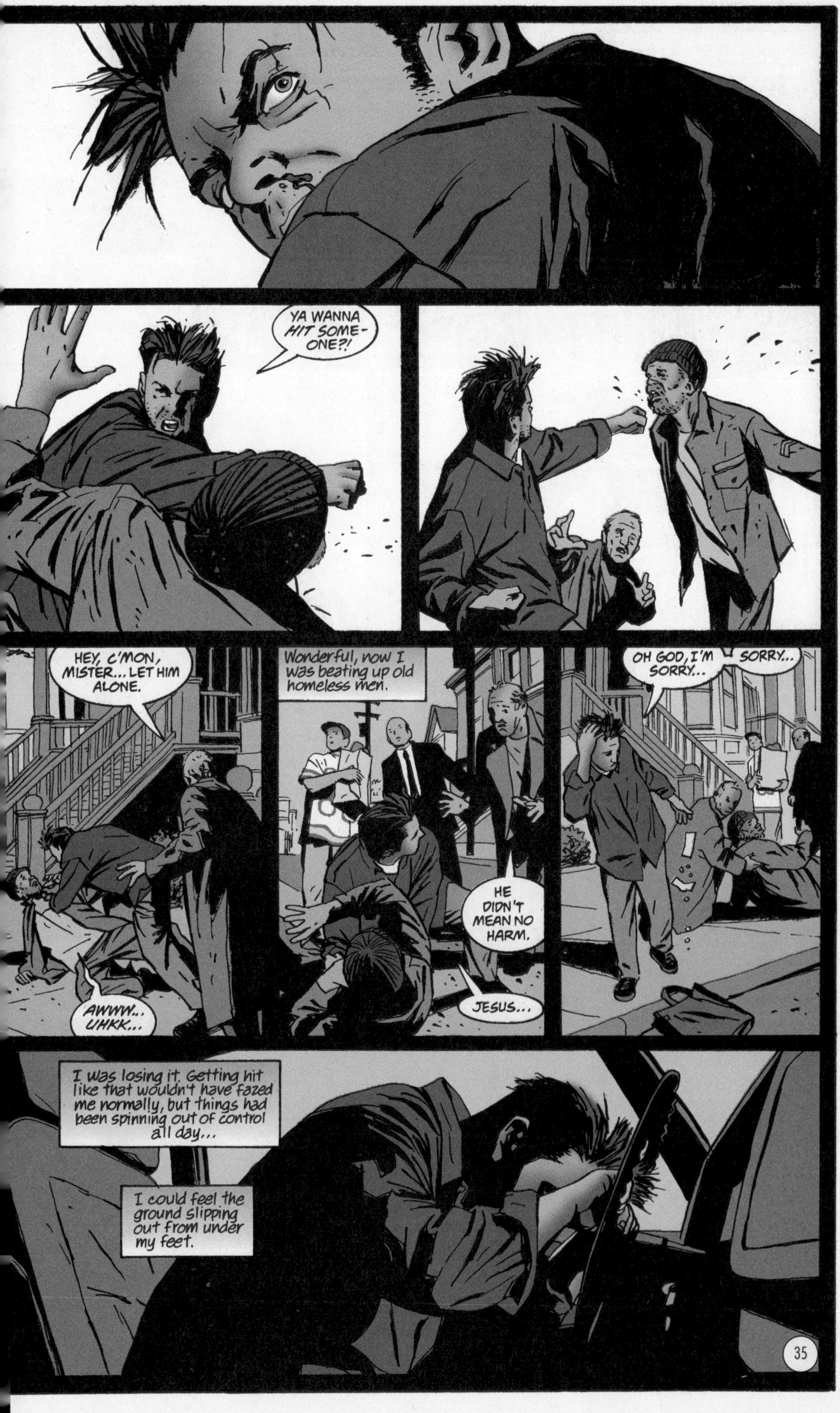
YA WANNA HIT SOME-ONE?!
HEY, C'MON, MISTER... LET HIM ALONE.
AWWW... UHKK...
Wonderful, now I was beating up old homeless men.
HE DIDN'T MEAN NO HARM.
JESUS...
OH GOD, I'M SORRY...
SORRY...
I was losing it. Getting hit like that wouldn't have fazed me normally, but things had been spinning out of control all day...
I could feel the ground slipping out from under my feet.

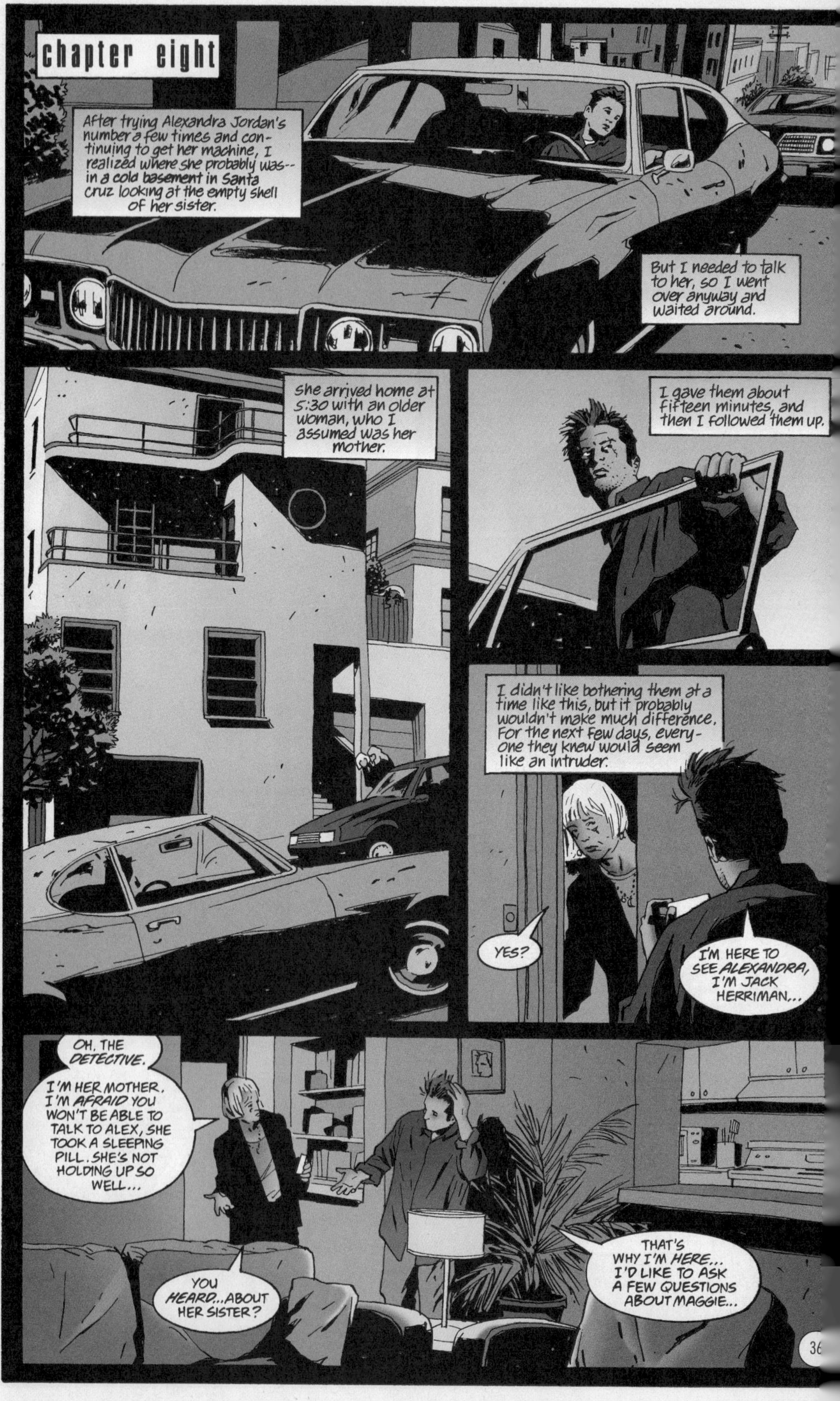
chapter eight
After trying Alexandra Jordan's number a few times and continuing to get her machine, I realized where she probably was--in a cold basement in Santa cruz looking at the empty shell of her sister.
But I needed to talk to her, so I went over anyway and waited around.
she arrived home at 5:30 with an older woman, who I assumed was her mother.
I gave them about fifteen minutes, and then I followed them up.
I didn't like bothering them at a time like this, but it probably wouldn't make much difference. For the next few days, everyone they knew would seem like an intruder.
YES?
I'M HERE TO SEE ALEXANDRA, I'M JACK HERRIMAN...
OH, THE DETECTIVE.
I'M HER MOTHER. I'M AFRAID YOU WON'T BE ABLE TO TALK TO ALEX, SHE TOOK A SLEEPING PILL. SHE'S NOT HOLDING UP SO WELL...
YOU HEARD...ABOUT HER SISTER?
THAT'S WHY I'M HERE... I'D LIKE TO ASK A FEW QUESTIONS ABOUT MAGGIE...

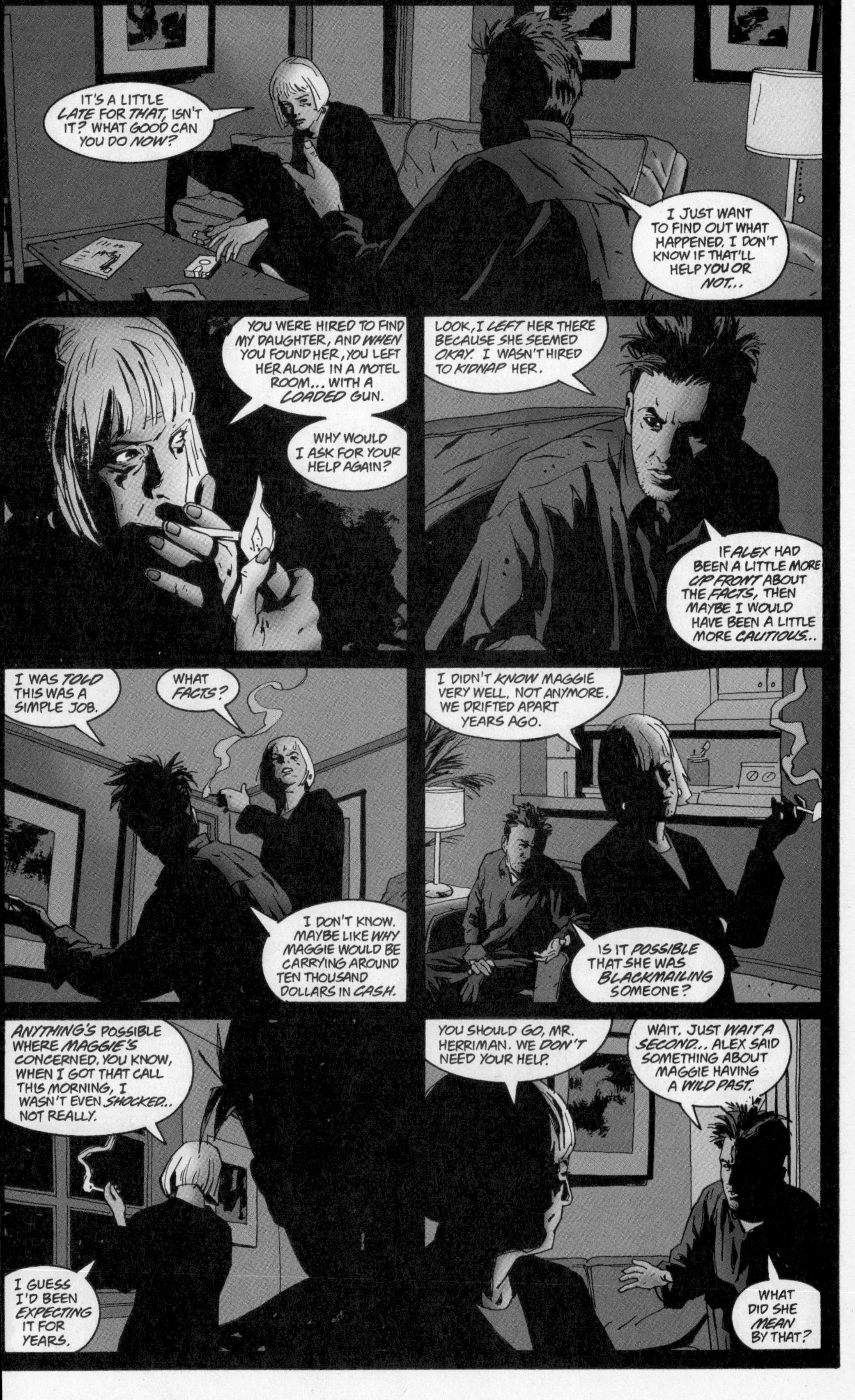
IT'S A LITTLE LATE FOR THAT, ISN'T IT? WHAT GOOD CAN YOU DO NOW?
I JUST WANT TO FIND OUT WHAT HAPPENED. I DON'T KNOW IF THAT'LL HELP YOU OR NOT...
YOU WERE HIRED TO FIND MY DAUGHTER, AND WHEN YOU FOUND HER, YOU LEFT HER ALONE IN A MOTEL ROOM... WITH A LOADED GUN.
WHY WOULD I ASK FOR YOUR HELP AGAIN?
LOOK, I LEFT HER THERE BECAUSE SHE SEEMED OKAY. I WASN'T HIRED TO KIDNAP HER.
IF ALEX HAD BEEN A LITTLE MORE UP FRONT ABOUT THE FACTS, THEN MAYBE I WOULD HAVE BEEN A LITTLE MORE CAUTIOUS...
I WAS TOLD THIS WAS A SIMPLE JOB.
WHAT FACTS?
I DON'T KNOW. MAYBE LIKE WHY MAGGIE WOULD BE CARRYING AROUND TEN THOUSAND DOLLARS IN CASH.
I DIDN'T KNOW MAGGIE VERY WELL, NOT ANYMORE. WE DRIFTED APART YEARS AGO.
IS IT POSSIBLE THAT SHE WAS BLACKMAILING SOMEONE?
ANYTHING'S POSSIBLE WHERE MAGGIE'S CONCERNED. YOU KNOW, WHEN I GOT THAT CALL THIS MORNING, I WASN'T EVEN SHOCKED... NOT REALLY.
I GUESS I'D BEEN EXPECTING IT FOR YEARS.
YOU SHOULD GO, MR. HERRIMAN. WE DON'T NEED YOUR HELP.
WAIT. JUST WAIT A SECOND... ALEX SAID SOMETHING ABOUT MAGGIE HAVING A WILD PAST.
WHAT DID SHE MEAN BY THAT?

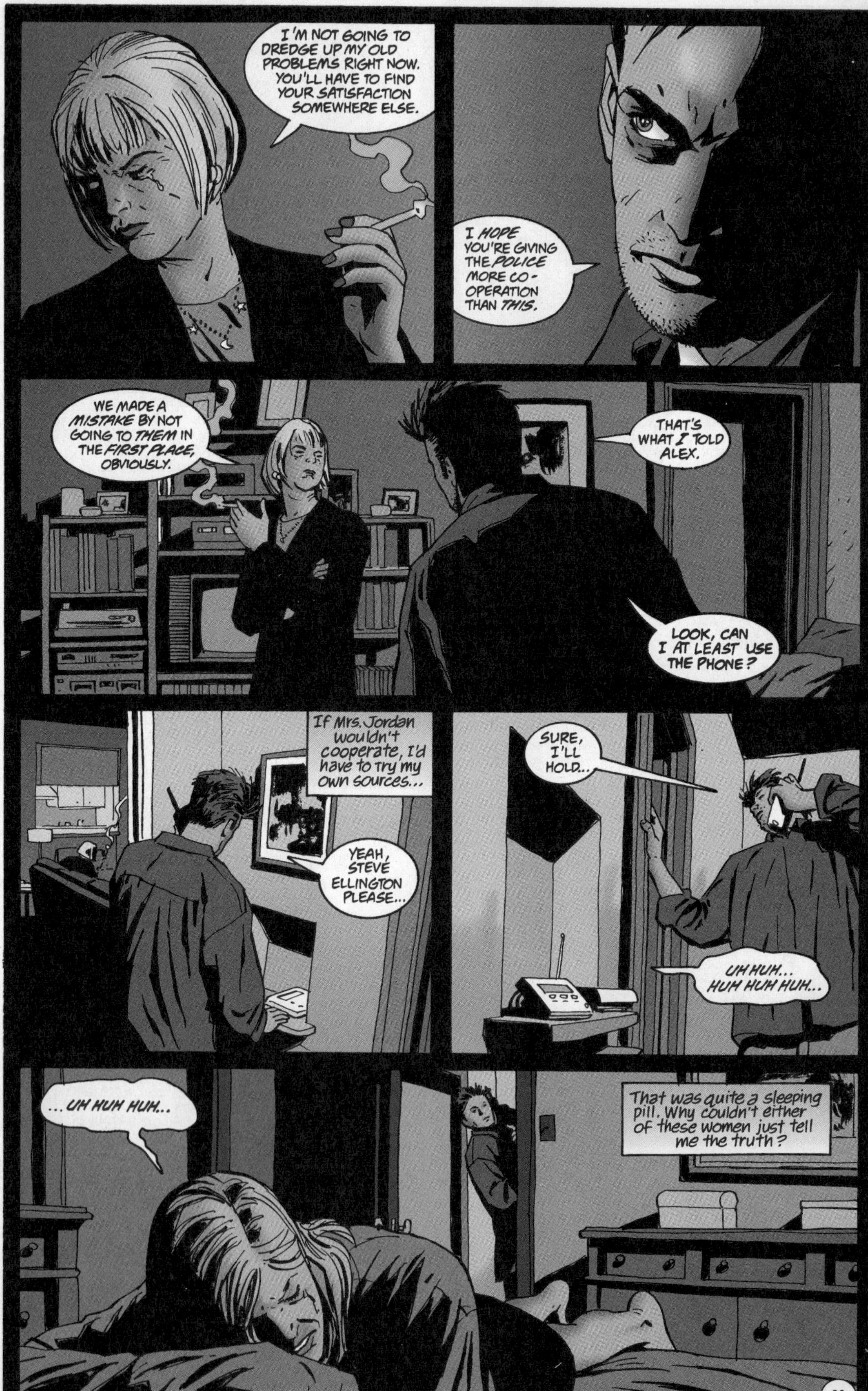

I'M NOT GOING TO DREDGE UP MY OLD PROBLEMS RIGHT NOW. YOU'LL HAVE TO FIND YOUR SATISFACTION SOMEWHERE ELSE.
I *HOPE* YOU'RE GIVING THE *POLICE* MORE CO-OPERATION THAN *THIS*.
WE MADE A *MISTAKE* BY NOT GOING TO *THEM* IN THE *FIRST PLACE*, OBVIOUSLY.
THAT'S WHAT *I* TOLD ALEX.
LOOK, CAN I AT LEAST USE THE PHONE?
If Mrs. Jordan wouldn't cooperate, I'd have to try my own sources...
YEAH, STEVE ELLINGTON PLEASE...
SURE, I'LL HOLD...
UH HUH... HUH HUH HUH...
...UH HUH HUH...
That was quite a sleeping pill. Why couldn't either of these women just tell me the truth?

chapter nine

I'd spent far too much time in courthouses and police stations while growing up to ever be comfortable in them now. I was always overcome with a fear that I wouldn't be allowed to leave--that I'd be put away for a crime only just discovered...

--Though long buried in my past.

Whitey had come up with some noteworthy items. Maggie Jordan had been arrested as a teenager for arson, possession of drugs, and even once for prostitution.

JESUS... SHE MUST'VE BEEN A NIGHTMARE.

As an adult she'd had a few busts for pot and coke, but nothing major. And certainly nothing that seemed to suggest a sudden leap to blackmail.

Technically her juvenile records were SEALED, but there was never a confidential file that Whitey couldn't access.

A patrolman until his back was broken in an accident a few years ago, he was now the best information tracker that the SFPD had. He followed a paper trail like a bloodhound.

NOW, HERE'S AN INTERESTING TIDBIT: IN '92 ALEXANDRA JORDAN WAS ARRESTED FOR STABBING HER MOTHER, MINOR WOUNDS INFLICTED, APPARENTLY, AND SHE GOT OFF WITH JUST PROBATION.

YOU'RE KIDDING...

I SHIT YOU NOT. BUT OTHER THAN THE ONE "PSYCHO" IMITATION, SHE'S CLEAN.

MAYBE I SHOULD BE MORE CAREFUL NEXT TIME I QUESTION HER.

JUST DON'T INTERROGATE HER WHILE SHE'S COOKING.

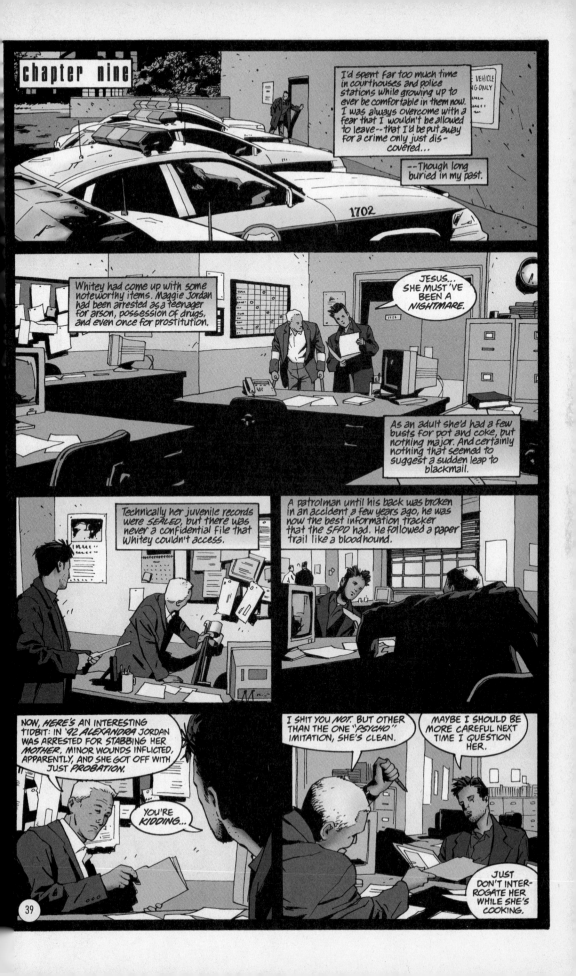

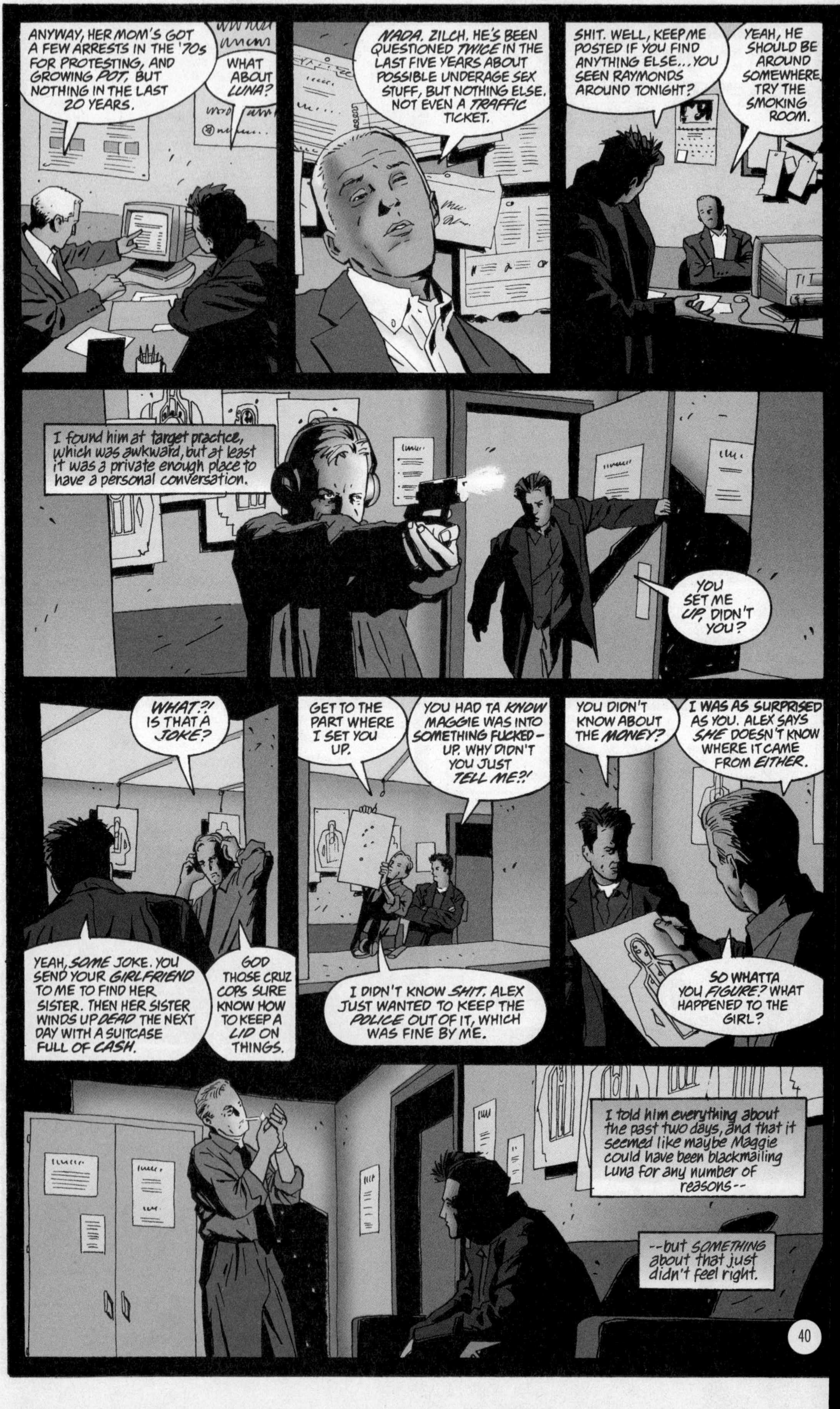
ANYWAY, HER MOM'S GOT A FEW ARRESTS IN THE '70s FOR PROTESTING, AND GROWING POT, BUT NOTHING IN THE LAST 20 YEARS.
WHAT ABOUT LUNA?
NADA. ZILCH. HE'S BEEN QUESTIONED TWICE IN THE LAST FIVE YEARS ABOUT POSSIBLE UNDERAGE SEX STUFF, BUT NOTHING ELSE. NOT EVEN A TRAFFIC TICKET.
SHIT. WELL, KEEP ME POSTED IF YOU FIND ANYTHING ELSE... YOU SEEN RAYMONDS AROUND TONIGHT?
YEAH, HE SHOULD BE AROUND SOMEWHERE. TRY THE SMOKING ROOM.
I found him at target practice, which was awkward, but at least it was a private enough place to have a personal conversation.
YOU SET ME UP, DIDN'T YOU?
WHAT?! IS THAT A JOKE?
YEAH, SOME JOKE. YOU SEND YOUR GIRLFRIEND TO ME TO FIND HER SISTER. THEN HER SISTER WINDS UP DEAD THE NEXT DAY WITH A SUITCASE FULL OF CASH.
GOD THOSE CRUZ COPS SURE KNOW HOW TO KEEP A LID ON THINGS.
GET TO THE PART WHERE I SET YOU UP.
YOU HAD TA KNOW MAGGIE WAS INTO SOMETHING FUCKED-UP. WHY DIDN'T YOU JUST TELL ME?!
I DIDN'T KNOW SHIT. ALEX JUST WANTED TO KEEP THE POLICE OUT OF IT, WHICH WAS FINE BY ME.
YOU DIDN'T KNOW ABOUT THE MONEY?
I WAS AS SURPRISED AS YOU. ALEX SAYS SHE DOESN'T KNOW WHERE IT CAME FROM EITHER.
SO WHATTA YOU FIGURE? WHAT HAPPENED TO THE GIRL?
I told him everything about the past two days, and that it seemed like maybe Maggie could have been blackmailing Luna for any number of reasons--
--but SOMETHING about that just didn't feel right.

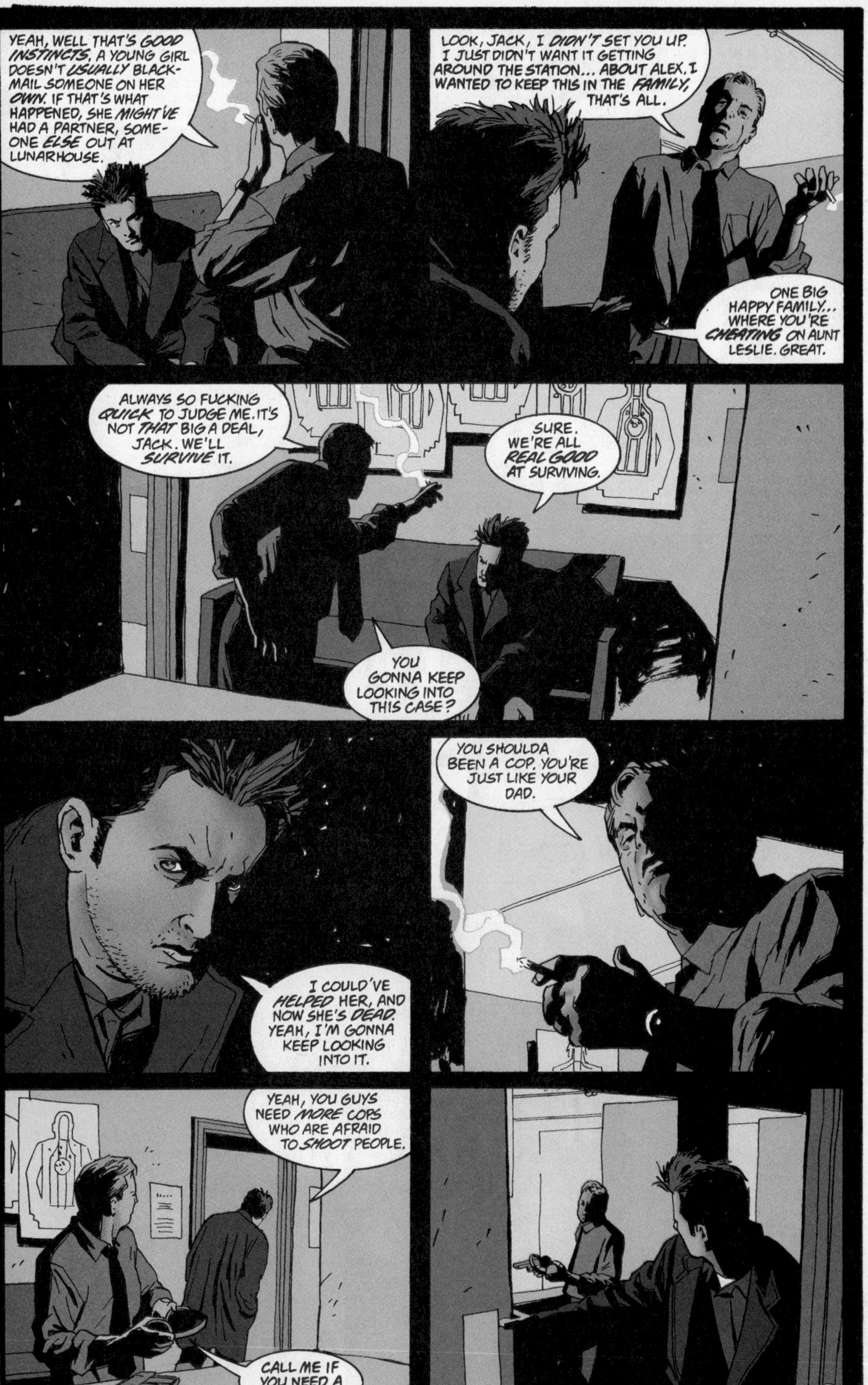
YEAH, WELL THAT'S GOOD INSTINCTS. A YOUNG GIRL DOESN'T USUALLY BLACKMAIL SOMEONE ON HER OWN. IF THAT'S WHAT HAPPENED, SHE MIGHT'VE HAD A PARTNER, SOMEONE ELSE OUT AT LUNARHOUSE.
LOOK, JACK, I DIDN'T SET YOU UP. I JUST DIDN'T WANT IT GETTING AROUND THE STATION... ABOUT ALEX. I WANTED TO KEEP THIS IN THE FAMILY, THAT'S ALL.
ONE BIG HAPPY FAMILY... WHERE YOU'RE CHEATING ON AUNT LESLIE. GREAT.
ALWAYS SO FUCKING QUICK TO JUDGE ME. IT'S NOT THAT BIG A DEAL, JACK. WE'LL SURVIVE IT.
SURE. WE'RE ALL REAL GOOD AT SURVIVING.
YOU GONNA KEEP LOOKING INTO THIS CASE?
I COULD'VE HELPED HER, AND NOW SHE'S DEAD. YEAH, I'M GONNA KEEP LOOKING INTO IT.
YOU SHOULDA BEEN A COP, YOU'RE JUST LIKE YOUR DAD.
YEAH, YOU GUYS NEED MORE COPS WHO ARE AFRAID TO SHOOT PEOPLE.
CALL ME IF YOU NEED A HEADS UP.

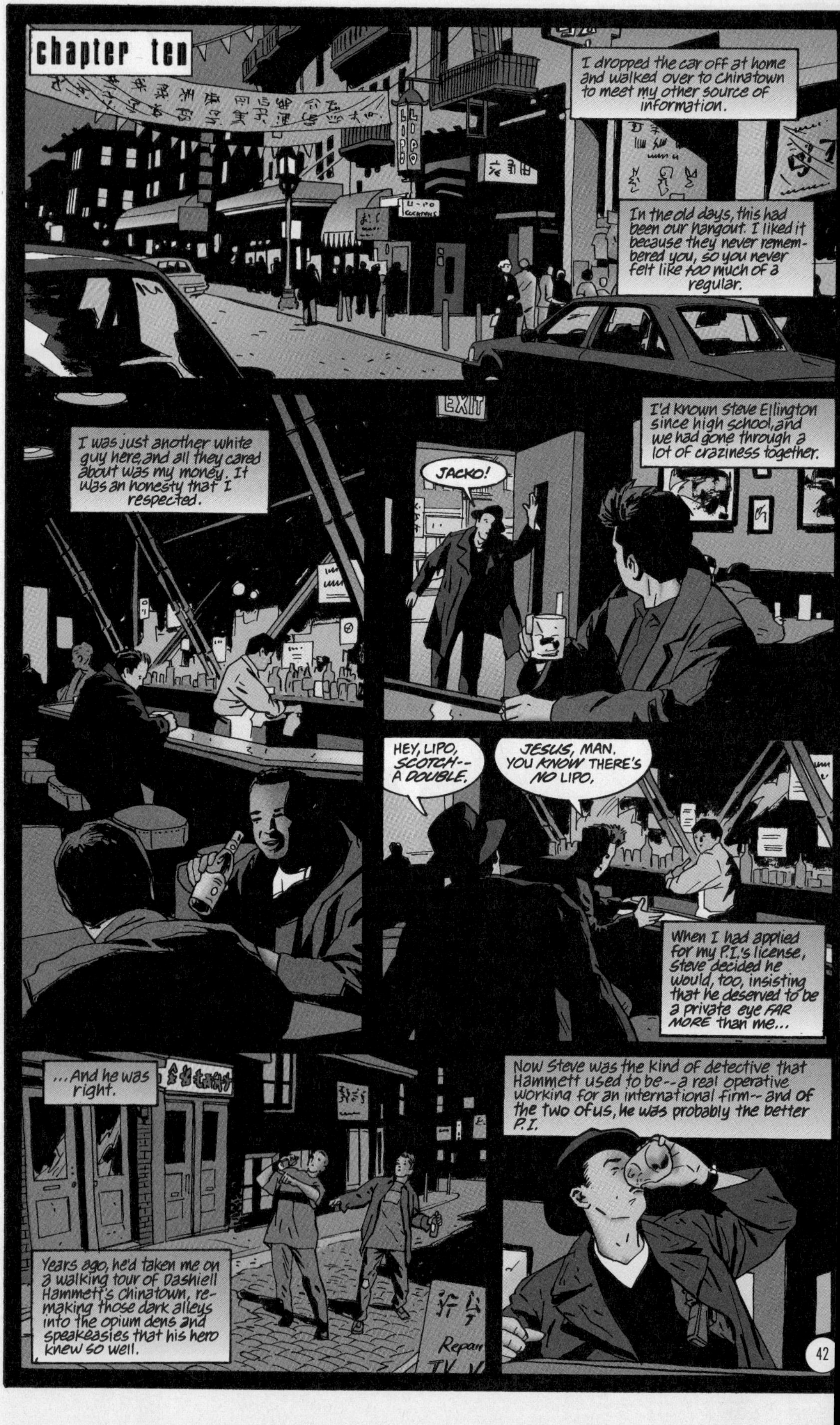
chapter ten
I dropped the car off at home and walked over to Chinatown to meet my other source of information.
In the old days, this had been our hangout. I liked it because they never remembered you, so you never felt like *too* much of a regular.
I was just another white guy here, and all they cared about was my money. It was an honesty that I respected.
I'd known Steve Ellington since high school, and we had gone through a lot of craziness together.
JACKO!
HEY, LIPO, SCOTCH-- A DOUBLE.
JESUS, MAN. YOU KNOW THERE'S NO LIPO.
When I had applied for my P.I.'s license, Steve decided he would, too, insisting that he deserved to be a private eye FAR MORE than me...
...And he was right.
Years ago, he'd taken me on a walking tour of Dashiell Hammett's Chinatown, remaking those dark alleys into the opium dens and speakeasies that his hero knew so well.
Now Steve was the kind of detective that Hammett used to be--a real operative working for an international firm--and of the two of us, he was probably the better P.I.
EXIT
Repair

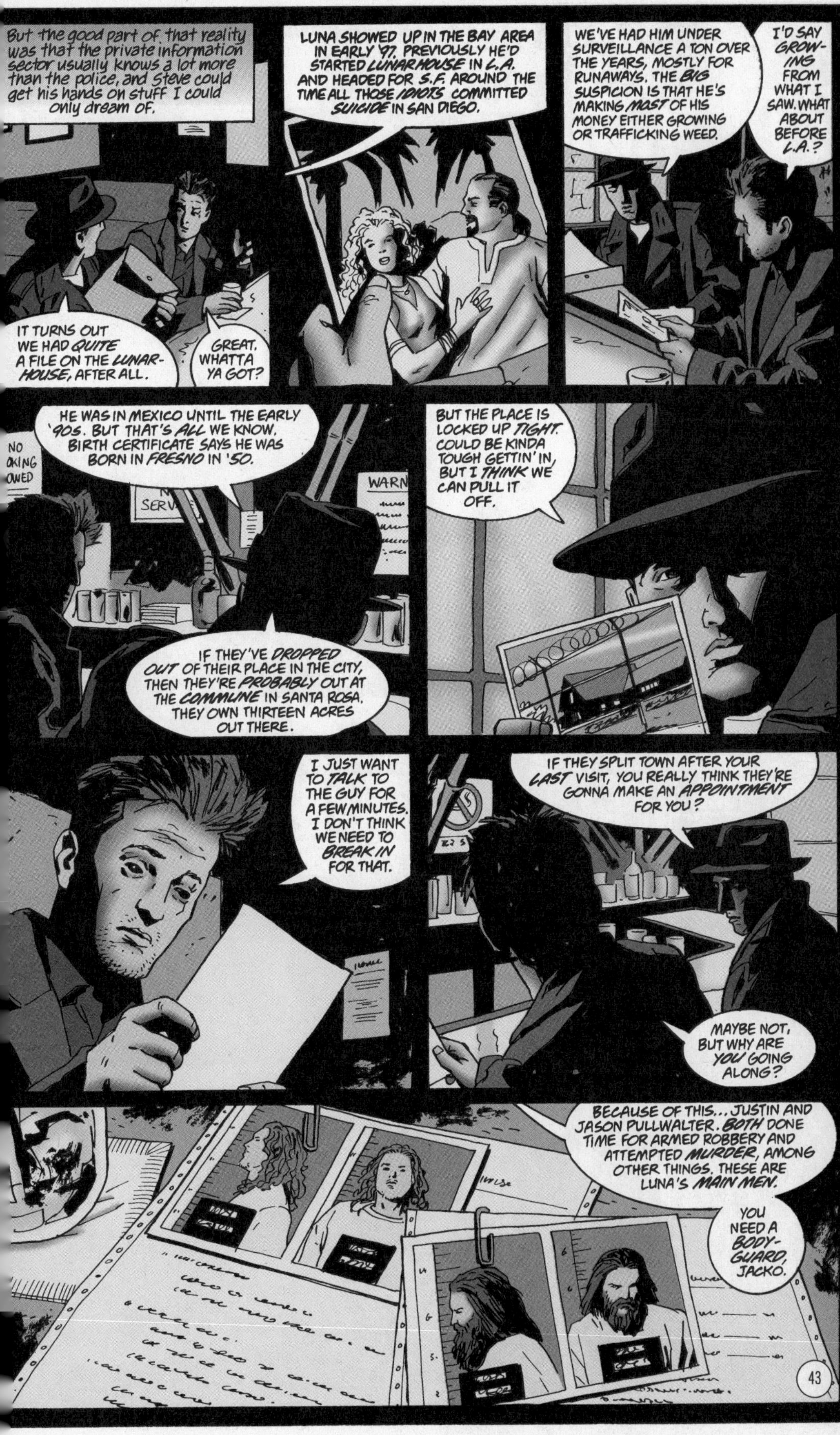
But the good part of that reality was that the private information sector usually knows a lot more than the police, and Steve could get his hands on stuff I could only dream of.
IT TURNS OUT WE HAD QUITE A FILE ON THE LUNAR-HOUSE, AFTER ALL.
GREAT. WHATTA YA GOT?
LUNA SHOWED UP IN THE BAY AREA IN EARLY '97. PREVIOUSLY HE'D STARTED LUNARHOUSE IN L.A. AND HEADED FOR S.F. AROUND THE TIME ALL THOSE IDIOTS COMMITTED SUICIDE IN SAN DIEGO.
WE'VE HAD HIM UNDER SURVEILLANCE A TON OVER THE YEARS, MOSTLY FOR RUNAWAYS. THE BIG SUSPICION IS THAT HE'S MAKING MOST OF HIS MONEY EITHER GROWING OR TRAFFICKING WEED.
I'D SAY GROWING FROM WHAT I SAW. WHAT ABOUT BEFORE L.A.?
HE WAS IN MEXICO UNTIL THE EARLY '90s. BUT THAT'S ALL WE KNOW. BIRTH CERTIFICATE SAYS HE WAS BORN IN FRESNO IN '50.
IF THEY'VE DROPPED OUT OF THEIR PLACE IN THE CITY, THEN THEY'RE PROBABLY OUT AT THE COMMUNE IN SANTA ROSA. THEY OWN THIRTEEN ACRES OUT THERE.
BUT THE PLACE IS LOCKED UP TIGHT. COULD BE KINDA TOUGH GETTIN' IN, BUT I THINK WE CAN PULL IT OFF.
I JUST WANT TO TALK TO THE GUY FOR A FEW MINUTES. I DON'T THINK WE NEED TO BREAK IN FOR THAT.
IF THEY SPLIT TOWN AFTER YOUR LAST VISIT, YOU REALLY THINK THEY'RE GONNA MAKE AN APPOINTMENT FOR YOU?
MAYBE NOT, BUT WHY ARE YOU GOING ALONG?
BECAUSE OF THIS... JUSTIN AND JASON PULLWALTER. BOTH DONE TIME FOR ARMED ROBBERY AND ATTEMPTED MURDER, AMONG OTHER THINGS. THESE ARE LUNA'S MAIN MEN.
YOU NEED A BODY-GUARD, JACKO.

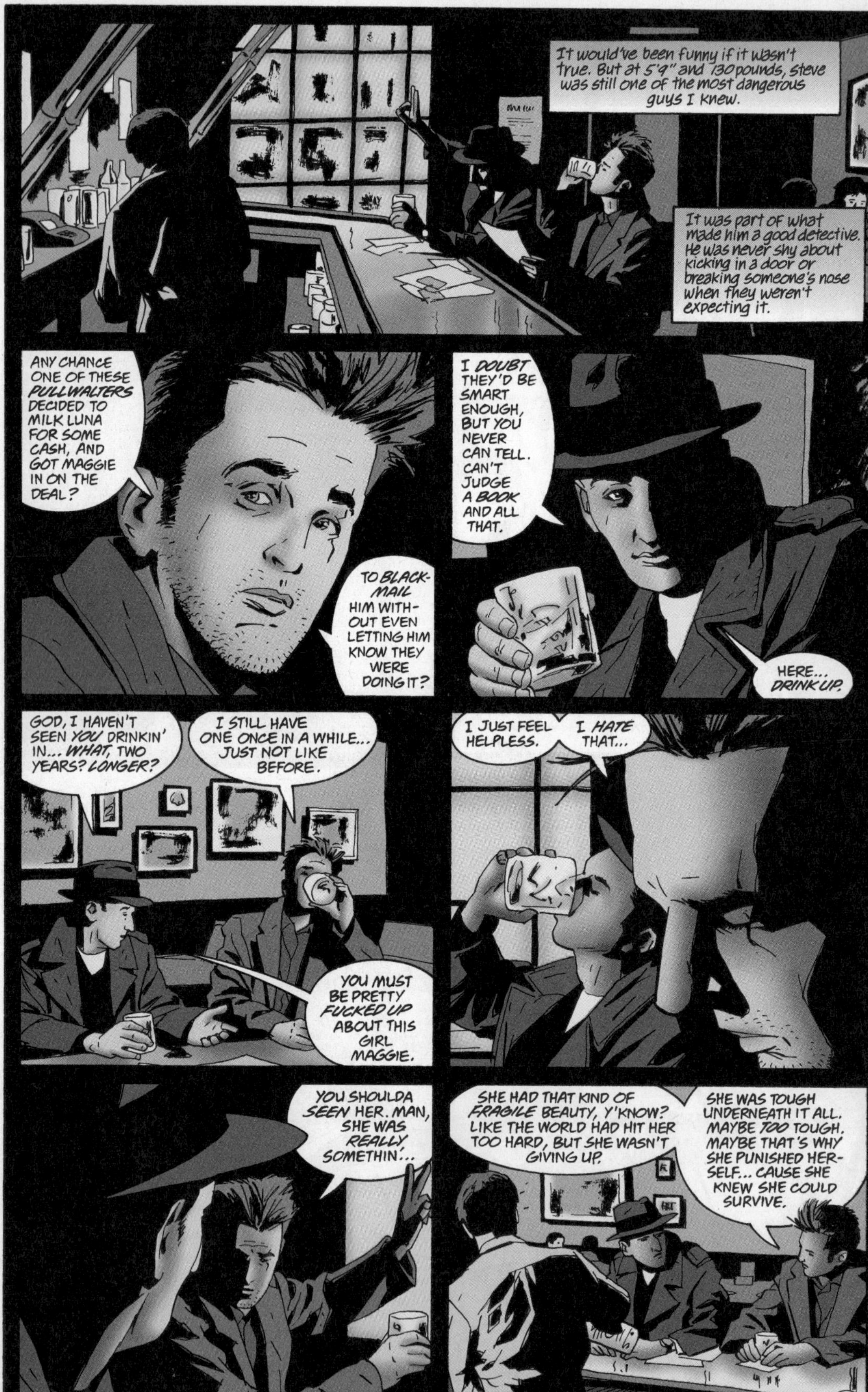

It would've been funny if it wasn't true. But at 5'9" and 130 pounds, Steve was still one of the most dangerous guys I knew.
It was part of what made him a good detective. He was never shy about kicking in a door or breaking someone's nose when they weren't expecting it.
ANY CHANCE ONE OF THESE PULLWALTERS DECIDED TO MILK LUNA FOR SOME CASH, AND GOT MAGGIE IN ON THE DEAL?
TO BLACKMAIL HIM WITHOUT EVEN LETTING HIM KNOW THEY WERE DOING IT?
I DOUBT THEY'D BE SMART ENOUGH, BUT YOU NEVER CAN TELL. CAN'T JUDGE A BOOK AND ALL THAT.
HERE... DRINK UP.
GOD, I HAVEN'T SEEN YOU DRINKIN' IN... WHAT, TWO YEARS? LONGER?
I STILL HAVE ONE ONCE IN A WHILE... JUST NOT LIKE BEFORE.
YOU MUST BE PRETTY FUCKED UP ABOUT THIS GIRL MAGGIE.
I JUST FEEL HELPLESS.
I HATE THAT...
YOU SHOULDA SEEN HER. MAN, SHE WAS REALLY SOMETHIN'...
SHE HAD THAT KIND OF FRAGILE BEAUTY, Y'KNOW? LIKE THE WORLD HAD HIT HER TOO HARD, BUT SHE WASN'T GIVING UP.
SHE WAS TOUGH UNDERNEATH IT ALL. MAYBE TOO TOUGH. MAYBE THAT'S WHY SHE PUNISHED HERSELF... CAUSE SHE KNEW SHE COULD SURVIVE.

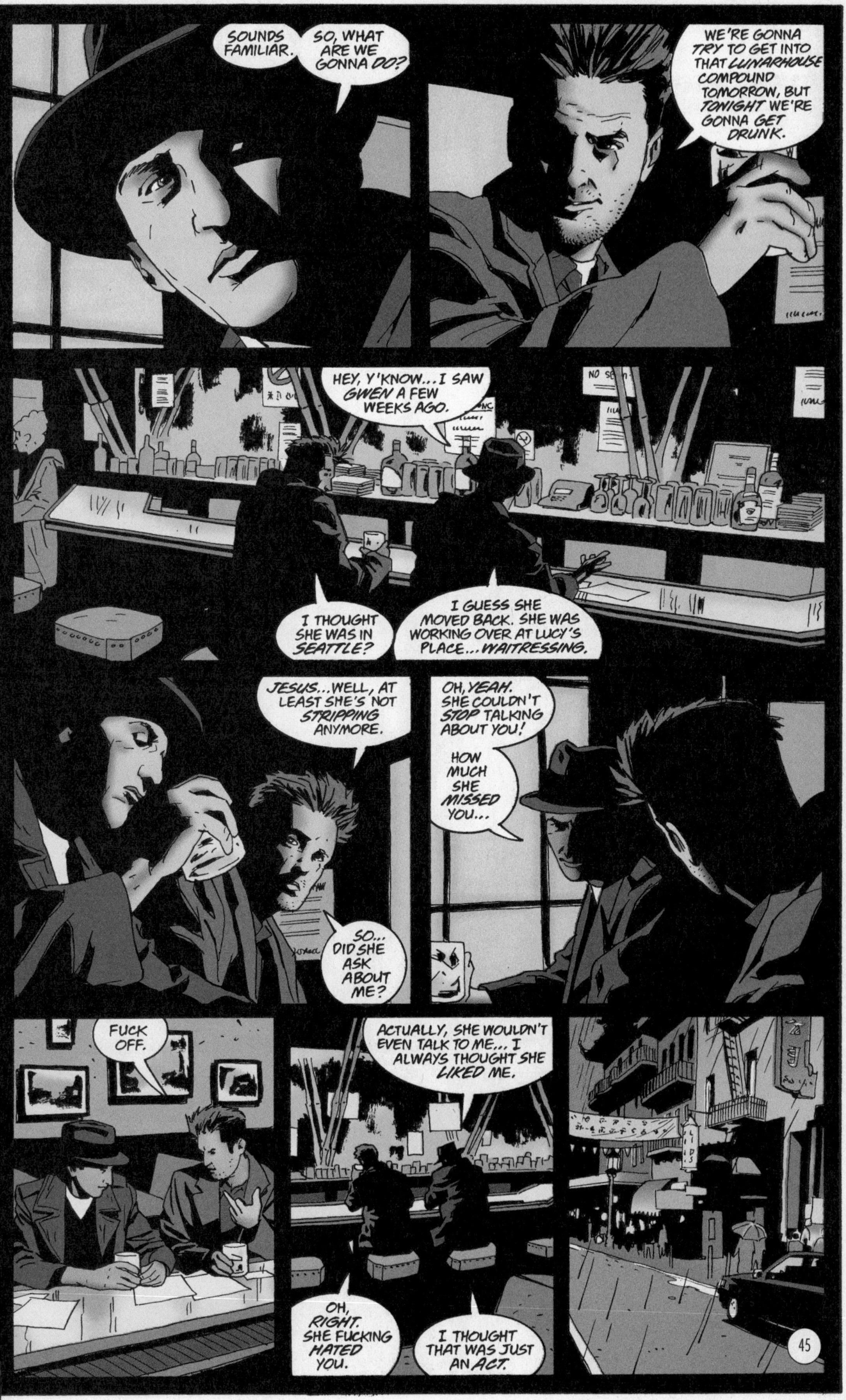
SOUNDS FAMILIAR.
SO, WHAT ARE WE GONNA DO?
WE'RE GONNA TRY TO GET INTO THAT LUNARHOUSE COMPOUND TOMORROW, BUT TONIGHT WE'RE GONNA GET DRUNK.
HEY, Y'KNOW... I SAW GWEN A FEW WEEKS AGO.
NO S
I THOUGHT SHE WAS IN SEATTLE?
I GUESS SHE MOVED BACK. SHE WAS WORKING OVER AT LUCY'S PLACE... WAITRESSING.
JESUS... WELL, AT LEAST SHE'S NOT STRIPPING ANYMORE.
OH, YEAH. SHE COULDN'T STOP TALKING ABOUT YOU!
HOW MUCH SHE MISSED YOU...
SO... DID SHE ASK ABOUT ME?
FUCK OFF.
ACTUALLY, SHE WOULDN'T EVEN TALK TO ME... I ALWAYS THOUGHT SHE LIKED ME.
OH, RIGHT. SHE FUCKING HATED YOU.
I THOUGHT THAT WAS JUST AN ACT.

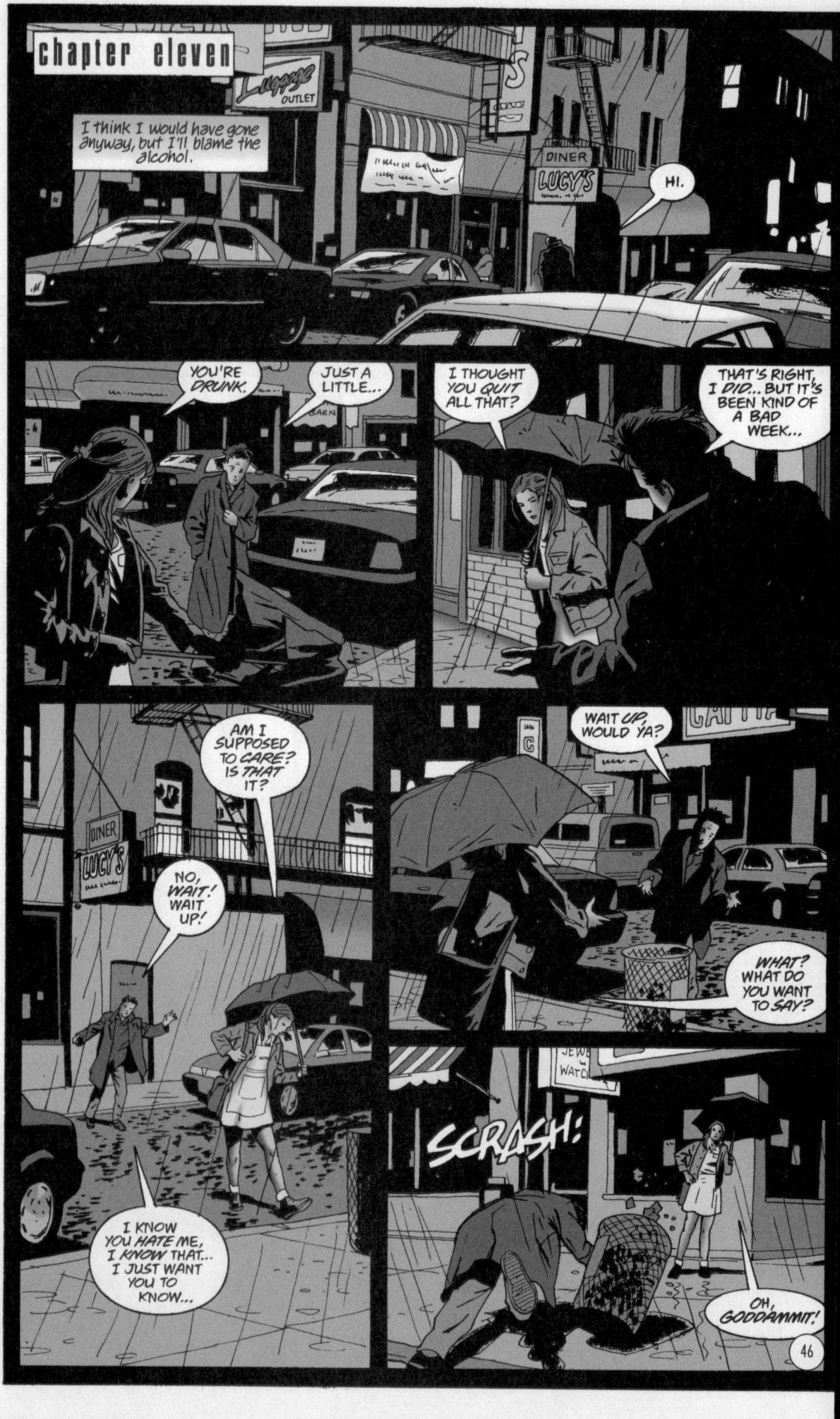
chapter eleven
Luggage OUTLET
I think I would have gone anyway, but I'll blame the alcohol.
DINER
LUCY'S
HI.
YOU'RE DRUNK.
JUST A LITTLE...
I THOUGHT YOU QUIT ALL THAT?
THAT'S RIGHT, I DID... BUT IT'S BEEN KIND OF A BAD WEEK...
AM I SUPPOSED TO CARE? IS THAT IT?
DINER
LUCY'S
NO, WAIT! WAIT UP!
I KNOW YOU HATE ME, I KNOW THAT... I JUST WANT YOU TO KNOW...
WAIT UP, WOULD YA?
WHAT? WHAT DO YOU WANT TO SAY?
SCRASH!
OH, GODDAMMIT!

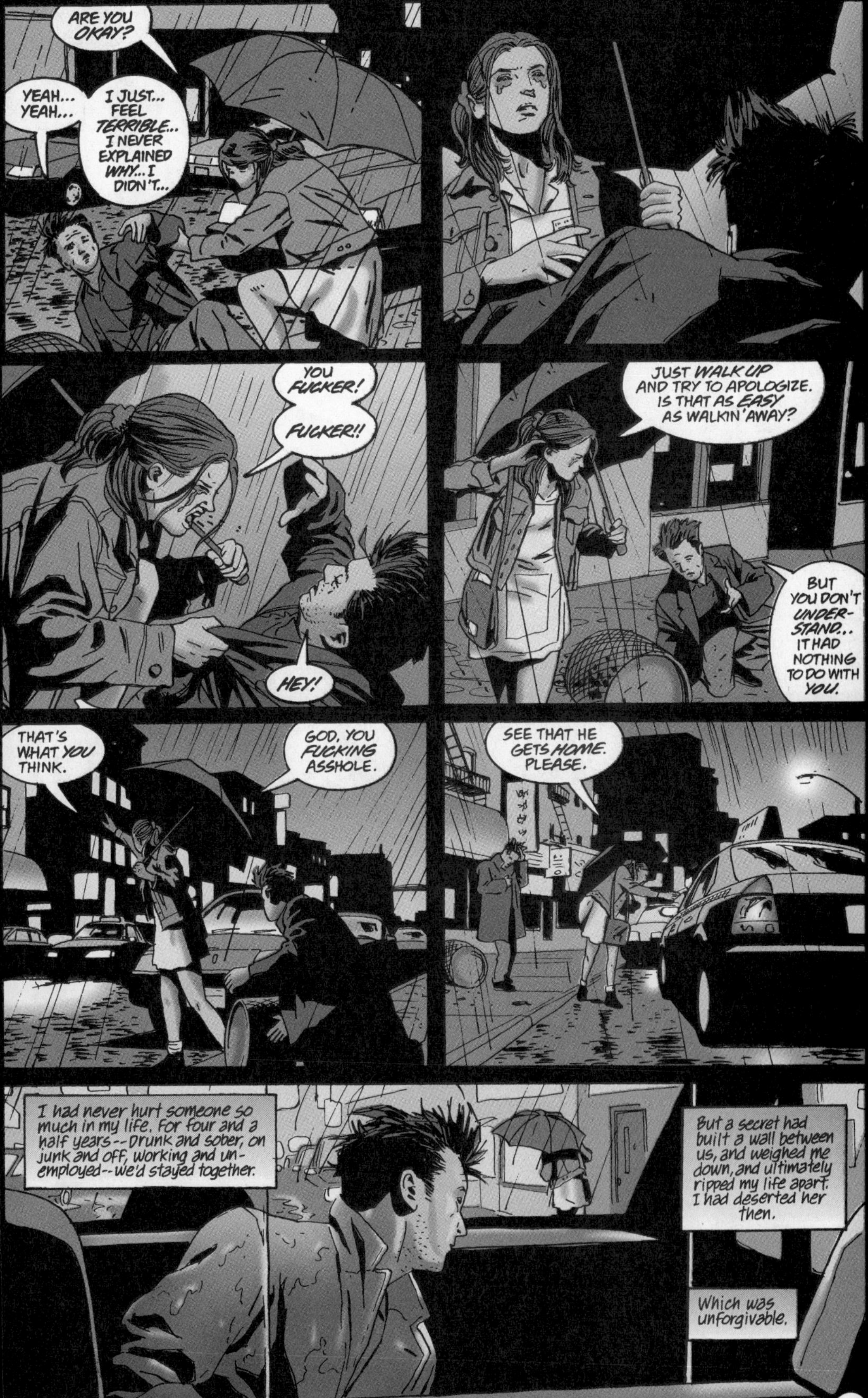

ARE YOU OKAY?
YEAH... YEAH...
I JUST... FEEL TERRIBLE... I NEVER EXPLAINED WHY... I DIDN'T...
YOU FUCKER!
FUCKER!!
HEY!
JUST WALK UP AND TRY TO APOLOGIZE. IS THAT AS EASY AS WALKIN' AWAY?
BUT YOU DON'T UNDER-STAND... IT HAD NOTHING TO DO WITH YOU.
THAT'S WHAT YOU THINK.
GOD, YOU FUCKING ASSHOLE.
SEE THAT HE GETS HOME. PLEASE.
I had never hurt someone so much in my life. For four and a half years--Drunk and sober, on junk and off, working and un-employed--we'd stayed together.
But a secret had built a wall between us, and weighed me down, and ultimately ripped my life apart. I had deserted her then.
Which was unforgivable.

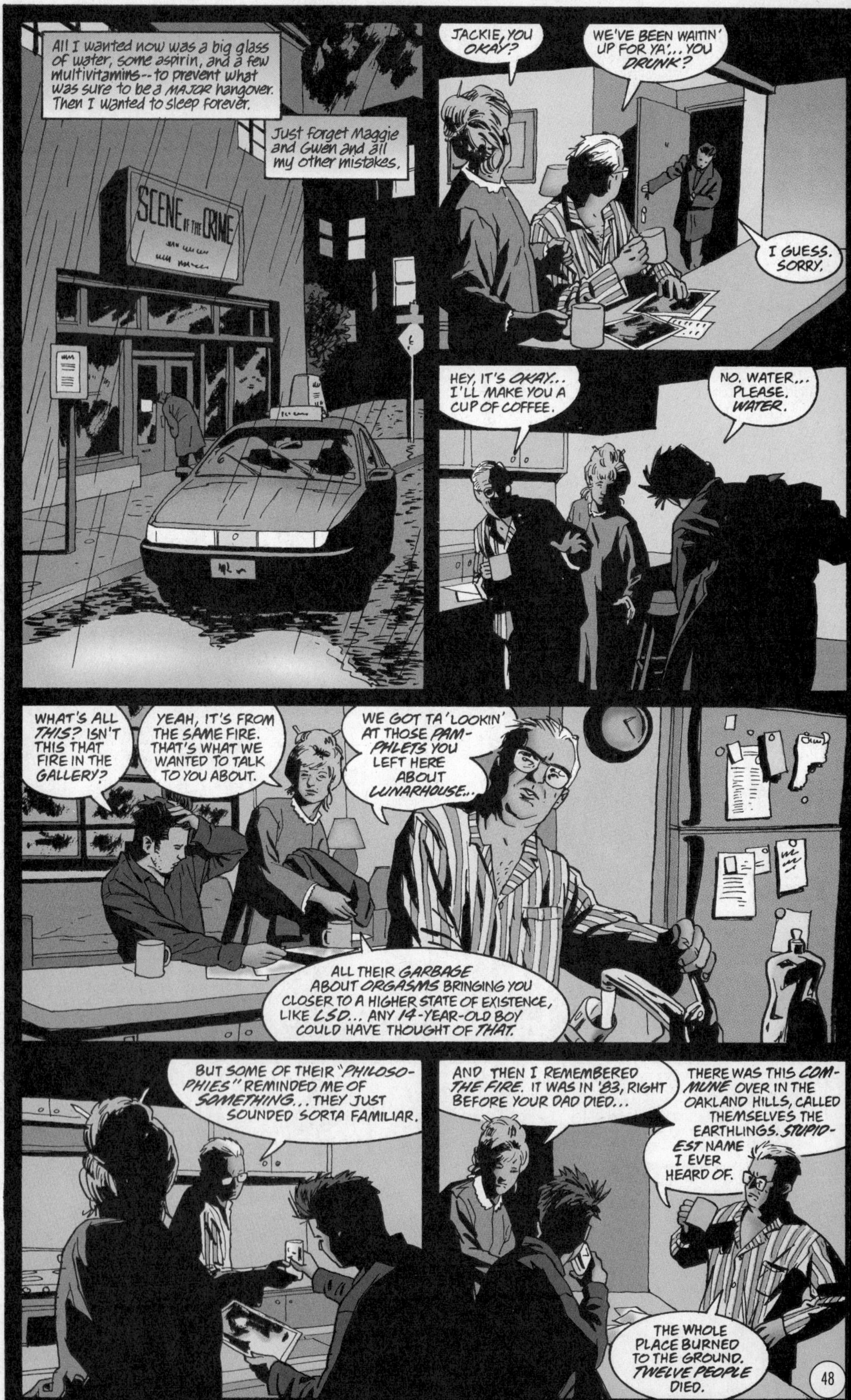

All I wanted now was a big glass of water, some aspirin, and a few multivitamins--to prevent what was sure to be a MAJOR hangover. Then I wanted to sleep forever.
Just forget Maggie and Gwen and all my other mistakes.
SCENE OF THE CRIME
JACKIE, YOU OKAY?
WE'VE BEEN WAITIN' UP FOR YA'... YOU DRUNK?
I GUESS. SORRY.
HEY, IT'S OKAY... I'LL MAKE YOU A CUP OF COFFEE.
NO. WATER... PLEASE. WATER.
WHAT'S ALL THIS? ISN'T THIS THAT FIRE IN THE GALLERY?
YEAH, IT'S FROM THE SAME FIRE. THAT'S WHAT WE WANTED TO TALK TO YOU ABOUT.
WE GOT TA 'LOOKIN' AT THOSE PAMPHLETS YOU LEFT HERE ABOUT LUNARHOUSE...
ALL THEIR GARBAGE ABOUT ORGASMS BRINGING YOU CLOSER TO A HIGHER STATE OF EXISTENCE, LIKE LSD... ANY 14-YEAR-OLD BOY COULD HAVE THOUGHT OF THAT.
BUT SOME OF THEIR "PHILOSOPHIES" REMINDED ME OF SOMETHING... THEY JUST SOUNDED SORTA FAMILIAR.
AND THEN I REMEMBERED THE FIRE. IT WAS IN '83, RIGHT BEFORE YOUR DAD DIED...
THERE WAS THIS COMMUNE OVER IN THE OAKLAND HILLS, CALLED THEMSELVES THE EARTHLINGS. STUPIDEST NAME I EVER HEARD OF.
THE WHOLE PLACE BURNED TO THE GROUND. TWELVE PEOPLE DIED.

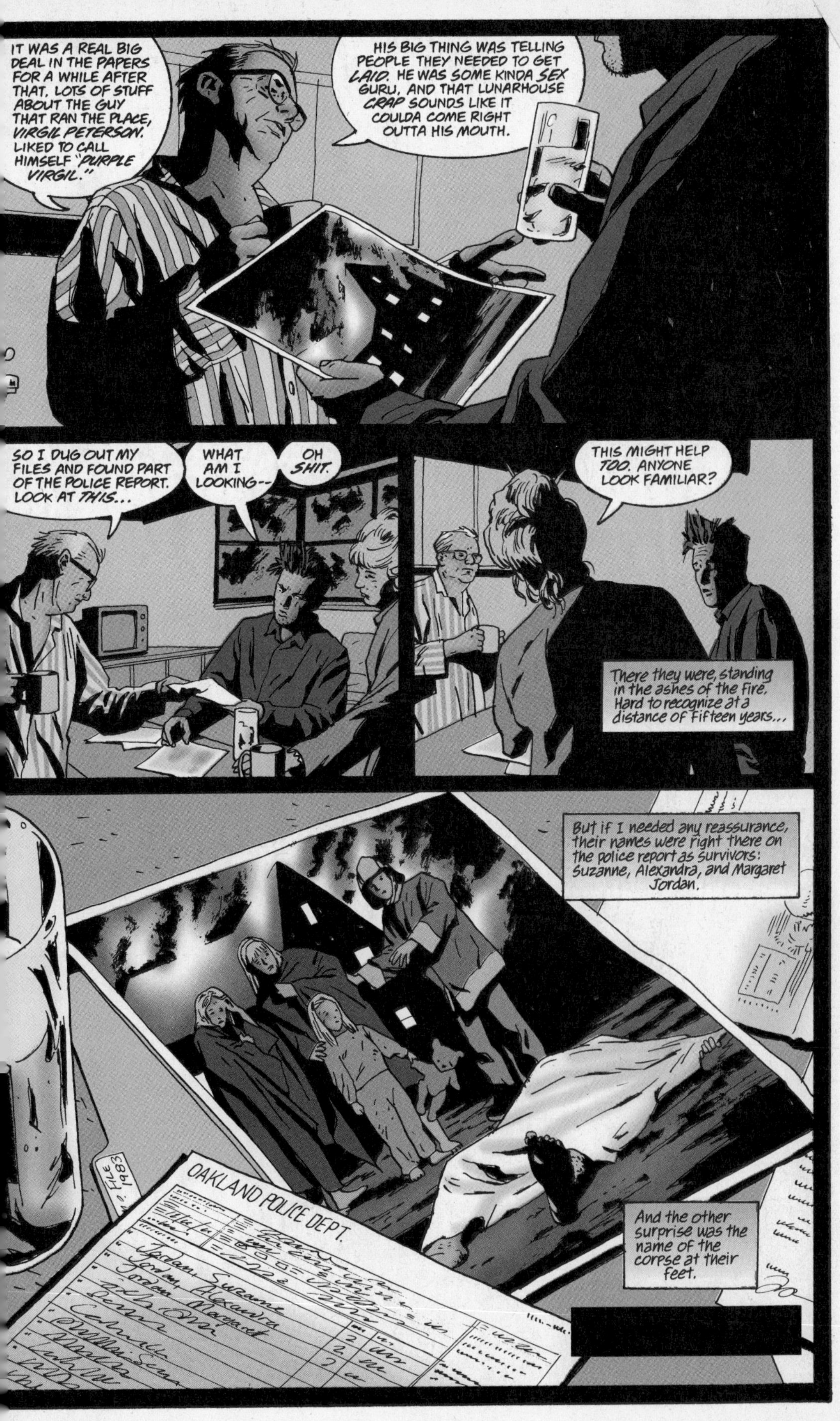
IT WAS A REAL BIG DEAL IN THE PAPERS FOR A WHILE AFTER THAT. LOTS OF STUFF ABOUT THE GUY THAT RAN THE PLACE, VIRGIL PETERSON. LIKED TO CALL HIMSELF "PURPLE VIRGIL."
HIS BIG THING WAS TELLING PEOPLE THEY NEEDED TO GET LAID. HE WAS SOME KINDA SEX GURU, AND THAT LUNARHOUSE CRAP SOUNDS LIKE IT COULDA COME RIGHT OUTTA HIS MOUTH.
SO I DUG OUT MY FILES AND FOUND PART OF THE POLICE REPORT. LOOK AT THIS...
WHAT AM I LOOKING--
OH SHIT.
THIS MIGHT HELP TOO. ANYONE LOOK FAMILIAR?
There they were, standing in the ashes of the fire. Hard to recognize at a distance of fifteen years...
But if I needed any reassurance, their names were right there on the police report as survivors: Suzanne, Alexandra, and Margaret Jordan.
FILE 1983
OAKLAND POLICE DEPT.
And the other surprise was the name of the corpse at their feet.

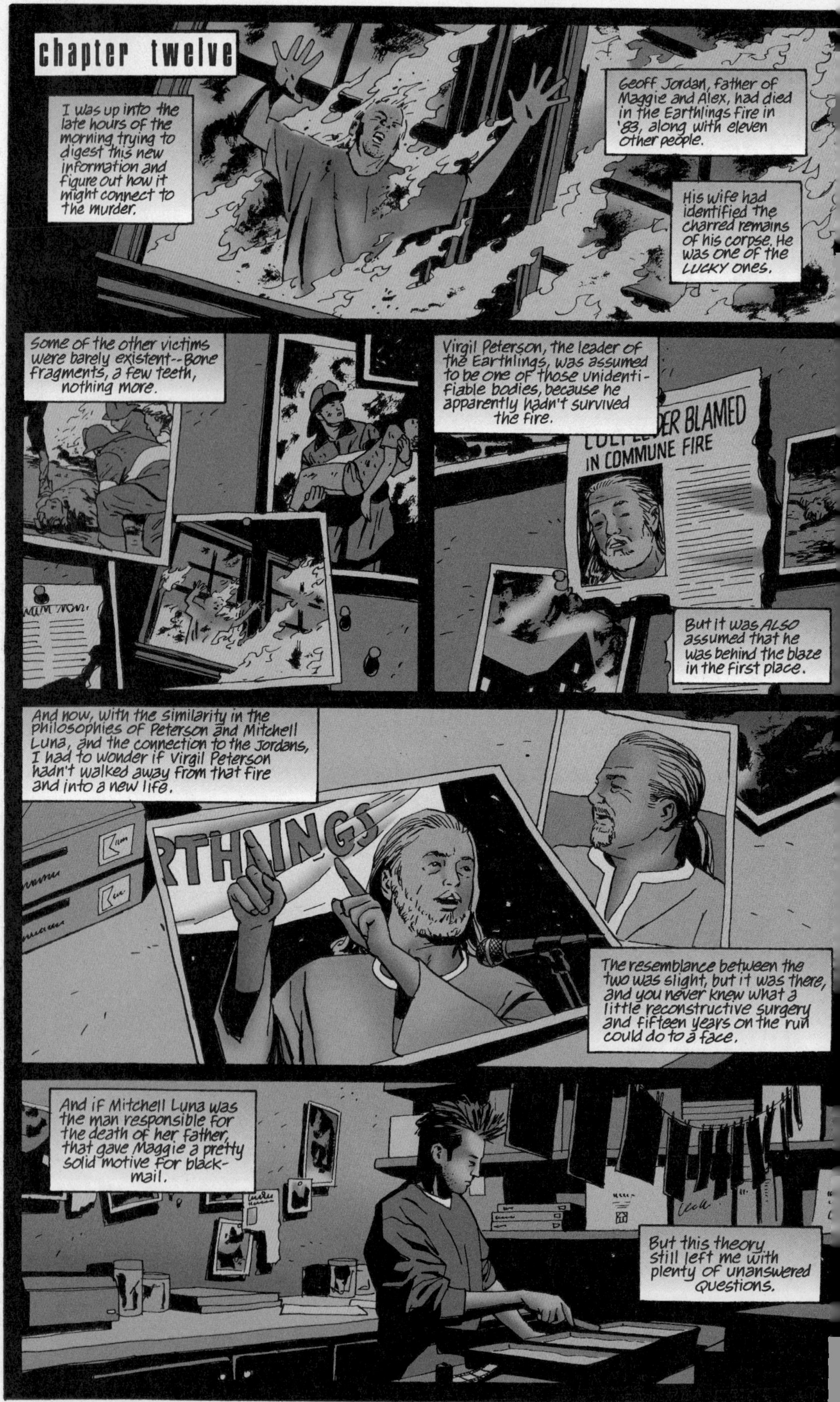
chapter twelve
I was up into the late hours of the morning trying to digest this new information and figure out how it might connect to the murder.
Geoff Jordan, father of Maggie and Alex, had died in the Earthlings fire in '83, along with eleven other people.
His wife had identified the charred remains of his corpse. He was one of the LUCKY ones.
Some of the other victims were barely existent--Bone fragments, a few teeth, nothing more.
Virgil Peterson, the leader of the Earthlings, was assumed to be one of those unidentifiable bodies, because he apparently hadn't survived the fire.
DER BLAMED
IN COMMUNE FIRE
But it was ALSO assumed that he was behind the blaze in the first place.
And now, with the similarity in the philosophies of Peterson and Mitchell Luna, and the connection to the Jordans, I had to wonder if Virgil Peterson hadn't walked away from that fire and into a new life.
RTHLINGS
The resemblance between the two was slight, but it was there, and you never knew what a little reconstructive surgery and fifteen years on the run could do to a face.
And if Mitchell Luna was the man responsible for the death of her father, that gave Maggie a pretty solid motive for blackmail.
But this theory still left me with plenty of unanswered questions.

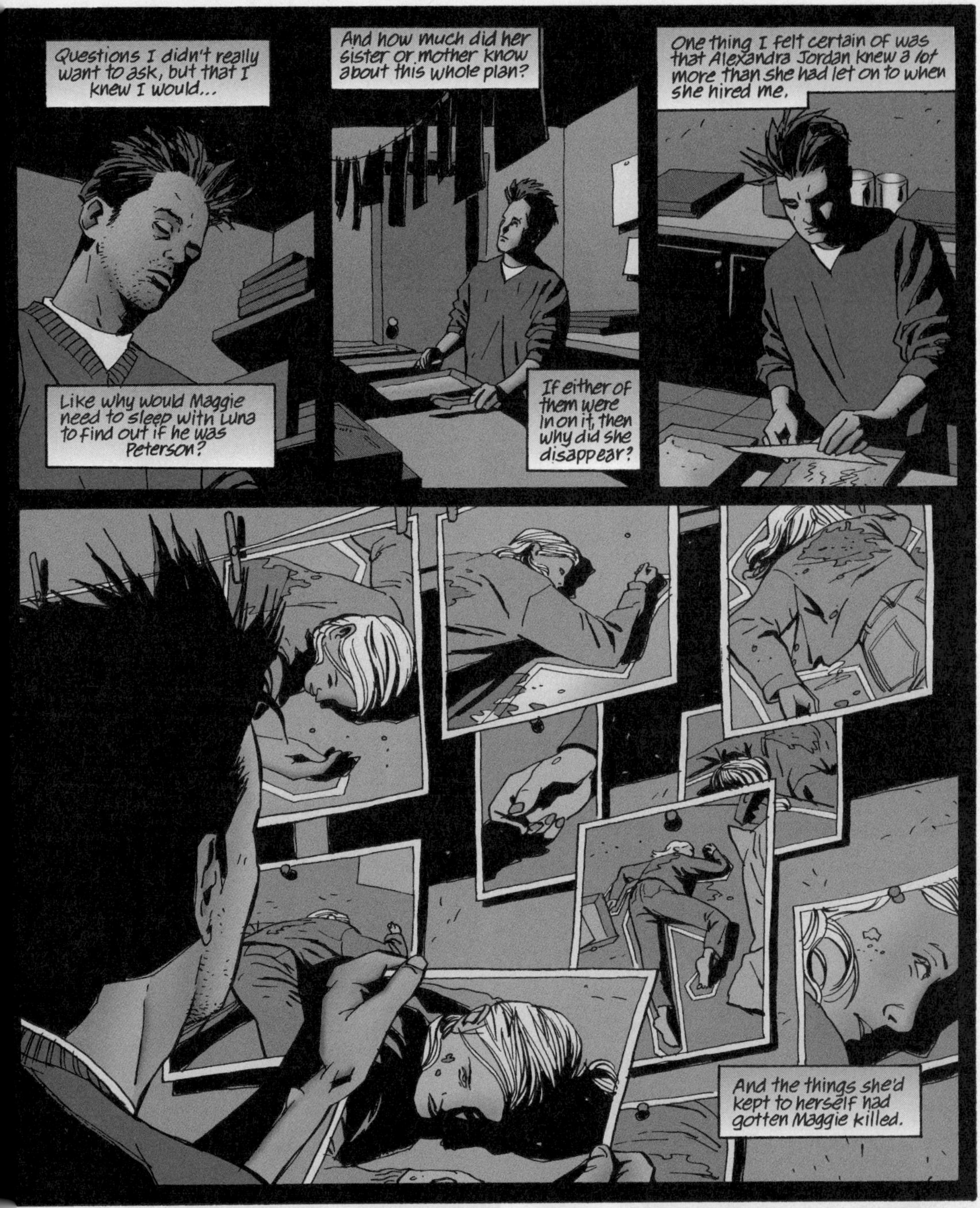

Questions I didn't really want to ask, but that I knew I would...
Like why would Maggie need to sleep with Luna to find out if he was Peterson?
And how much did her sister or mother know about this whole plan?
If either of them were in on it, then why did she disappear?
One thing I felt certain of was that Alexandra Jordan knew a lot more than she had let on to when she hired me.
And the things she'd kept to herself had gotten Maggie killed.

A LITTLE PIECE OF GOODNIGHT

part three of four

ED BRUBAKER writer MICHAEL LARK pencils SEAN PHILLIPS inks

JOHN COSTANZA letters JAMES SINCLAIR colors JENNIFER LEE asst. editor SHELLY ROEBERG editor

SCENE OF THE CRIME created by BRUBAKER and LARK

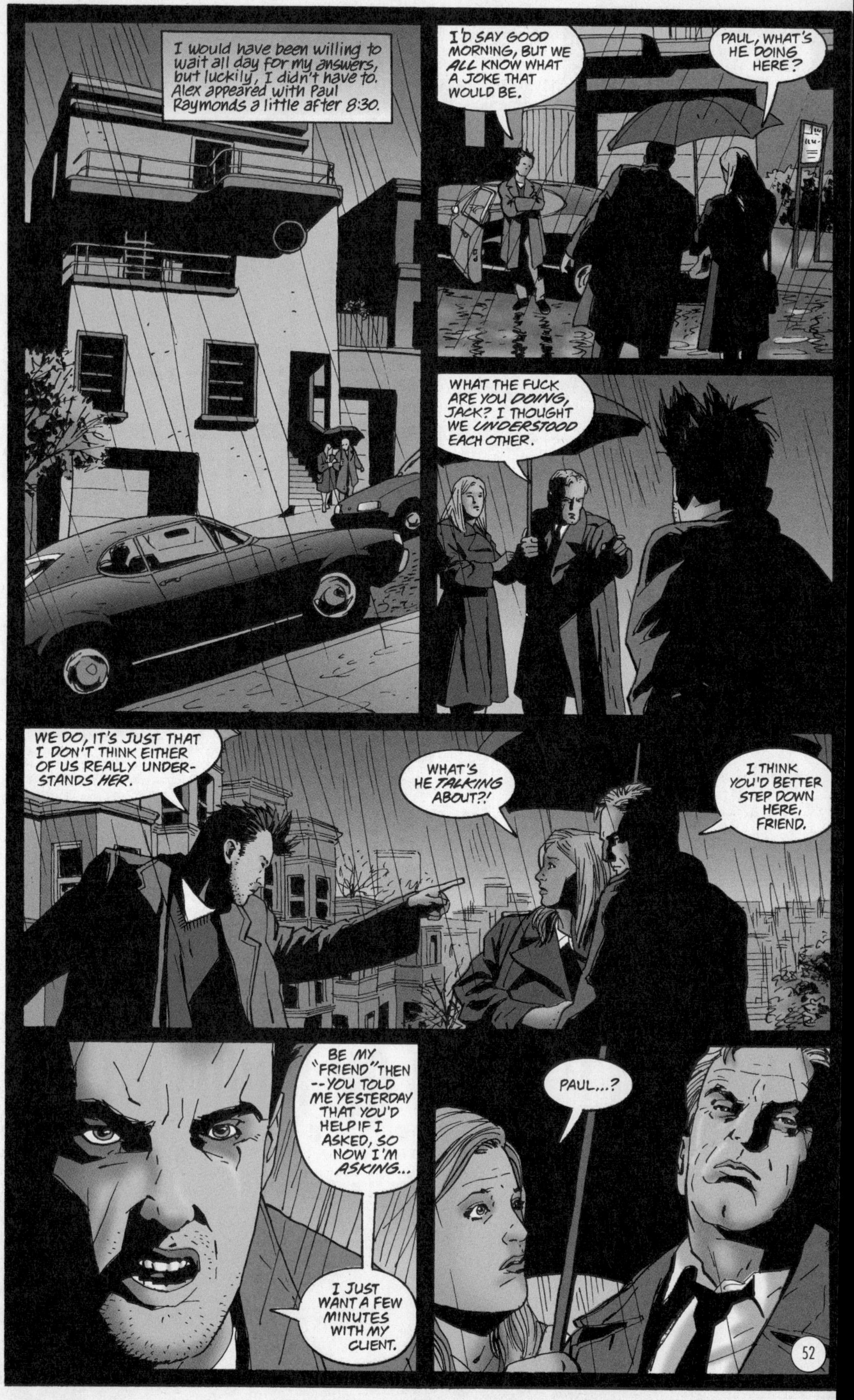
I would have been willing to wait all day for my answers, but luckily, I didn't have to. Alex appeared with Paul Raymonds a little after 8:30.
I'D SAY GOOD MORNING, BUT WE ALL KNOW WHAT A JOKE THAT WOULD BE.
PAUL, WHAT'S HE DOING HERE?
WHAT THE FUCK ARE YOU DOING, JACK? I THOUGHT WE UNDERSTOOD EACH OTHER.
WE DO, IT'S JUST THAT I DON'T THINK EITHER OF US REALLY UNDER-STANDS HER.
WHAT'S HE TALKING ABOUT?!
I THINK YOU'D BETTER STEP DOWN HERE, FRIEND.
BE MY "FRIEND" THEN --YOU TOLD ME YESTERDAY THAT YOU'D HELP IF I ASKED, SO NOW I'M ASKING...
I JUST WANT A FEW MINUTES WITH MY CLIENT.
PAUL...?

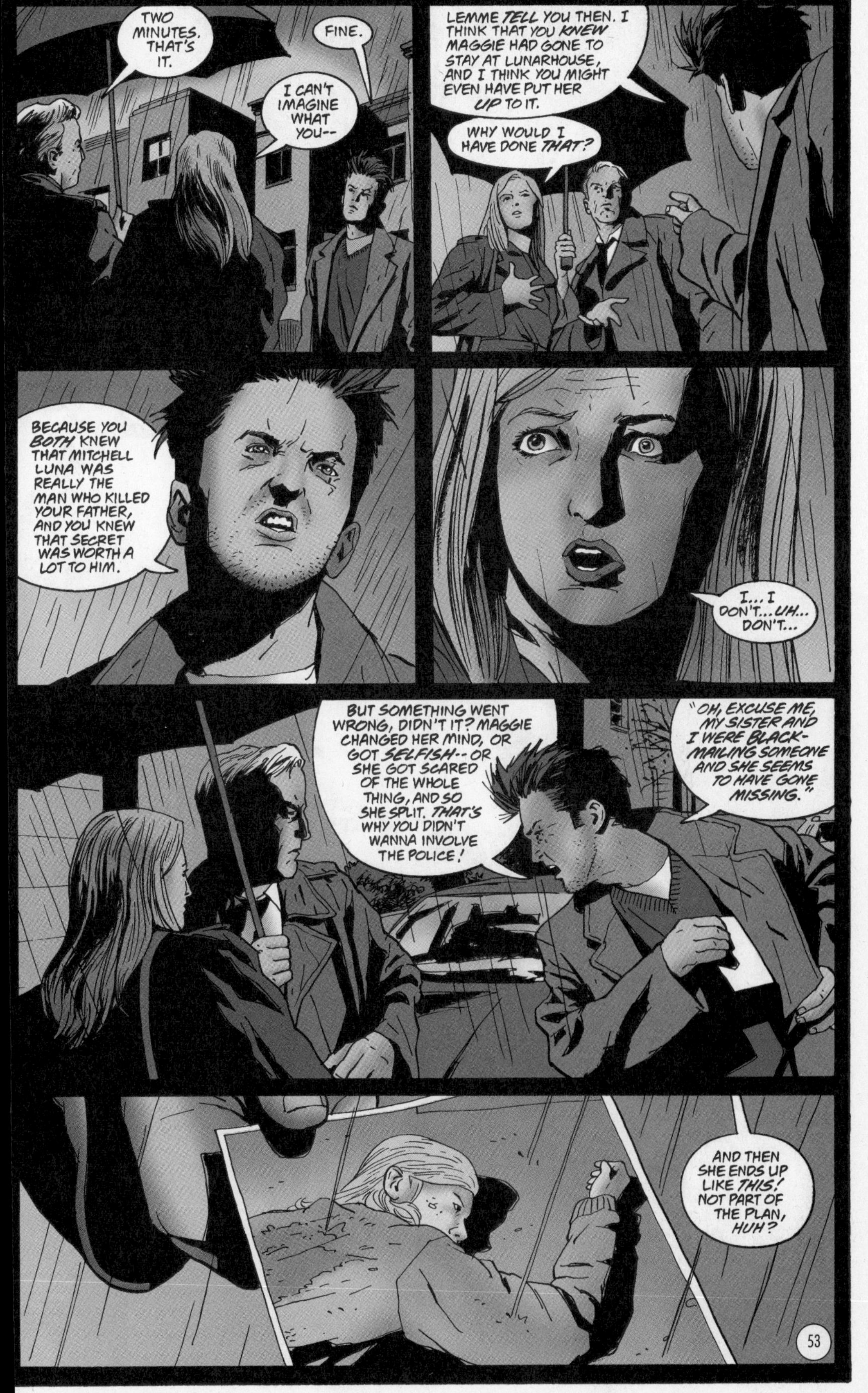

TWO MINUTES. THAT'S IT.
FINE.
I CAN'T IMAGINE WHAT YOU--
LEMME TELL YOU THEN. I THINK THAT YOU KNEW MAGGIE HAD GONE TO STAY AT LUNARHOUSE, AND I THINK YOU MIGHT EVEN HAVE PUT HER UP TO IT.
WHY WOULD I HAVE DONE THAT?
BECAUSE YOU BOTH KNEW THAT MITCHELL LUNA WAS REALLY THE MAN WHO KILLED YOUR FATHER, AND YOU KNEW THAT SECRET WAS WORTH A LOT TO HIM.
I... I DON'T... UH... DON'T...
BUT SOMETHING WENT WRONG, DIDN'T IT? MAGGIE CHANGED HER MIND, OR GOT SELFISH-- OR SHE GOT SCARED OF THE WHOLE THING, AND SO SHE SPLIT. THAT'S WHY YOU DIDN'T WANNA INVOLVE THE POLICE!
"OH, EXCUSE ME, MY SISTER AND I WERE BLACK-MAILING SOMEONE AND SHE SEEMS TO HAVE GONE MISSING."
AND THEN SHE ENDS UP LIKE THIS! NOT PART OF THE PLAN, HUH?

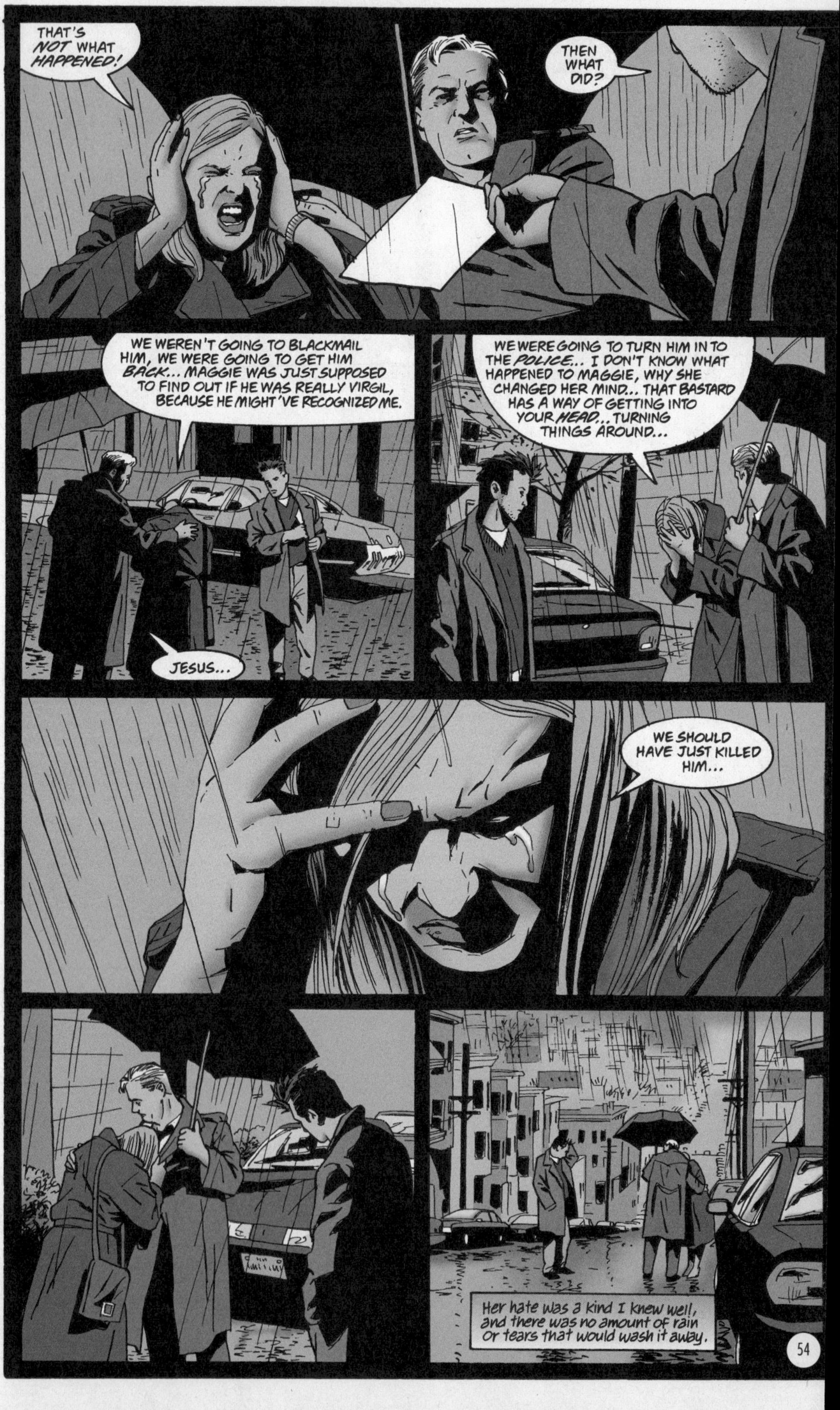
THAT'S NOT WHAT HAPPENED!
THEN WHAT DID?
WE WEREN'T GOING TO BLACKMAIL HIM, WE WERE GOING TO GET HIM BACK... MAGGIE WAS JUST SUPPOSED TO FIND OUT IF HE WAS REALLY VIRGIL, BECAUSE HE MIGHT'VE RECOGNIZED ME.
JESUS...
WE WERE GOING TO TURN HIM IN TO THE POLICE... I DON'T KNOW WHAT HAPPENED TO MAGGIE, WHY SHE CHANGED HER MIND... THAT BASTARD HAS A WAY OF GETTING INTO YOUR HEAD... TURNING THINGS AROUND...
WE SHOULD HAVE JUST KILLED HIM...
Her hate was a kind I knew well, and there was no amount of rain or tears that would wash it away.

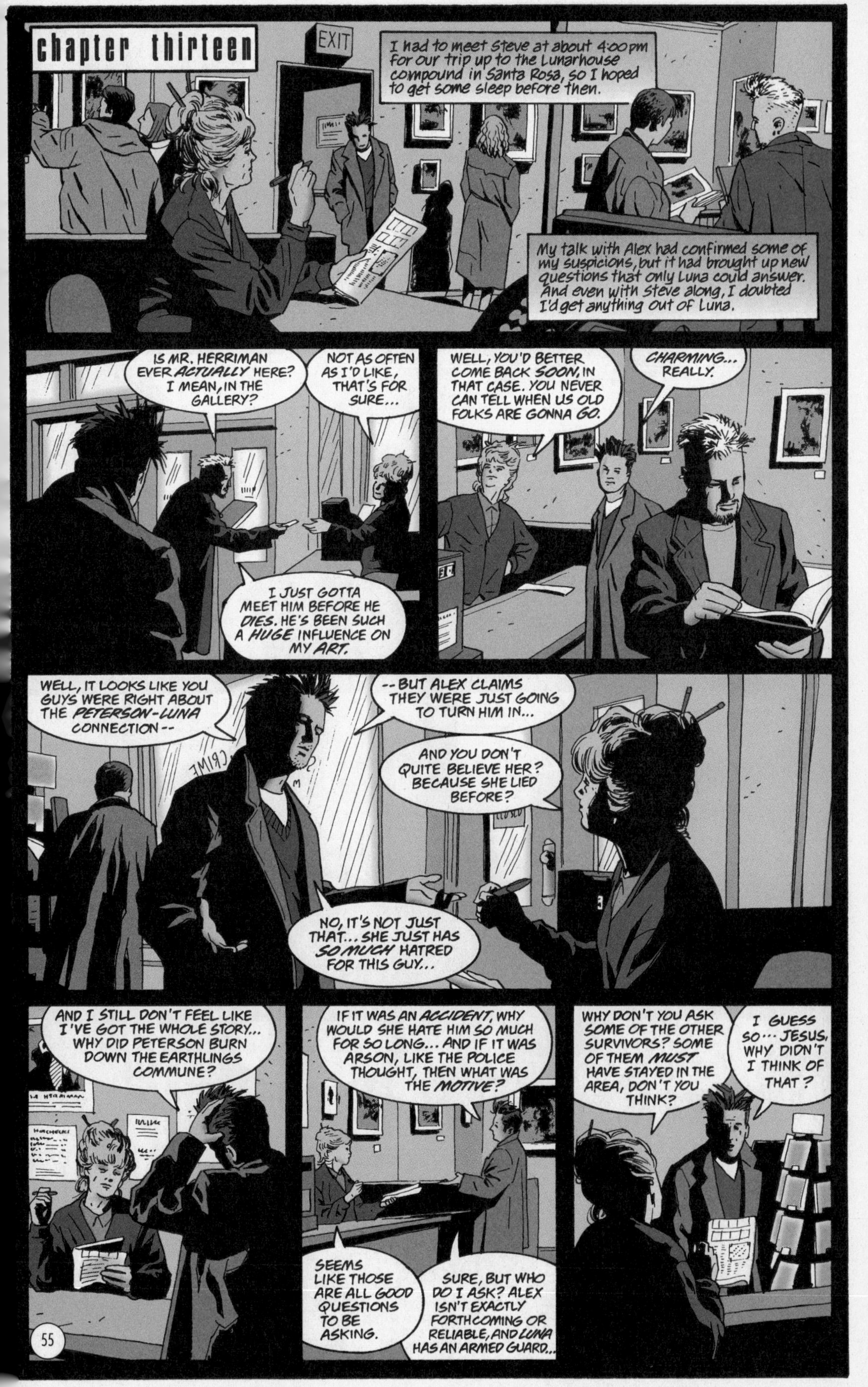

chapter thirteen
EXIT
I had to meet Steve at about 4:00 pm for our trip up to the Lunarhouse compound in Santa Rosa, so I hoped to get some sleep before then.
My talk with Alex had confirmed some of my suspicions, but it had brought up new questions that only Luna could answer. And even with Steve along, I doubted I'd get anything out of Luna.
IS MR. HERRIMAN EVER ACTUALLY HERE? I MEAN, IN THE GALLERY?
NOT AS OFTEN AS I'D LIKE, THAT'S FOR SURE...
I JUST GOTTA MEET HIM BEFORE HE DIES. HE'S BEEN SUCH A HUGE INFLUENCE ON MY ART.
WELL, YOU'D BETTER COME BACK SOON, IN THAT CASE. YOU NEVER CAN TELL WHEN US OLD FOLKS ARE GONNA GO.
CHARMING... REALLY.
WELL, IT LOOKS LIKE YOU GUYS WERE RIGHT ABOUT THE PETERSON-LUNA CONNECTION--
--BUT ALEX CLAIMS THEY WERE JUST GOING TO TURN HIM IN...
AND YOU DON'T QUITE BELIEVE HER? BECAUSE SHE LIED BEFORE?
NO, IT'S NOT JUST THAT... SHE JUST HAS SO MUCH HATRED FOR THIS GUY...
AND I STILL DON'T FEEL LIKE I'VE GOT THE WHOLE STORY... WHY DID PETERSON BURN DOWN THE EARTHLINGS COMMUNE?
IF IT WAS AN ACCIDENT, WHY WOULD SHE HATE HIM SO MUCH FOR SO LONG... AND IF IT WAS ARSON, LIKE THE POLICE THOUGHT, THEN WHAT WAS THE MOTIVE?
SEEMS LIKE THOSE ARE ALL GOOD QUESTIONS TO BE ASKING.
SURE, BUT WHO DO I ASK? ALEX ISN'T EXACTLY FORTHCOMING OR RELIABLE, AND LUNA HAS AN ARMED GUARD...
WHY DON'T YOU ASK SOME OF THE OTHER SURVIVORS? SOME OF THEM MUST HAVE STAYED IN THE AREA, DON'T YOU THINK?
I GUESS SO... JESUS, WHY DIDN'T I THINK OF THAT?

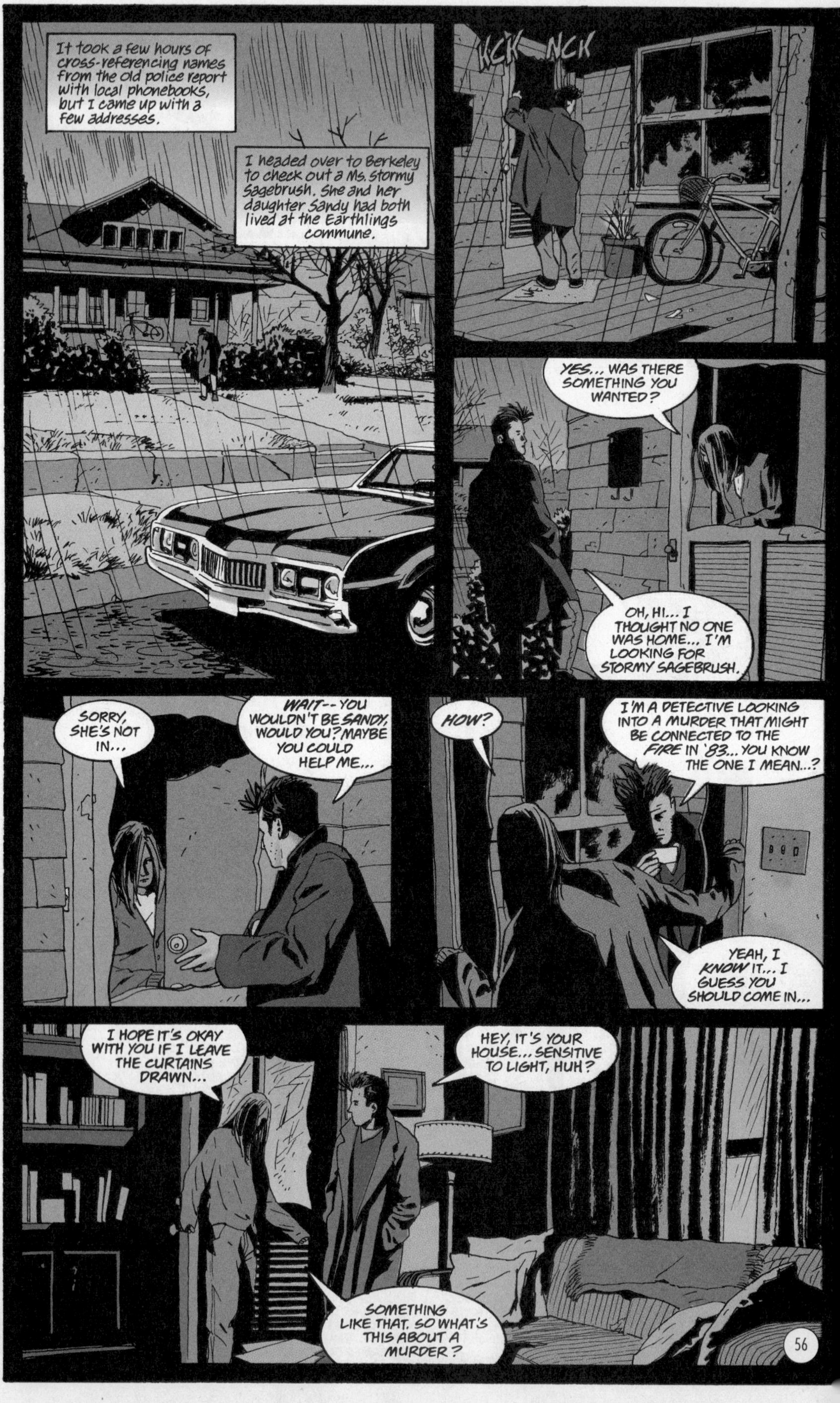

It took a few hours of cross-referencing names from the old police report with local phonebooks, but I came up with a few addresses.
I headed over to Berkeley to check out a Ms. Stormy Sagebrush. She and her daughter Sandy had both lived at the Earthlings commune.
KNCK KNCK
YES... WAS THERE SOMETHING YOU WANTED?
OH, HI... I THOUGHT NO ONE WAS HOME... I'M LOOKING FOR STORMY SAGEBRUSH.
SORRY, SHE'S NOT IN...
WAIT-- YOU WOULDN'T BE SANDY, WOULD YOU? MAYBE YOU COULD HELP ME...
HOW?
I'M A DETECTIVE LOOKING INTO A MURDER THAT MIGHT BE CONNECTED TO THE FIRE IN '83... YOU KNOW THE ONE I MEAN...?
YEAH, I KNOW IT... I GUESS YOU SHOULD COME IN...
I HOPE IT'S OKAY WITH YOU IF I LEAVE THE CURTAINS DRAWN...
HEY, IT'S YOUR HOUSE... SENSITIVE TO LIGHT, HUH?
SOMETHING LIKE THAT. SO WHAT'S THIS ABOUT A MURDER?

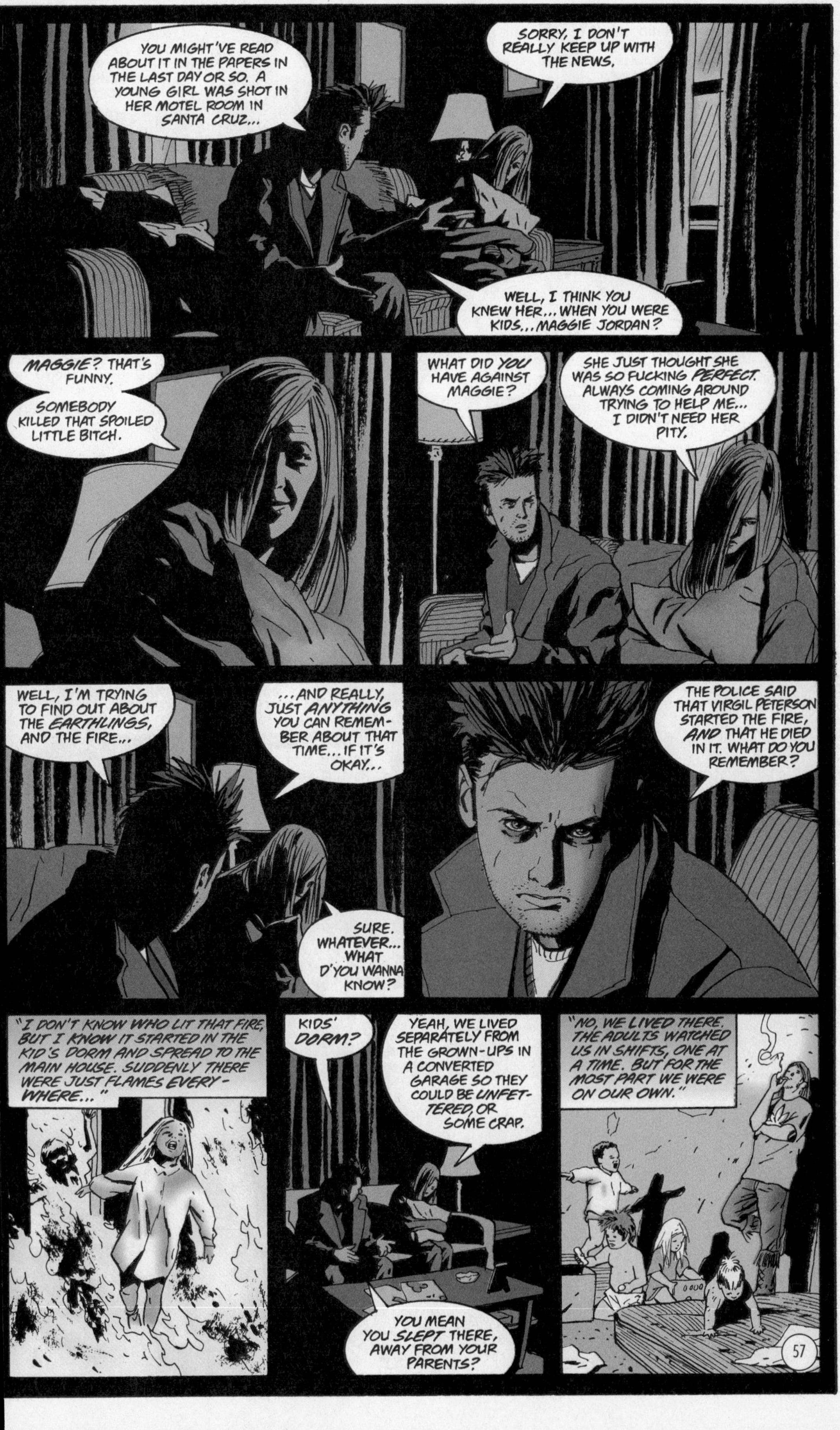
YOU MIGHT'VE READ ABOUT IT IN THE PAPERS IN THE LAST DAY OR SO. A YOUNG GIRL WAS SHOT IN HER MOTEL ROOM IN SANTA CRUZ...
SORRY, I DON'T REALLY KEEP UP WITH THE NEWS.
WELL, I THINK YOU KNEW HER... WHEN YOU WERE KIDS... MAGGIE JORDAN?
MAGGIE? THAT'S FUNNY.
SOMEBODY KILLED THAT SPOILED LITTLE BITCH.
WHAT DID YOU HAVE AGAINST MAGGIE?
SHE JUST THOUGHT SHE WAS SO FUCKING PERFECT. ALWAYS COMING AROUND TRYING TO HELP ME... I DIDN'T NEED HER PITY.
WELL, I'M TRYING TO FIND OUT ABOUT THE EARTHLINGS, AND THE FIRE...
...AND REALLY, JUST ANYTHING YOU CAN REMEMBER ABOUT THAT TIME... IF IT'S OKAY...
SURE. WHATEVER... WHAT D'YOU WANNA KNOW?
THE POLICE SAID THAT VIRGIL PETERSON STARTED THE FIRE, AND THAT HE DIED IN IT. WHAT DO YOU REMEMBER?
"I DON'T KNOW WHO LIT THAT FIRE, BUT I KNOW IT STARTED IN THE KID'S DORM AND SPREAD TO THE MAIN HOUSE. SUDDENLY THERE WERE JUST FLAMES EVERY-WHERE..."
KIDS' DORM?
YEAH, WE LIVED SEPARATELY FROM THE GROWN-UPS IN A CONVERTED GARAGE SO THEY COULD BE UNFET-TERED, OR SOME CRAP.
YOU MEAN YOU SLEPT THERE, AWAY FROM YOUR PARENTS?
"NO, WE LIVED THERE. THE ADULTS WATCHED US IN SHIFTS, ONE AT A TIME. BUT FOR THE MOST PART WE WERE ON OUR OWN."

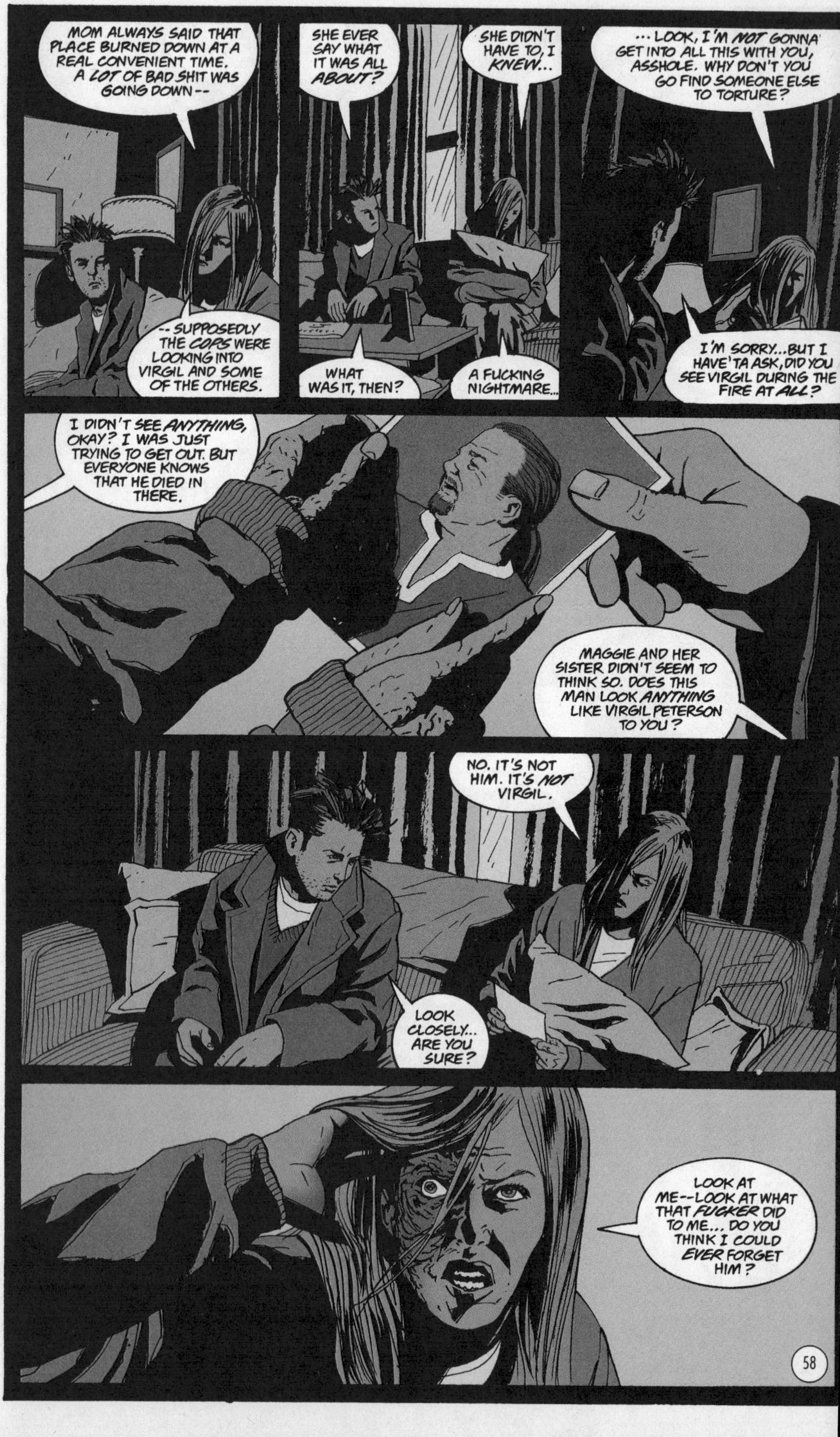
MOM ALWAYS SAID THAT PLACE BURNED DOWN AT A REAL CONVENIENT TIME. A LOT OF BAD SHIT WAS GOING DOWN--
--SUPPOSEDLY THE COPS WERE LOOKING INTO VIRGIL AND SOME OF THE OTHERS.
SHE EVER SAY WHAT IT WAS ALL ABOUT?
SHE DIDN'T HAVE TO, I KNEW...
WHAT WAS IT, THEN?
A FUCKING NIGHTMARE...
...LOOK, I'M NOT GONNA GET INTO ALL THIS WITH YOU, ASSHOLE. WHY DON'T YOU GO FIND SOMEONE ELSE TO TORTURE?
I'M SORRY...BUT I HAVE'TA ASK, DID YOU SEE VIRGIL DURING THE FIRE AT ALL?
I DIDN'T SEE ANYTHING, OKAY? I WAS JUST TRYING TO GET OUT. BUT EVERYONE KNOWS THAT HE DIED IN THERE.
MAGGIE AND HER SISTER DIDN'T SEEM TO THINK SO. DOES THIS MAN LOOK ANYTHING LIKE VIRGIL PETERSON TO YOU?
NO. IT'S NOT HIM. IT'S NOT VIRGIL.
LOOK CLOSELY... ARE YOU SURE?
LOOK AT ME--LOOK AT WHAT THAT FUCKER DID TO ME... DO YOU THINK I COULD EVER FORGET HIM?

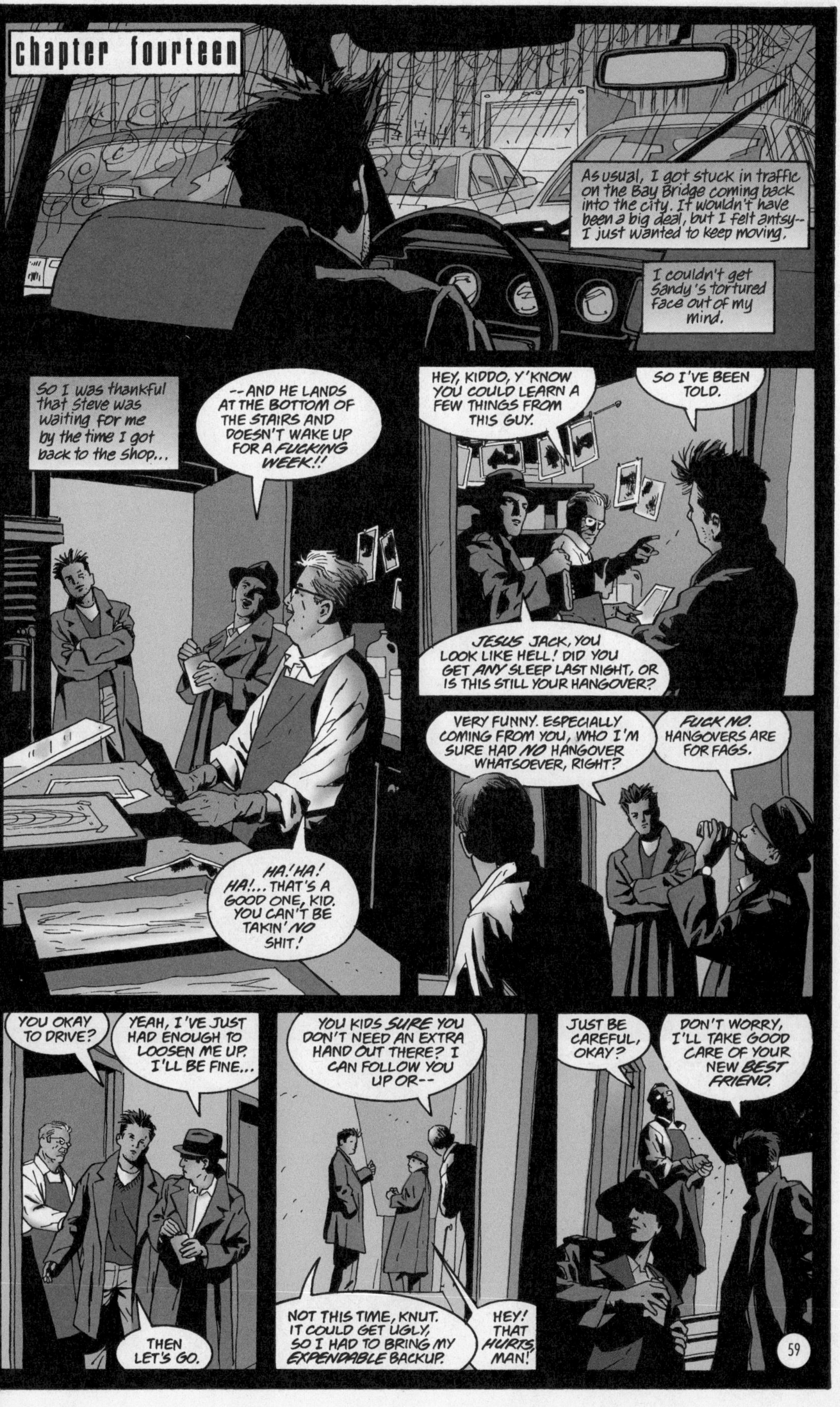
chapter fourteen
As usual, I got stuck in traffic on the Bay Bridge coming back into the city. It wouldn't have been a big deal, but I felt antsy-- I just wanted to keep moving.
I couldn't get Sandy's tortured face out of my mind.
So I was thankful that Steve was waiting for me by the time I got back to the shop...
--AND HE LANDS AT THE BOTTOM OF THE STAIRS AND DOESN'T WAKE UP FOR A FUCKING WEEK!!
HA! HA! HA!... THAT'S A GOOD ONE, KID. YOU CAN'T BE TAKIN' NO SHIT!
HEY, KIDDO, Y'KNOW YOU COULD LEARN A FEW THINGS FROM THIS GUY.
SO I'VE BEEN TOLD.
JESUS JACK, YOU LOOK LIKE HELL! DID YOU GET ANY SLEEP LAST NIGHT, OR IS THIS STILL YOUR HANGOVER?
VERY FUNNY. ESPECIALLY COMING FROM YOU, WHO I'M SURE HAD NO HANGOVER WHATSOEVER, RIGHT?
FUCK NO. HANGOVERS ARE FOR FAGS.
YOU OKAY TO DRIVE?
YEAH, I'VE JUST HAD ENOUGH TO LOOSEN ME UP. I'LL BE FINE...
THEN LET'S GO.
YOU KIDS SURE YOU DON'T NEED AN EXTRA HAND OUT THERE? I CAN FOLLOW YOU UP OR--
NOT THIS TIME, KNUT. IT COULD GET UGLY, SO I HAD TO BRING MY EXPENDABLE BACKUP.
HEY! THAT HURTS, MAN!
JUST BE CAREFUL, OKAY?
DON'T WORRY, I'LL TAKE GOOD CARE OF YOUR NEW BEST FRIEND.

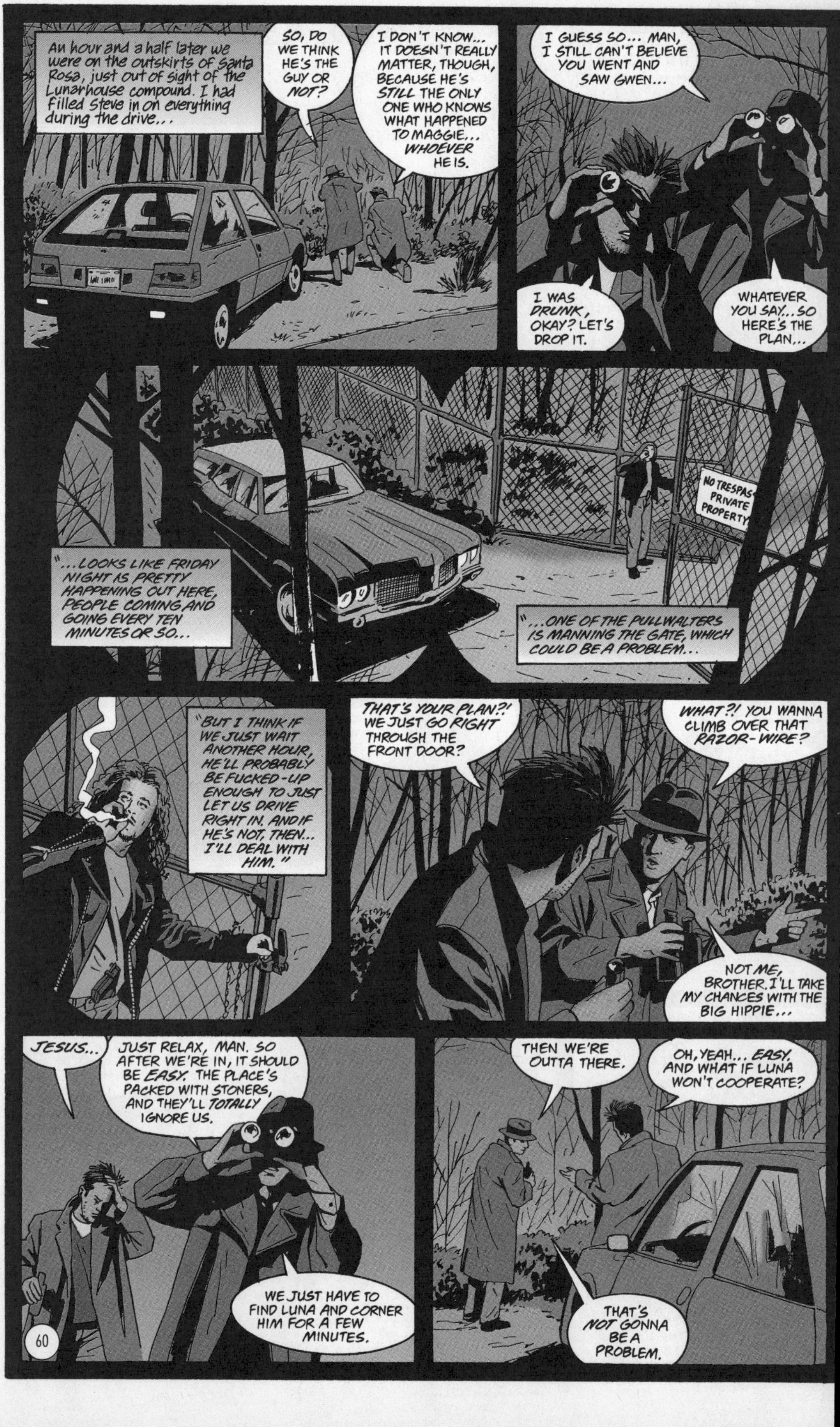

An hour and a half later we were on the outskirts of Santa Rosa, just out of sight of the Lunarhouse compound. I had filled Steve in on everything during the drive...
SO, DO WE THINK HE'S THE GUY OR NOT?
I DON'T KNOW... IT DOESN'T REALLY MATTER, THOUGH, BECAUSE HE'S STILL THE ONLY ONE WHO KNOWS WHAT HAPPENED TO MAGGIE... WHOEVER HE IS.
I GUESS SO... MAN, I STILL CAN'T BELIEVE YOU WENT AND SAW GWEN...
I WAS DRUNK, OKAY? LET'S DROP IT.
WHATEVER YOU SAY... SO HERE'S THE PLAN...
"...LOOKS LIKE FRIDAY NIGHT IS PRETTY HAPPENING OUT HERE, PEOPLE COMING AND GOING EVERY TEN MINUTES OR SO...
NO TRESPAS PRIVATE PROPERTY
"...ONE OF THE PULLWALTERS IS MANNING THE GATE, WHICH COULD BE A PROBLEM...
"BUT I THINK IF WE JUST WAIT ANOTHER HOUR, HE'LL PROBABLY BE FUCKED-UP ENOUGH TO JUST LET US DRIVE RIGHT IN. AND IF HE'S NOT, THEN... I'LL DEAL WITH HIM."
THAT'S YOUR PLAN?! WE JUST GO RIGHT THROUGH THE FRONT DOOR?
WHAT?! YOU WANNA CLIMB OVER THAT RAZOR-WIRE?
NOT ME, BROTHER. I'LL TAKE MY CHANCES WITH THE BIG HIPPIE...
JESUS...
JUST RELAX, MAN. SO AFTER WE'RE IN, IT SHOULD BE EASY. THE PLACE'S PACKED WITH STONERS, AND THEY'LL TOTALLY IGNORE US.
WE JUST HAVE TO FIND LUNA AND CORNER HIM FOR A FEW MINUTES.
THEN WE'RE OUTTA THERE.
OH, YEAH... EASY. AND WHAT IF LUNA WON'T COOPERATE?
THAT'S NOT GONNA BE A PROBLEM.

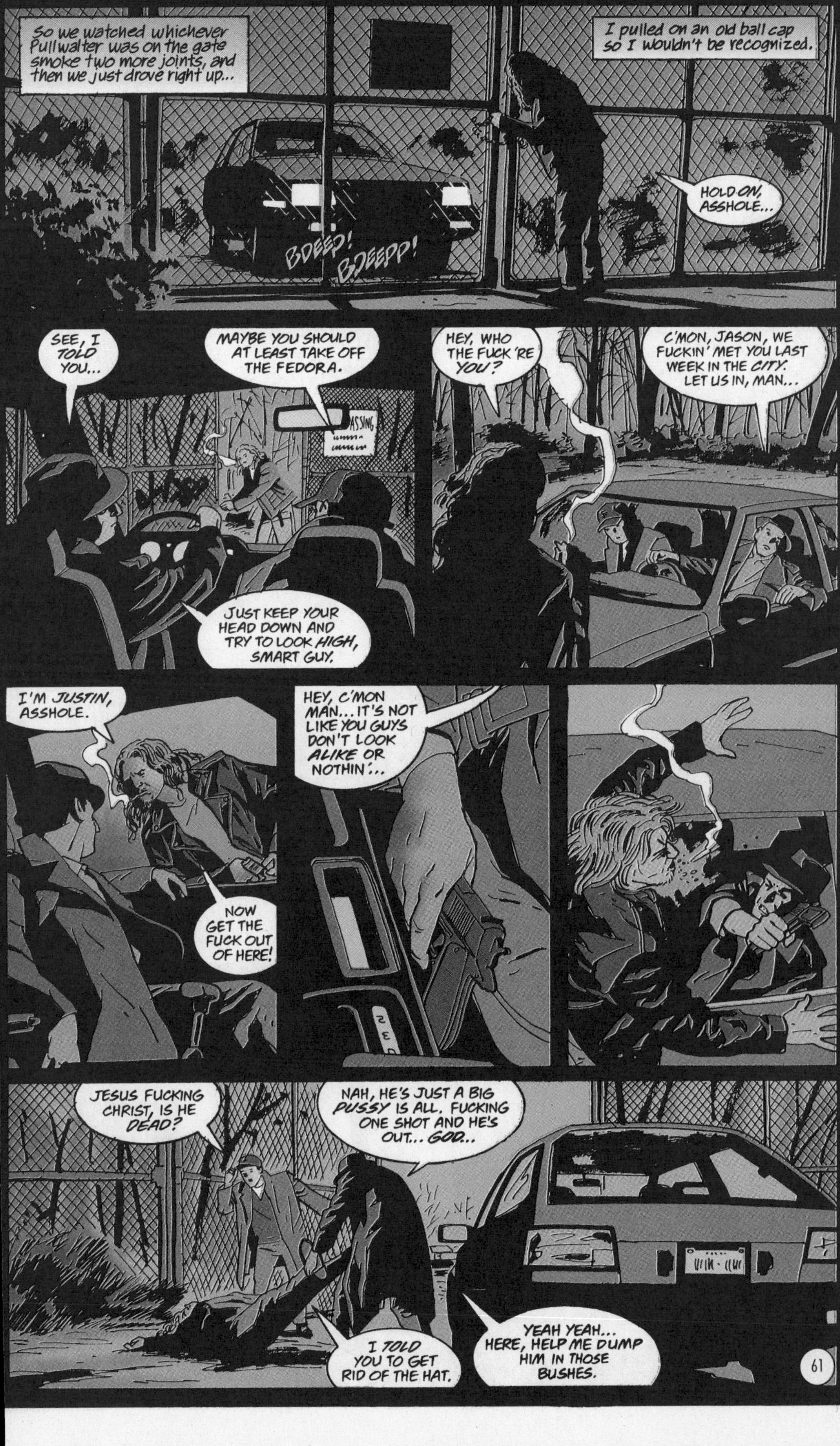

So we watched whichever Pullwalter was on the gate smoke two more joints, and then we just drove right up...
I pulled on an old ball cap so I wouldn't be recognized.
BDEEP! BDEEPP!
HOLD ON, ASSHOLE...
SEE, I TOLD YOU...
MAYBE YOU SHOULD AT LEAST TAKE OFF THE FEDORA.
JUST KEEP YOUR HEAD DOWN AND TRY TO LOOK HIGH, SMART GUY.
HEY, WHO THE FUCK 'RE YOU?
C'MON, JASON, WE FUCKIN' MET YOU LAST WEEK IN THE CITY. LET US IN, MAN...
I'M JUSTIN, ASSHOLE.
NOW GET THE FUCK OUT OF HERE!
HEY, C'MON MAN... IT'S NOT LIKE YOU GUYS DON'T LOOK ALIKE OR NOTHIN'...
JESUS FUCKING CHRIST, IS HE DEAD?
NAH, HE'S JUST A BIG PUSSY IS ALL. FUCKING ONE SHOT AND HE'S OUT... GOD...
I TOLD YOU TO GET RID OF THE HAT.
YEAH YEAH... HERE, HELP ME DUMP HIM IN THOSE BUSHES.

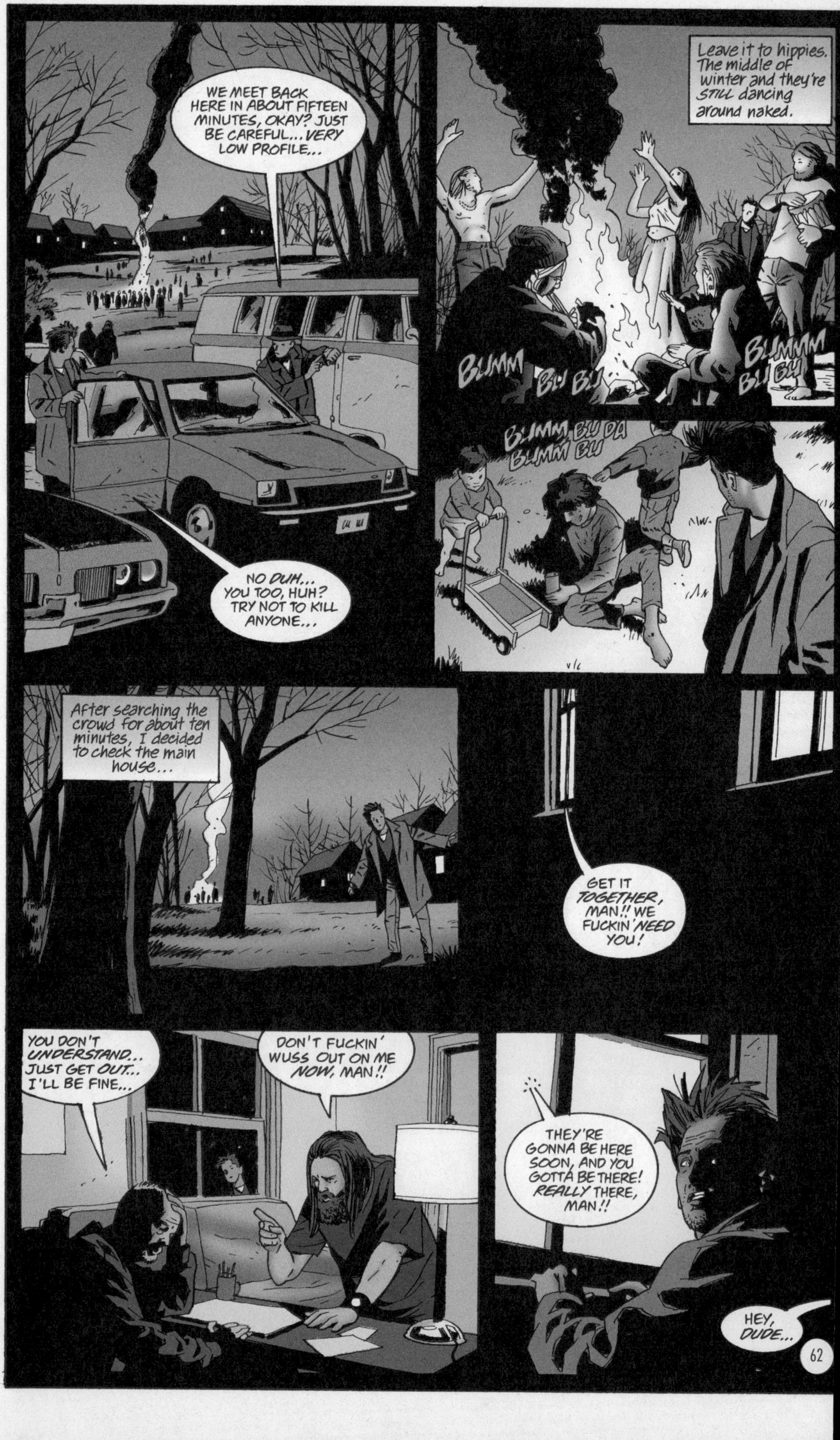
WE MEET BACK HERE IN ABOUT FIFTEEN MINUTES, OKAY? JUST BE CAREFUL... VERY LOW PROFILE...
NO DUH... YOU TOO, HUH? TRY NOT TO KILL ANYONE...
Leave it to hippies. The middle of winter and they're STILL dancing around naked.
BUMM BU BU
BUMMM BU BU
BUMM BU DA BUMM BU
After searching the crowd for about ten minutes, I decided to check the main house...
GET IT TOGETHER, MAN!! WE FUCKIN' NEED YOU!
YOU DON'T UNDERSTAND... JUST GET OUT... I'LL BE FINE...
DON'T FUCKIN' WUSS OUT ON ME NOW, MAN!!
THEY'RE GONNA BE HERE SOON, AND YOU GOTTA BE THERE! REALLY THERE, MAN!!
HEY, DUDE...

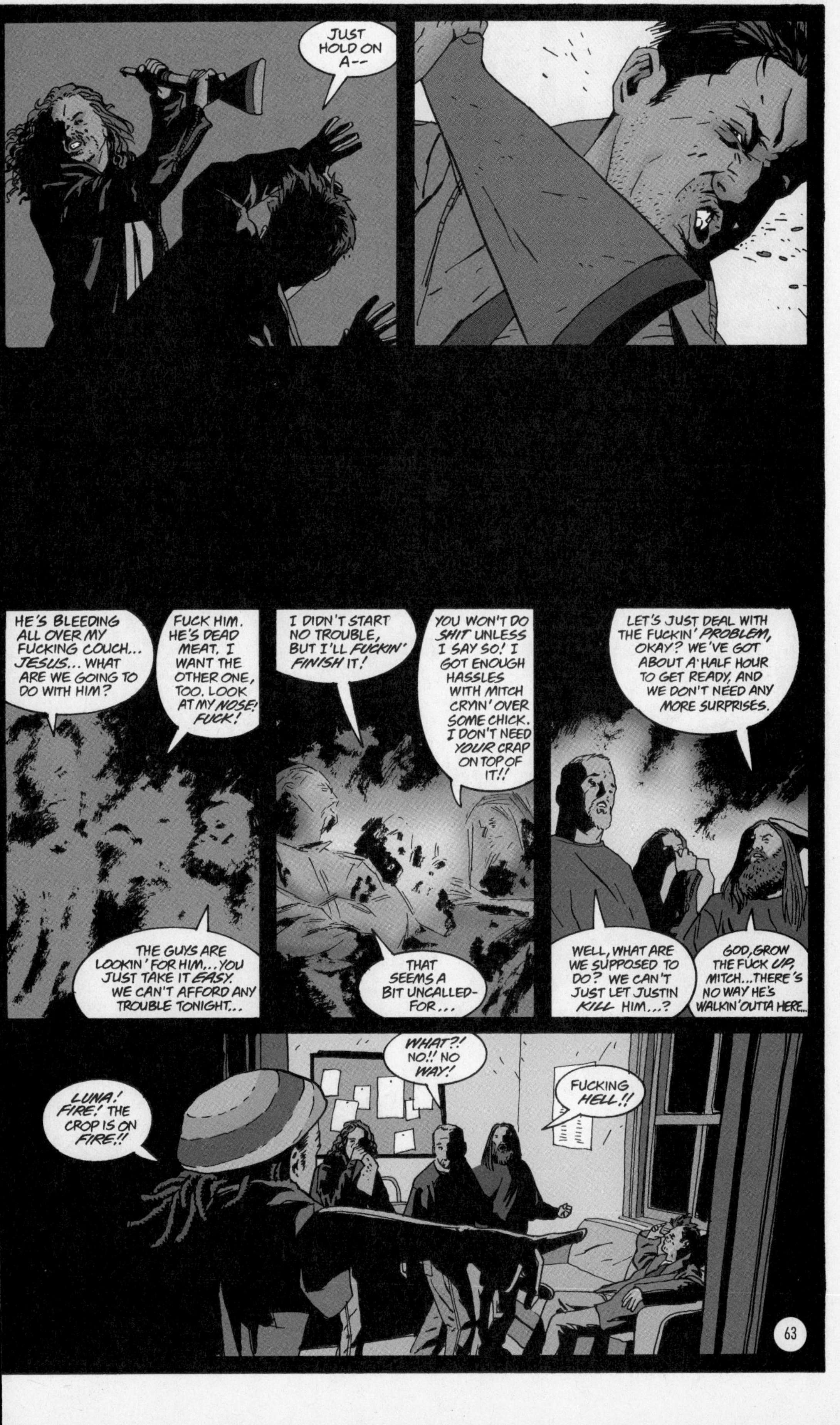
JUST HOLD ON A--
HE'S BLEEDING ALL OVER MY FUCKING COUCH... JESUS... WHAT ARE WE GOING TO DO WITH HIM?
FUCK HIM. HE'S DEAD MEAT. I WANT THE OTHER ONE, TOO. LOOK AT MY NOSE! FUCK!
THE GUYS ARE LOOKIN' FOR HIM... YOU JUST TAKE IT EASY. WE CAN'T AFFORD ANY TROUBLE TONIGHT...
I DIDN'T START NO TROUBLE, BUT I'LL FUCKIN' FINISH IT!
YOU WON'T DO SHIT UNLESS I SAY SO! I GOT ENOUGH HASSLES WITH MITCH CRYIN' OVER SOME CHICK. I DON'T NEED YOUR CRAP ON TOP OF IT!!
THAT SEEMS A BIT UNCALLED-FOR...
LET'S JUST DEAL WITH THE FUCKIN' PROBLEM, OKAY? WE'VE GOT ABOUT A HALF HOUR TO GET READY, AND WE DON'T NEED ANY MORE SURPRISES.
WELL, WHAT ARE WE SUPPOSED TO DO? WE CAN'T JUST LET JUSTIN KILL HIM...?
GOD, GROW THE FUCK UP, MITCH... THERE'S NO WAY HE'S WALKIN' OUTTA HERE...
LUNA! FIRE! THE CROP IS ON FIRE!!
WHAT?! NO!! NO WAY!
FUCKING HELL!!

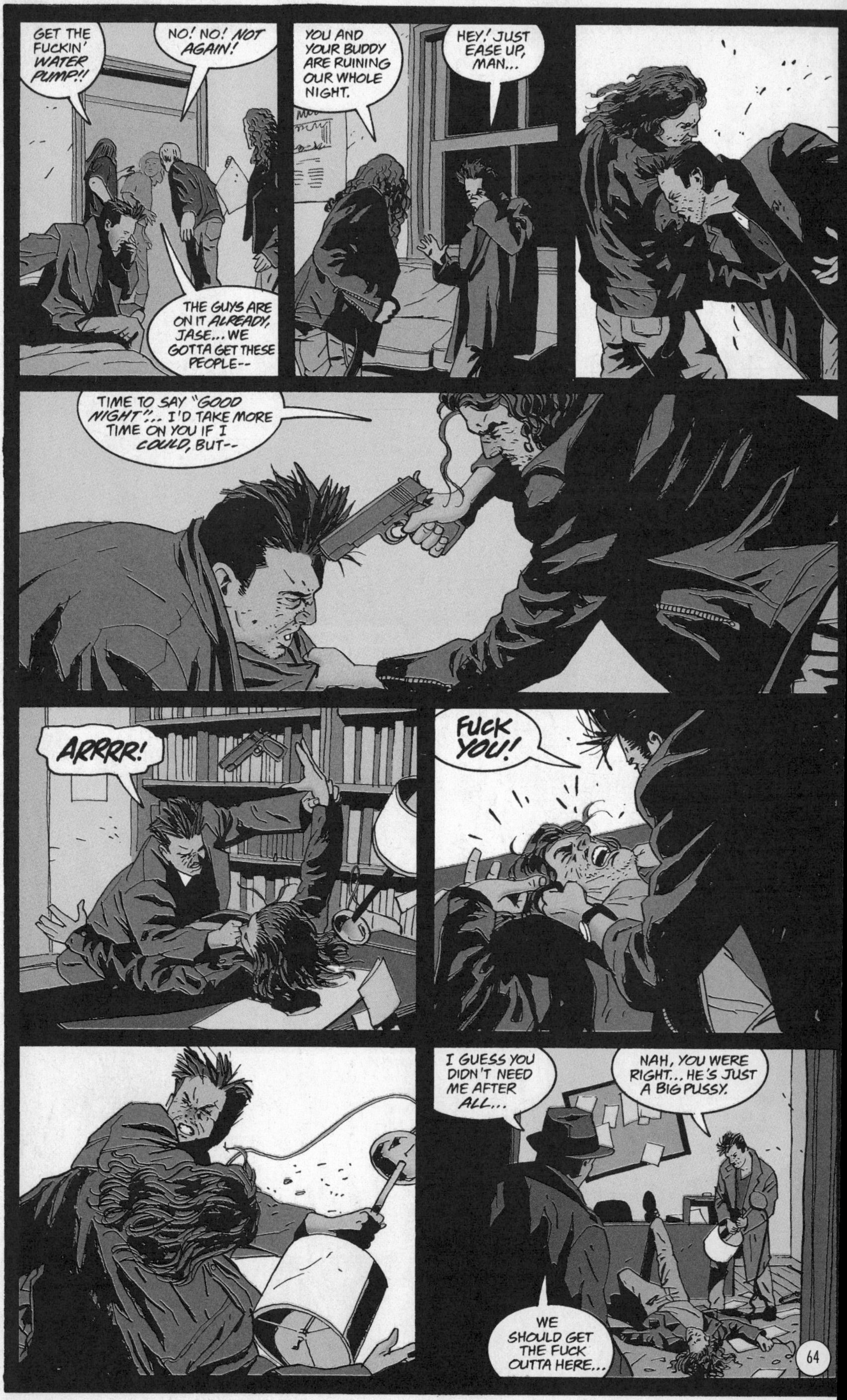
GET THE FUCKIN' WATER PUMP!!
NO! NO! NOT AGAIN!
THE GUYS ARE ON IT ALREADY, JASE... WE GOTTA GET THESE PEOPLE--
YOU AND YOUR BUDDY ARE RUINING OUR WHOLE NIGHT.
HEY! JUST EASE UP, MAN...
TIME TO SAY "GOOD NIGHT"... I'D TAKE MORE TIME ON YOU IF I COULD, BUT--
ARRRR!
FUCK YOU!
I GUESS YOU DIDN'T NEED ME AFTER ALL...
NAH, YOU WERE RIGHT... HE'S JUST A BIG PUSSY.
WE SHOULD GET THE FUCK OUTTA HERE...

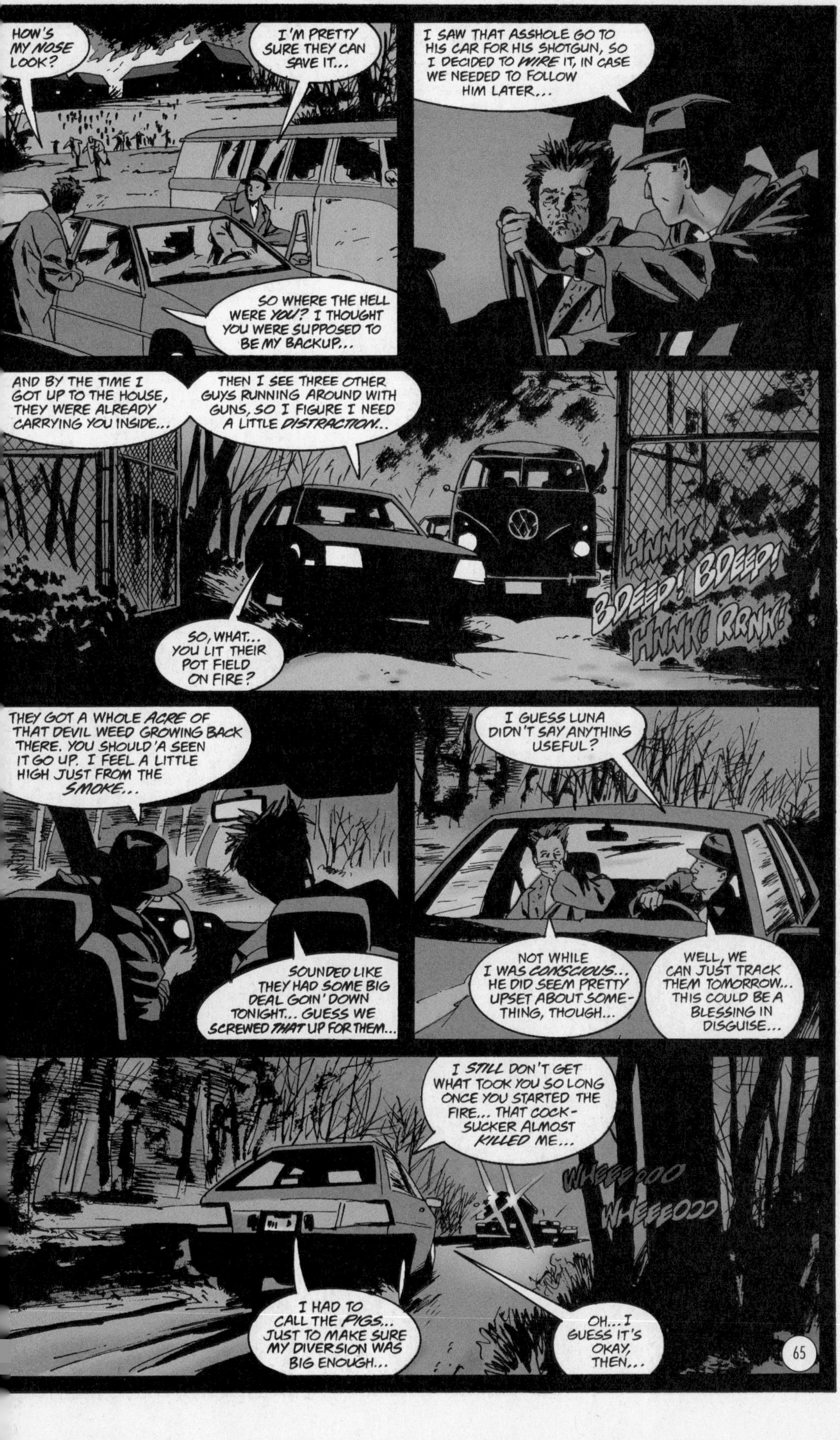
HOW'S MY NOSE LOOK?
I'M PRETTY SURE THEY CAN SAVE IT...
SO WHERE THE HELL WERE YOU? I THOUGHT YOU WERE SUPPOSED TO BE MY BACKUP...
I SAW THAT ASSHOLE GO TO HIS CAR FOR HIS SHOTGUN, SO I DECIDED TO WIRE IT, IN CASE WE NEEDED TO FOLLOW HIM LATER...
AND BY THE TIME I GOT UP TO THE HOUSE, THEY WERE ALREADY CARRYING YOU INSIDE...
THEN I SEE THREE OTHER GUYS RUNNING AROUND WITH GUNS, SO I FIGURE I NEED A LITTLE DISTRACTION...
HNNK
BDEEP! BDEEP!
HNNK! RRNK!
SO, WHAT... YOU LIT THEIR POT FIELD ON FIRE?
THEY GOT A WHOLE ACRE OF THAT DEVIL WEED GROWING BACK THERE. YOU SHOULD'A SEEN IT GO UP. I FEEL A LITTLE HIGH JUST FROM THE SMOKE...
SOUNDED LIKE THEY HAD SOME BIG DEAL GOIN' DOWN TONIGHT... GUESS WE SCREWED THAT UP FOR THEM...
I GUESS LUNA DIDN'T SAY ANYTHING USEFUL?
NOT WHILE I WAS CONSCIOUS... HE DID SEEM PRETTY UPSET ABOUT SOME-THING, THOUGH...
WELL, WE CAN JUST TRACK THEM TOMORROW... THIS COULD BE A BLESSING IN DISGUISE...
I STILL DON'T GET WHAT TOOK YOU SO LONG ONCE YOU STARTED THE FIRE... THAT COCK-SUCKER ALMOST KILLED ME...
WHEEEOOO
WHEEEOOO
I HAD TO CALL THE PIGS... JUST TO MAKE SURE MY DIVERSION WAS BIG ENOUGH...
OH... I GUESS IT'S OKAY, THEN...
65

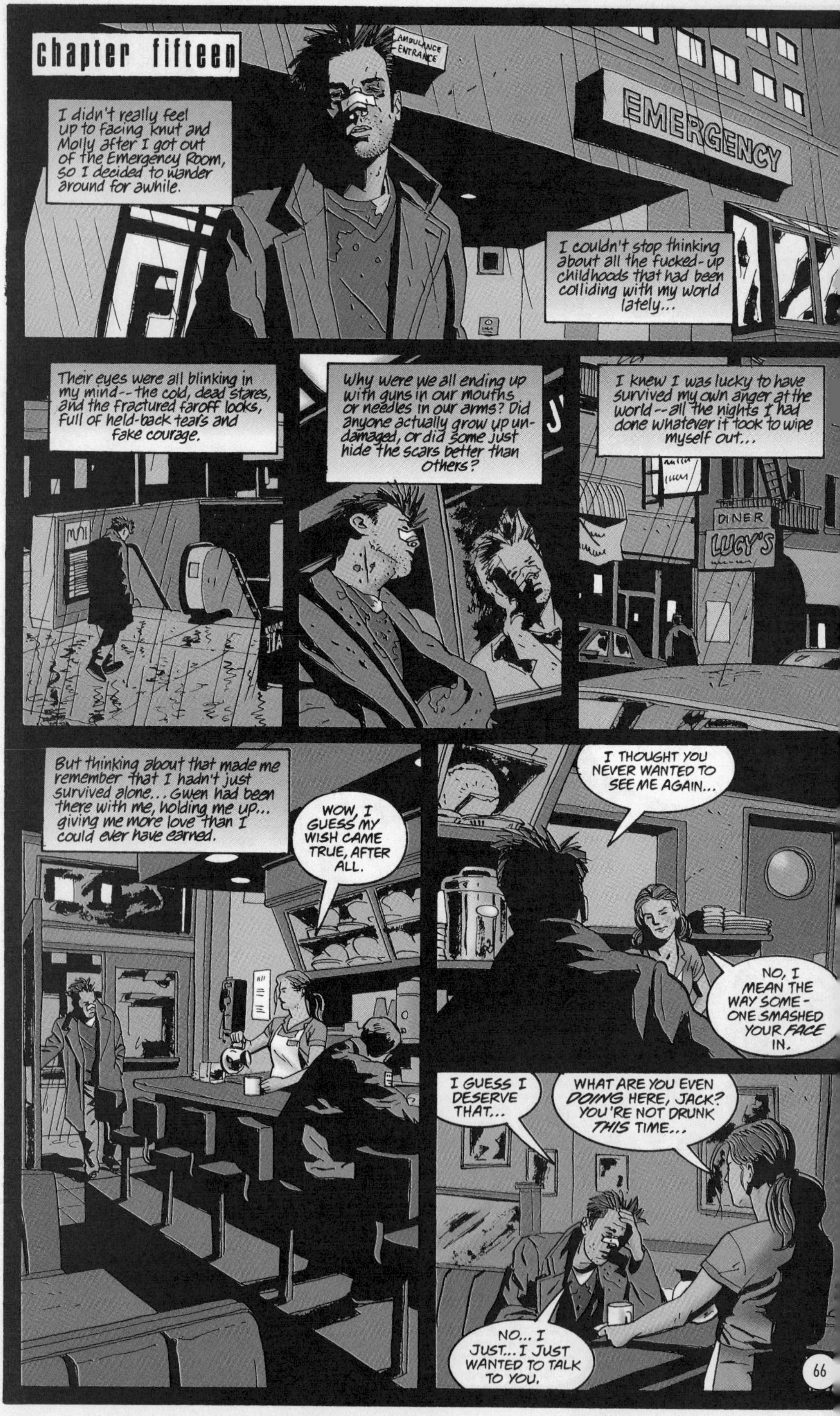
chapter fifteen
AMBULANCE ENTRANCE
EMERGENCY
I didn't really feel up to facing Knut and Molly after I got out of the Emergency Room, so I decided to wander around for awhile.
I couldn't stop thinking about all the fucked-up childhoods that had been colliding with my world lately...
Their eyes were all blinking in my mind-- the cold, dead stares, and the fractured faroff looks, full of held-back tears and fake courage.
Why were we all ending up with guns in our mouths or needles in our arms? Did anyone actually grow up un-damaged, or did some just hide the scars better than others?
I knew I was lucky to have survived my own anger at the world--all the nights I had done whatever it took to wipe myself out...
DINER
LUCY'S
But thinking about that made me remember that I hadn't just survived alone... Gwen had been there with me, holding me up... giving me more love than I could ever have earned.
WOW, I GUESS MY WISH CAME TRUE, AFTER ALL.
I THOUGHT YOU NEVER WANTED TO SEE ME AGAIN...
NO, I MEAN THE WAY SOME-ONE SMASHED YOUR *FACE* IN.
I GUESS I DESERVE THAT...
WHAT ARE YOU EVEN *DOING* HERE, JACK? YOU'RE NOT DRUNK *THIS* TIME...
NO... I JUST... I JUST WANTED TO TALK TO YOU.

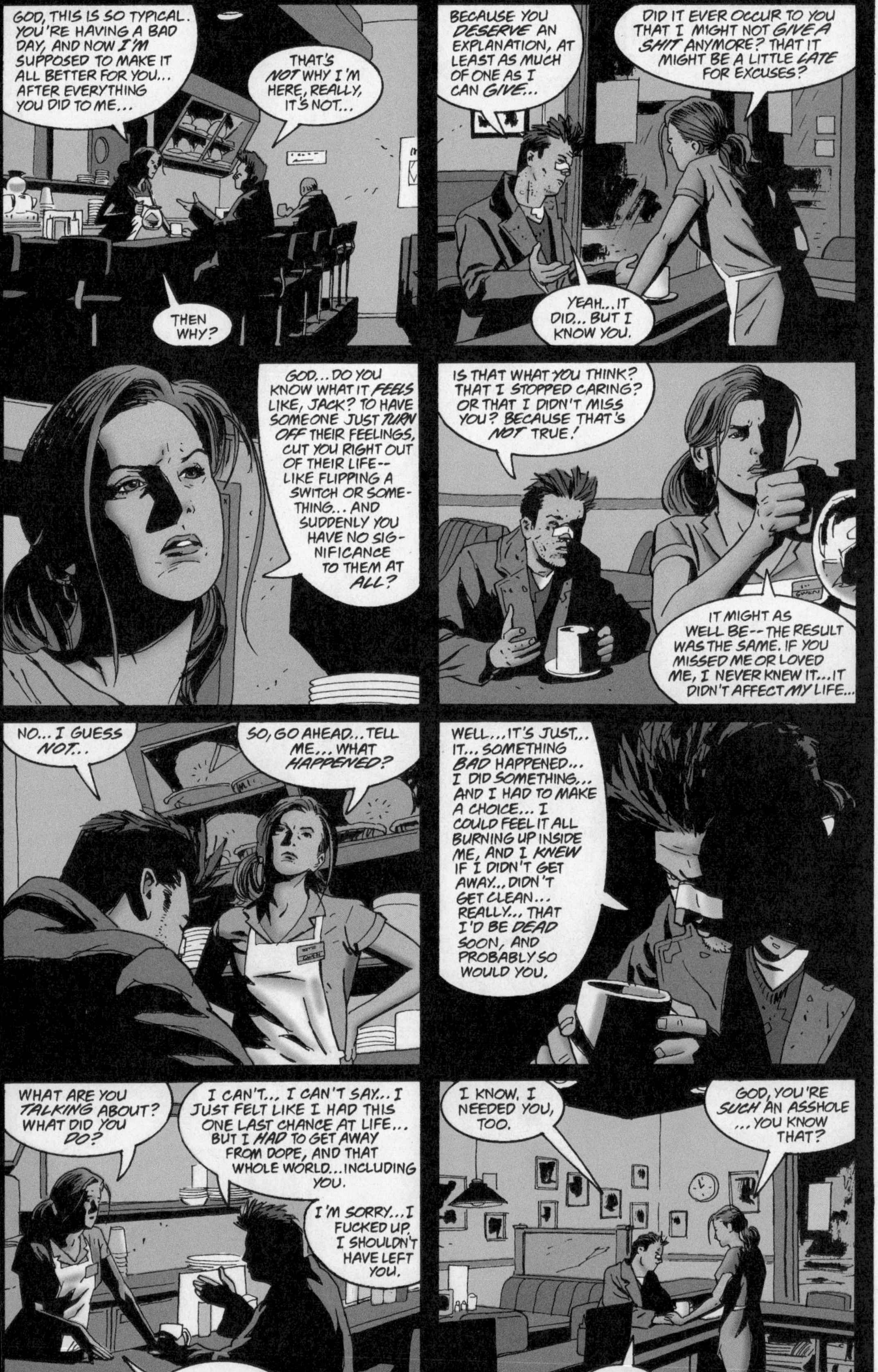
GOD, THIS IS SO TYPICAL. YOU'RE HAVING A BAD DAY, AND NOW I'M SUPPOSED TO MAKE IT ALL BETTER FOR YOU... AFTER EVERYTHING YOU DID TO ME...
THAT'S NOT WHY I'M HERE, REALLY, IT'S NOT...
THEN WHY?
BECAUSE YOU DESERVE AN EXPLANATION, AT LEAST AS MUCH OF ONE AS I CAN GIVE...
DID IT EVER OCCUR TO YOU THAT I MIGHT NOT GIVE A SHIT ANYMORE? THAT IT MIGHT BE A LITTLE LATE FOR EXCUSES?
YEAH...IT DID... BUT I KNOW YOU.
GOD... DO YOU KNOW WHAT IT FEELS LIKE, JACK? TO HAVE SOMEONE JUST TURN OFF THEIR FEELINGS, CUT YOU RIGHT OUT OF THEIR LIFE-- LIKE FLIPPING A SWITCH OR SOMETHING... AND SUDDENLY YOU HAVE NO SIGNIFICANCE TO THEM AT ALL?
IS THAT WHAT YOU THINK? THAT I STOPPED CARING? OR THAT I DIDN'T MISS YOU? BECAUSE THAT'S NOT TRUE!
IT MIGHT AS WELL BE-- THE RESULT WAS THE SAME. IF YOU MISSED ME OR LOVED ME, I NEVER KNEW IT... IT DIDN'T AFFECT MY LIFE...
NO... I GUESS NOT...
SO, GO AHEAD... TELL ME... WHAT HAPPENED?
WELL... IT'S JUST... IT... SOMETHING BAD HAPPENED... I DID SOMETHING... AND I HAD TO MAKE A CHOICE... I COULD FEEL IT ALL BURNING UP INSIDE ME, AND I KNEW IF I DIDN'T GET AWAY... DIDN'T GET CLEAN... REALLY... THAT I'D BE DEAD SOON, AND PROBABLY SO WOULD YOU.
WHAT ARE YOU TALKING ABOUT? WHAT DID YOU DO?
I CAN'T... I CAN'T SAY... I JUST FELT LIKE I HAD THIS ONE LAST CHANCE AT LIFE... BUT I HAD TO GET AWAY FROM DOPE, AND THAT WHOLE WORLD... INCLUDING YOU.
I'M SORRY... I FUCKED UP. I SHOULDN'T HAVE LEFT YOU.
NO... YOU SHOULDN'T HAVE... I NEEDED YOU.
I KNOW. I NEEDED YOU, TOO.
GOD, YOU'RE SUCH AN ASSHOLE ...YOU KNOW THAT?
YEAH, I DO.

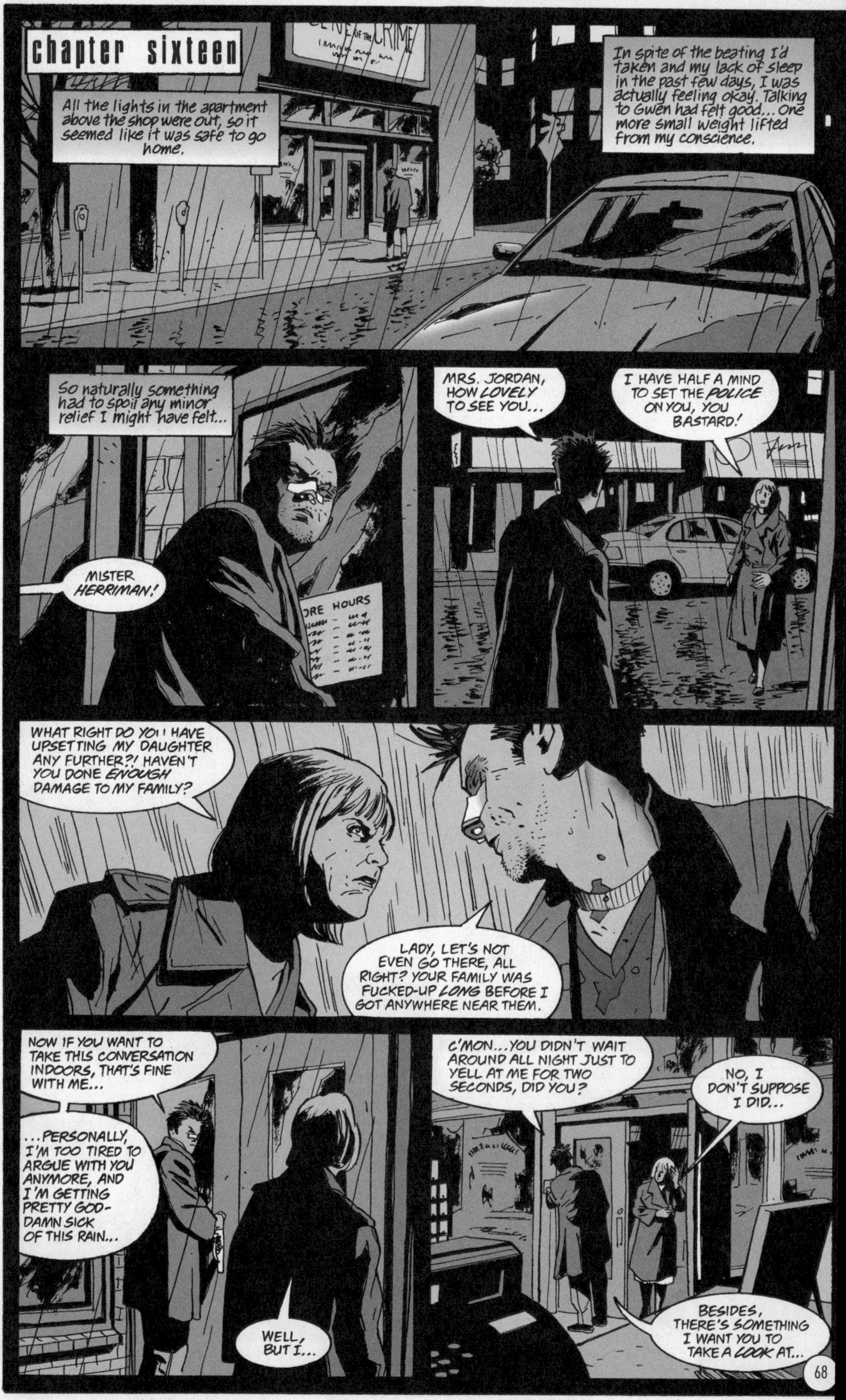

chapter sixteen
All the lights in the apartment above the shop were out, so it seemed like it was safe to go home.
In spite of the beating I'd taken and my lack of sleep in the past few days, I was actually feeling okay. Talking to Gwen had felt good... One more small weight lifted from my conscience.
So naturally something had to spoil any minor relief I might have felt...
MISTER HERRIMAN!
MRS. JORDAN, HOW LOVELY TO SEE YOU...
I HAVE HALF A MIND TO SET THE POLICE ON YOU, YOU BASTARD!
WHAT RIGHT DO YOU HAVE UPSETTING MY DAUGHTER ANY FURTHER?! HAVEN'T YOU DONE ENOUGH DAMAGE TO MY FAMILY?
LADY, LET'S NOT EVEN GO THERE, ALL RIGHT? YOUR FAMILY WAS FUCKED-UP LONG BEFORE I GOT ANYWHERE NEAR THEM.
NOW IF YOU WANT TO TAKE THIS CONVERSATION INDOORS, THAT'S FINE WITH ME...
...PERSONALLY, I'M TOO TIRED TO ARGUE WITH YOU ANYMORE, AND I'M GETTING PRETTY GOD-DAMN SICK OF THIS RAIN...
WELL, BUT I...
C'MON...YOU DIDN'T WAIT AROUND ALL NIGHT JUST TO YELL AT ME FOR TWO SECONDS, DID YOU?
NO, I DON'T SUPPOSE I DID...
BESIDES, THERE'S SOMETHING I WANT YOU TO TAKE A LOOK AT...

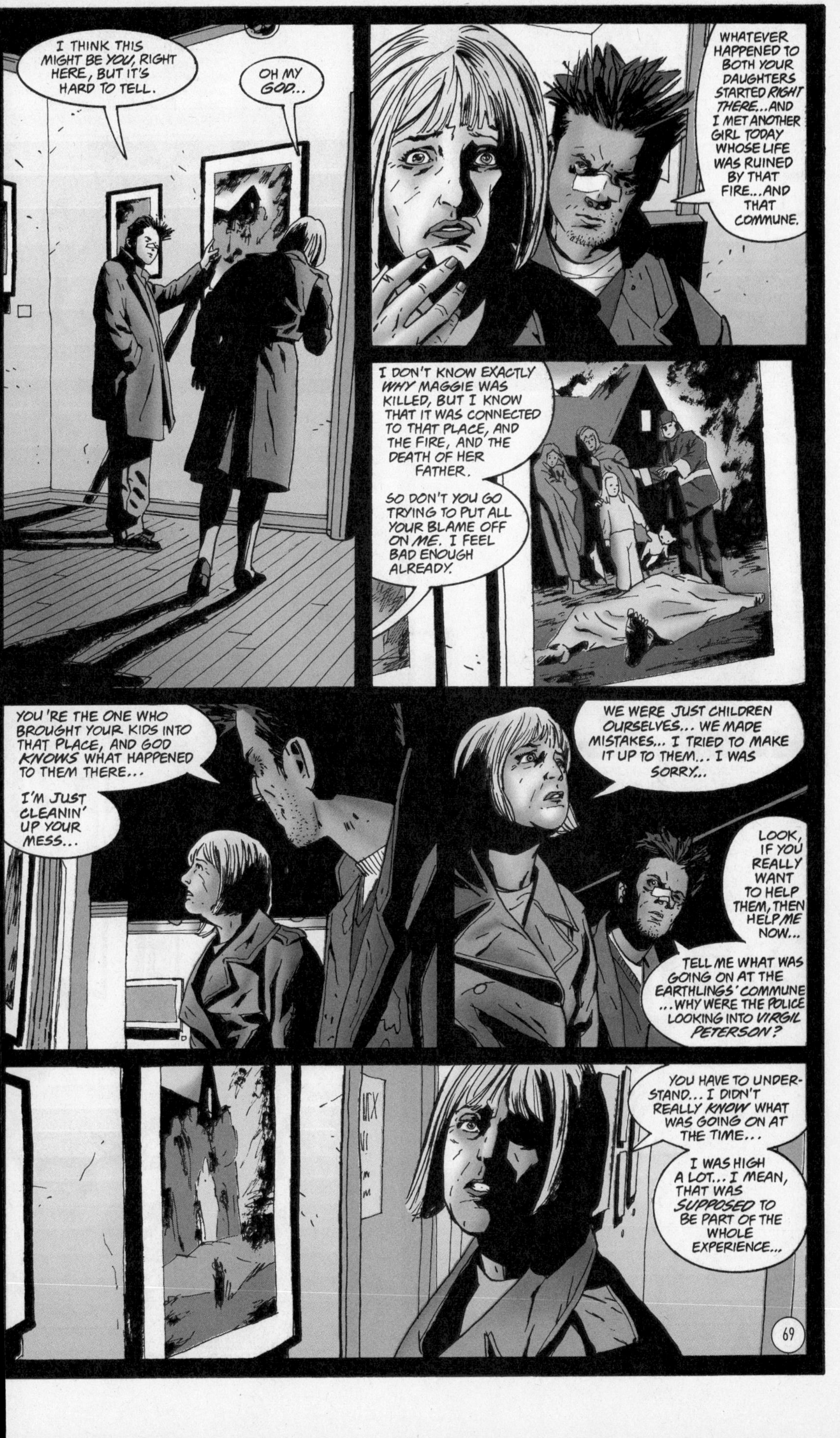
I THINK THIS MIGHT BE YOU, RIGHT HERE, BUT IT'S HARD TO TELL.
OH MY GOD...
WHATEVER HAPPENED TO BOTH YOUR DAUGHTERS STARTED RIGHT THERE...AND I MET ANOTHER GIRL TODAY WHOSE LIFE WAS RUINED BY THAT FIRE...AND THAT COMMUNE.
I DON'T KNOW EXACTLY WHY MAGGIE WAS KILLED, BUT I KNOW THAT IT WAS CONNECTED TO THAT PLACE, AND THE FIRE, AND THE DEATH OF HER FATHER.
SO DON'T YOU GO TRYING TO PUT ALL YOUR BLAME OFF ON ME. I FEEL BAD ENOUGH ALREADY.
YOU'RE THE ONE WHO BROUGHT YOUR KIDS INTO THAT PLACE, AND GOD KNOWS WHAT HAPPENED TO THEM THERE...
I'M JUST CLEANIN' UP YOUR MESS...
WE WERE JUST CHILDREN OURSELVES... WE MADE MISTAKES... I TRIED TO MAKE IT UP TO THEM... I WAS SORRY...
LOOK, IF YOU REALLY WANT TO HELP THEM, THEN HELP ME NOW...
TELL ME WHAT WAS GOING ON AT THE EARTHLINGS' COMMUNE ...WHY WERE THE POLICE LOOKING INTO VIRGIL PETERSON?
YOU HAVE TO UNDERSTAND... I DIDN'T REALLY KNOW WHAT WAS GOING ON AT THE TIME...
I WAS HIGH A LOT... I MEAN, THAT WAS SUPPOSED TO BE PART OF THE WHOLE EXPERIENCE...

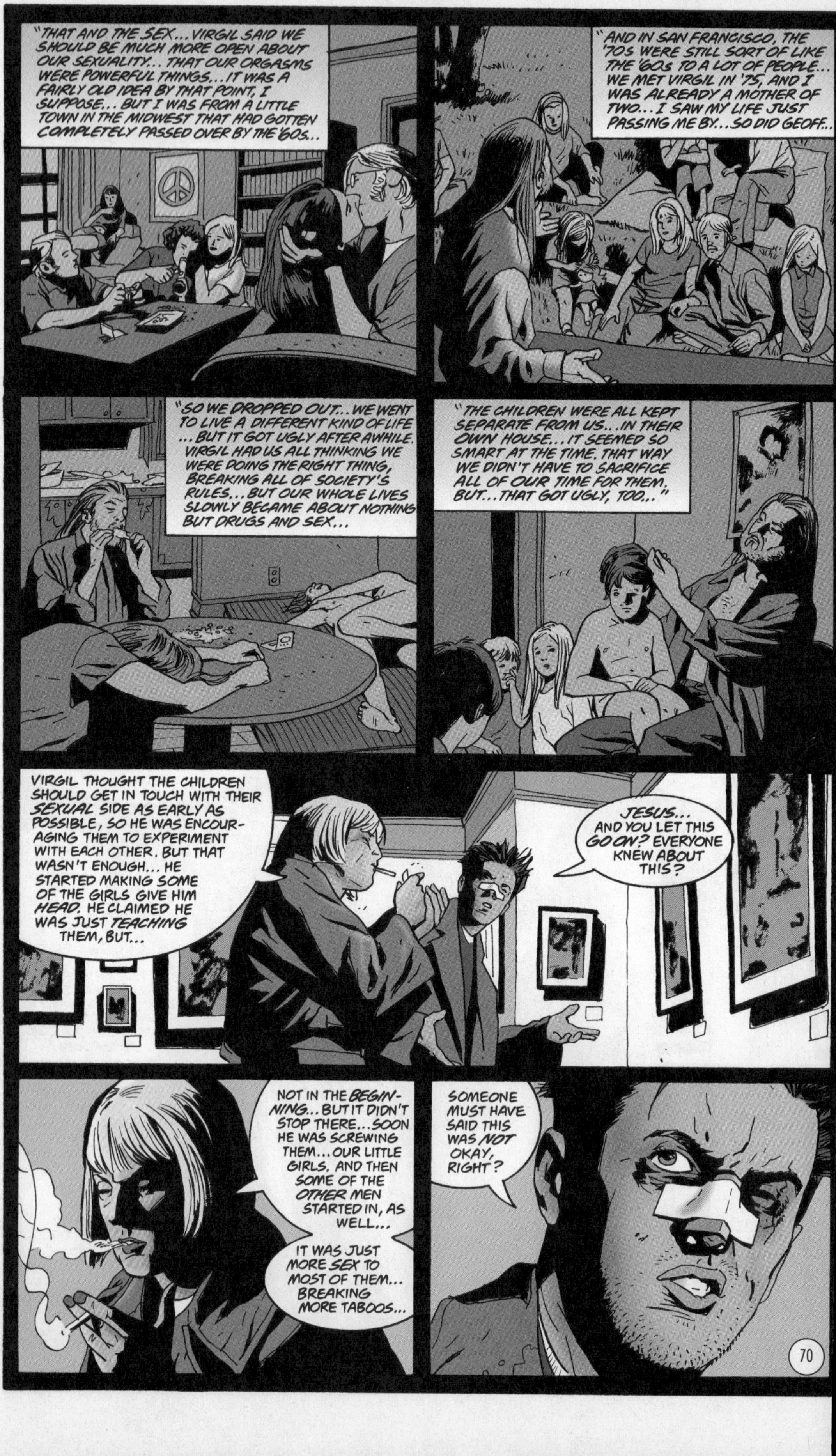
"THAT AND THE SEX... VIRGIL SAID WE SHOULD BE MUCH MORE OPEN ABOUT OUR SEXUALITY... THAT OUR ORGASMS WERE POWERFUL THINGS... IT WAS A FAIRLY OLD IDEA BY THAT POINT, I SUPPOSE... BUT I WAS FROM A LITTLE TOWN IN THE MIDWEST THAT HAD GOTTEN COMPLETELY PASSED OVER BY THE '60s...
"AND IN SAN FRANCISCO, THE '70s WERE STILL SORT OF LIKE THE '60s TO A LOT OF PEOPLE... WE MET VIRGIL IN '75, AND I WAS ALREADY A MOTHER OF TWO... I SAW MY LIFE JUST PASSING ME BY... SO DID GEOFF...
"SO WE DROPPED OUT... WE WENT TO LIVE A DIFFERENT KIND OF LIFE ... BUT IT GOT UGLY AFTER AWHILE. VIRGIL HAD US ALL THINKING WE WERE DOING THE RIGHT THING, BREAKING ALL OF SOCIETY'S RULES... BUT OUR WHOLE LIVES SLOWLY BECAME ABOUT NOTHING BUT DRUGS AND SEX...
"THE CHILDREN WERE ALL KEPT SEPARATE FROM US... IN THEIR OWN HOUSE... IT SEEMED SO SMART AT THE TIME. THAT WAY WE DIDN'T HAVE TO SACRIFICE ALL OF OUR TIME FOR THEM. BUT... THAT GOT UGLY, TOO..."
VIRGIL THOUGHT THE CHILDREN SHOULD GET IN TOUCH WITH THEIR SEXUAL SIDE AS EARLY AS POSSIBLE, SO HE WAS ENCOURAGING THEM TO EXPERIMENT WITH EACH OTHER. BUT THAT WASN'T ENOUGH... HE STARTED MAKING SOME OF THE GIRLS GIVE HIM HEAD. HE CLAIMED HE WAS JUST TEACHING THEM, BUT...
JESUS... AND YOU LET THIS GO ON? EVERYONE KNEW ABOUT THIS?
NOT IN THE BEGINNING... BUT IT DIDN'T STOP THERE... SOON HE WAS SCREWING THEM... OUR LITTLE GIRLS. AND THEN SOME OF THE OTHER MEN STARTED IN, AS WELL...
IT WAS JUST MORE SEX TO MOST OF THEM... BREAKING MORE TABOOS...
SOMEONE MUST HAVE SAID THIS WAS NOT OKAY, RIGHT?

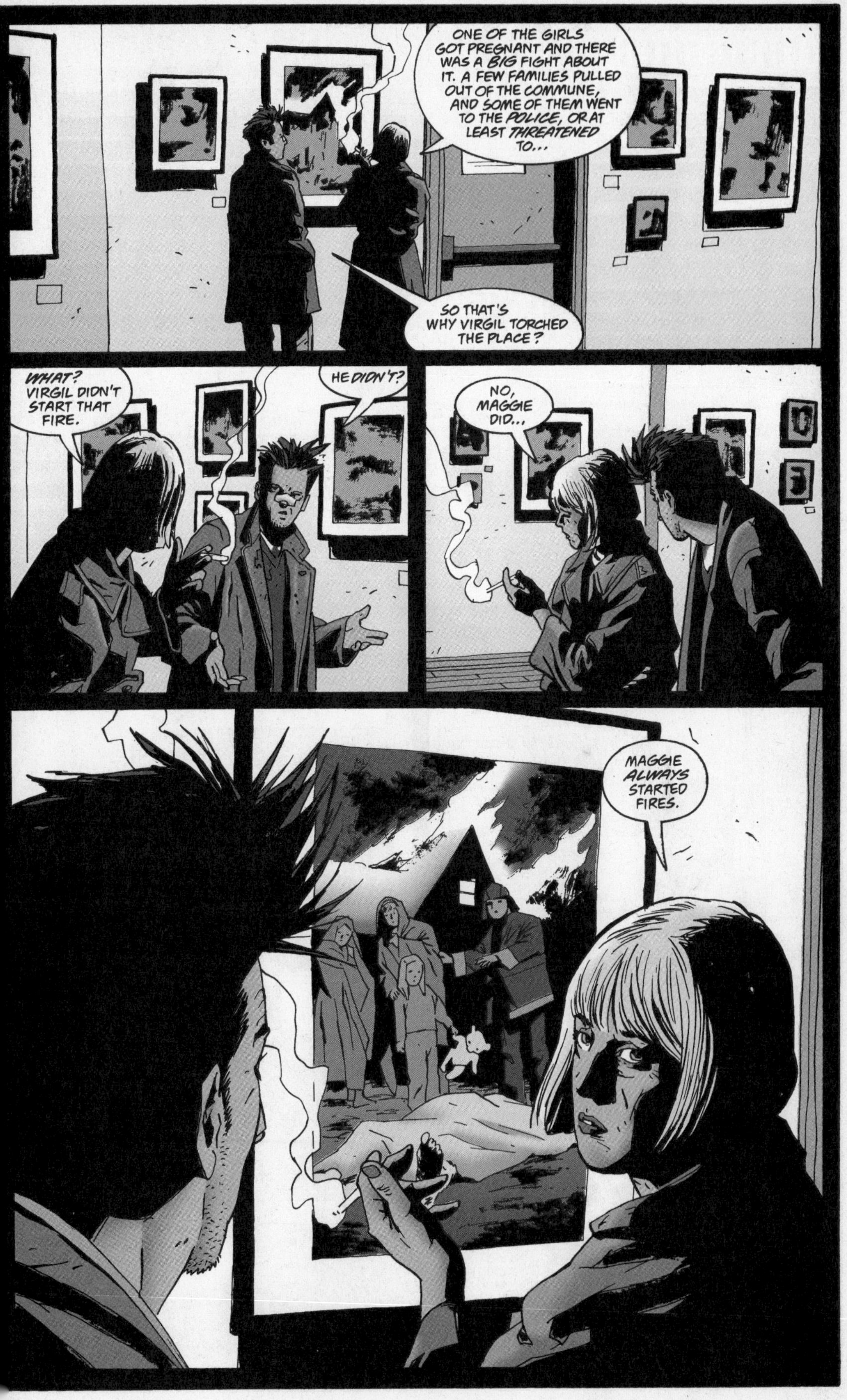
ONE OF THE GIRLS GOT PREGNANT AND THERE WAS A *BIG* FIGHT ABOUT IT. A FEW FAMILIES PULLED OUT OF THE COMMUNE, AND SOME OF THEM WENT TO THE *POLICE*, OR AT LEAST *THREATENED* TO...
SO THAT'S WHY VIRGIL TORCHED THE PLACE?
WHAT? VIRGIL DIDN'T START THAT FIRE.
HE *DIDN'T?*
NO, MAGGIE DID...
MAGGIE *ALWAYS* STARTED FIRES.

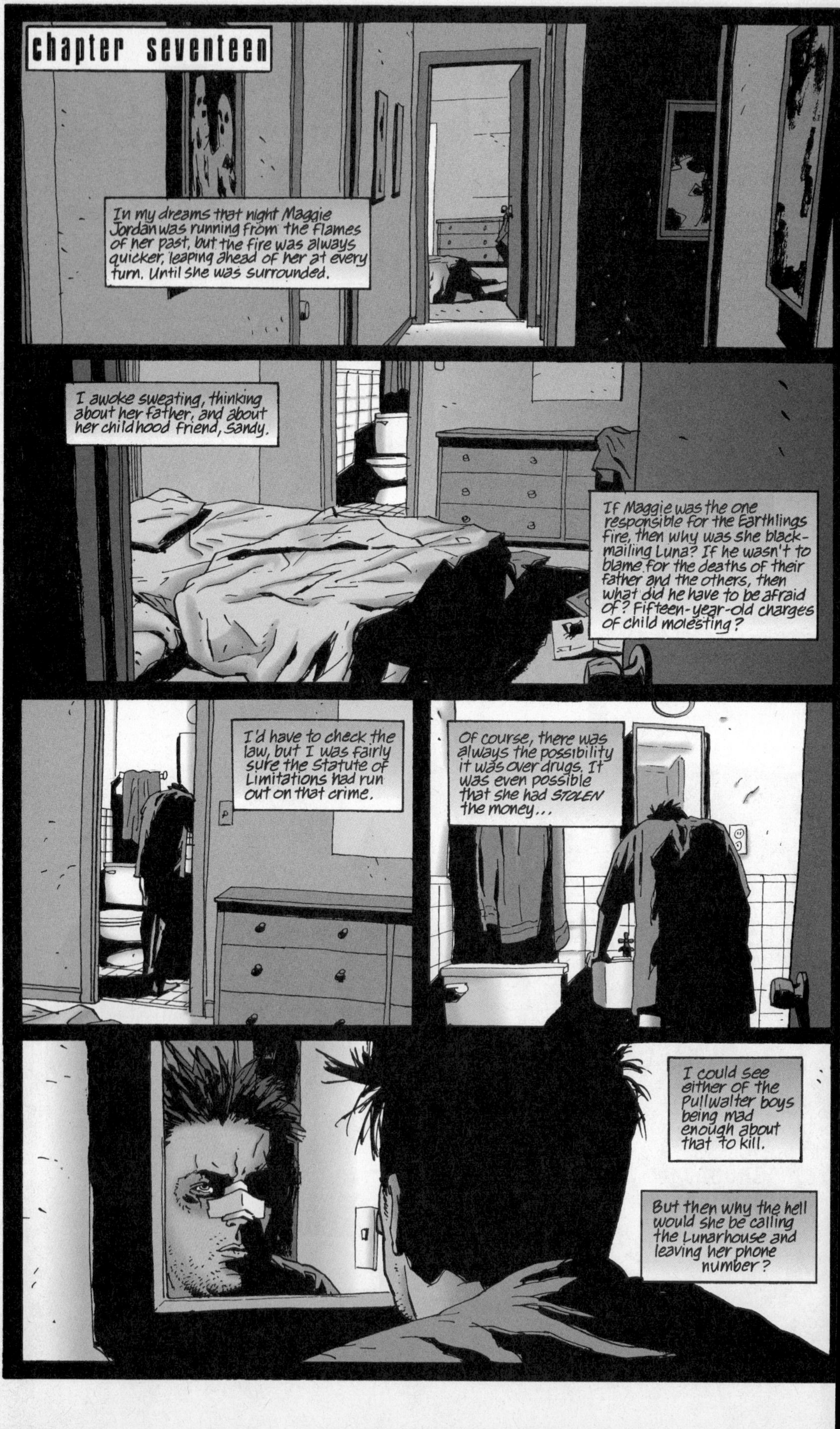
chapter seventeen
In my dreams that night Maggie Jordan was running from the flames of her past, but the fire was always quicker, leaping ahead of her at every turn. Until she was surrounded.
I awoke sweating, thinking about her father, and about her childhood friend, Sandy.
If Maggie was the one responsible for the Earthlings fire, then why was she black-mailing Luna? If he wasn't to blame for the deaths of their father and the others, then what did he have to be afraid of? Fifteen-year-old charges of child molesting?
I'd have to check the law, but I was fairly sure the Statute of Limitations had run out on that crime.
Of course, there was always the possibility it was over drugs. It was even possible that she had STOLEN the money...
I could see either of the Pullwalter boys being mad enough about that to kill.
But then why the hell would she be calling the Lunarhouse and leaving her phone number?

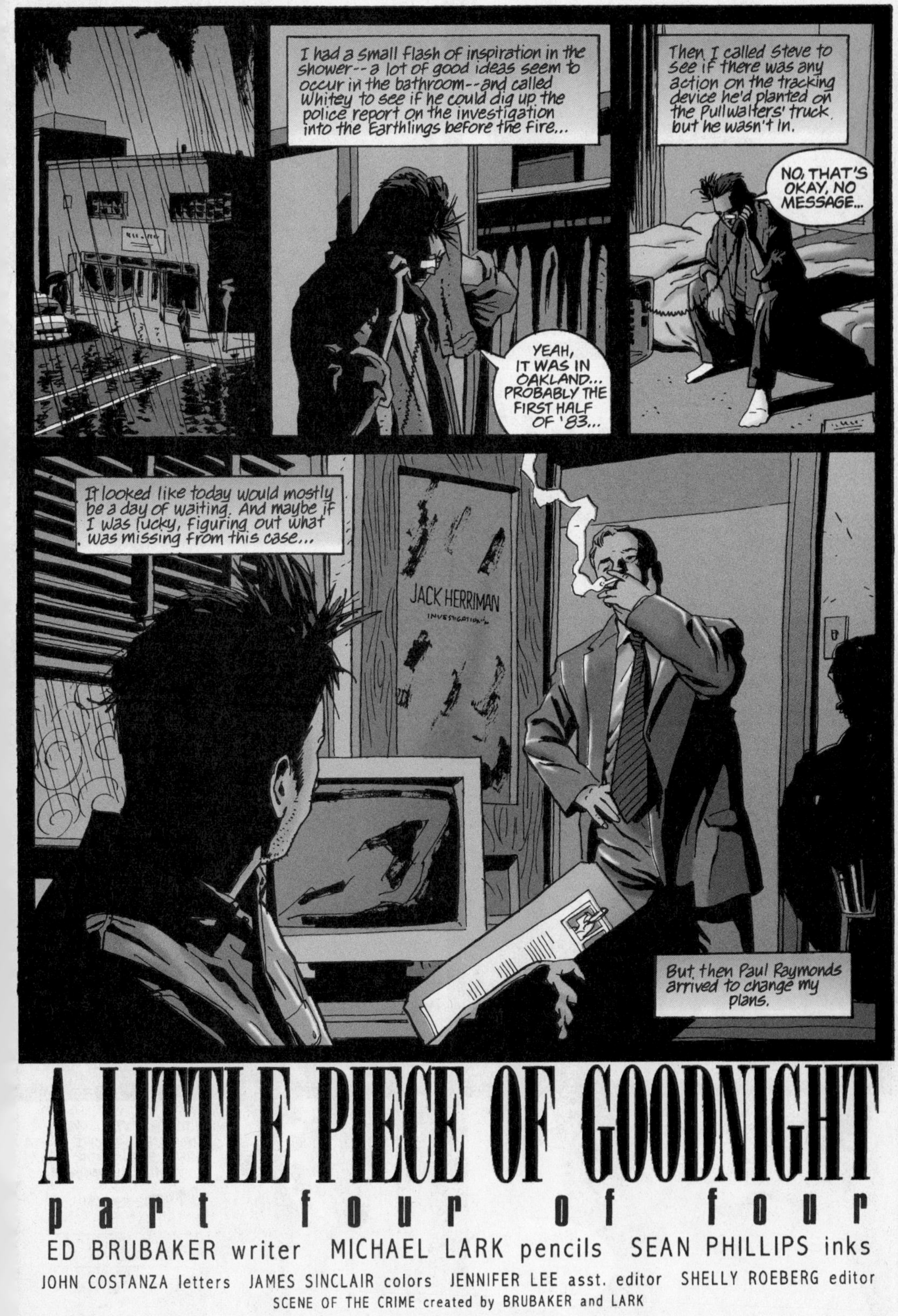

I had a small flash of inspiration in the shower-- a lot of good ideas seem to occur in the bathroom--and called Whitey to see if he could dig up the police report on the investigation into the Earthlings before the fire...
YEAH, IT WAS IN OAKLAND... PROBABLY THE FIRST HALF OF '83...
Then I called Steve to see if there was any action on the tracking device he'd planted on the Pullwalters' truck but he wasn't in.
NO, THAT'S OKAY, NO MESSAGE...
It looked like today would mostly be a day of waiting. And maybe if I was lucky, figuring out what was missing from this case...
JACK HERRIMAN
But, then Paul Raymonds arrived to change my plans.

A LITTLE PIECE OF GOODNIGHT

part four of four

ED BRUBAKER writer MICHAEL LARK pencils SEAN PHILLIPS inks

JOHN COSTANZA letters JAMES SINCLAIR colors JENNIFER LEE asst. editor SHELLY ROEBERG editor

SCENE OF THE CRIME created by BRUBAKER and LARK

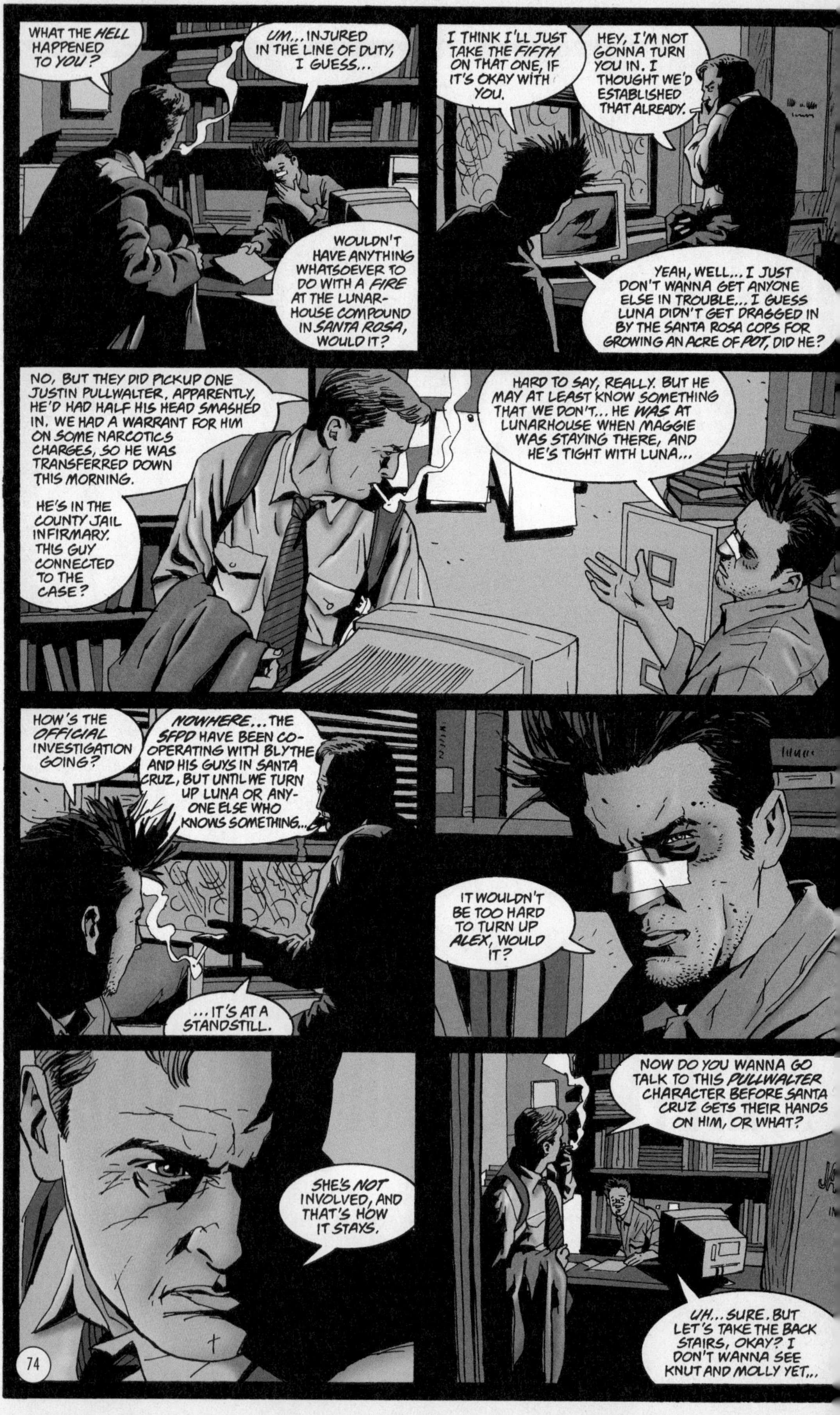
WHAT THE HELL HAPPENED TO YOU?
UM... INJURED IN THE LINE OF DUTY, I GUESS...
WOULDN'T HAVE ANYTHING WHATSOEVER TO DO WITH A FIRE AT THE LUNAR-HOUSE COMPOUND IN SANTA ROSA, WOULD IT?
I THINK I'LL JUST TAKE THE FIFTH ON THAT ONE, IF IT'S OKAY WITH YOU.
HEY, I'M NOT GONNA TURN YOU IN. I THOUGHT WE'D ESTABLISHED THAT ALREADY.
YEAH, WELL... I JUST DON'T WANNA GET ANYONE ELSE IN TROUBLE... I GUESS LUNA DIDN'T GET DRAGGED IN BY THE SANTA ROSA COPS FOR GROWING AN ACRE OF POT, DID HE?
NO, BUT THEY DID PICKUP ONE JUSTIN PULLWALTER, APPARENTLY. HE'D HAD HALF HIS HEAD SMASHED IN. WE HAD A WARRANT FOR HIM ON SOME NARCOTICS CHARGES, SO HE WAS TRANSFERRED DOWN THIS MORNING.
HE'S IN THE COUNTY JAIL INFIRMARY. THIS GUY CONNECTED TO THE CASE?
HARD TO SAY, REALLY. BUT HE MAY AT LEAST KNOW SOMETHING THAT WE DON'T... HE WAS AT LUNARHOUSE WHEN MAGGIE WAS STAYING THERE, AND HE'S TIGHT WITH LUNA...
HOW'S THE OFFICIAL INVESTIGATION GOING?
NOWHERE... THE SFPD HAVE BEEN CO-OPERATING WITH BLYTHE AND HIS GUYS IN SANTA CRUZ, BUT UNTIL WE TURN UP LUNA OR ANY-ONE ELSE WHO KNOWS SOMETHING...
...IT'S AT A STANDSTILL.
IT WOULDN'T BE TOO HARD TO TURN UP ALEX, WOULD IT?
SHE'S NOT INVOLVED, AND THAT'S HOW IT STAYS.
NOW DO YOU WANNA GO TALK TO THIS PULLWALTER CHARACTER BEFORE SANTA CRUZ GETS THEIR HANDS ON HIM, OR WHAT?
UH... SURE. BUT LET'S TAKE THE BACK STAIRS, OKAY? I DON'T WANNA SEE KNUT AND MOLLY YET...

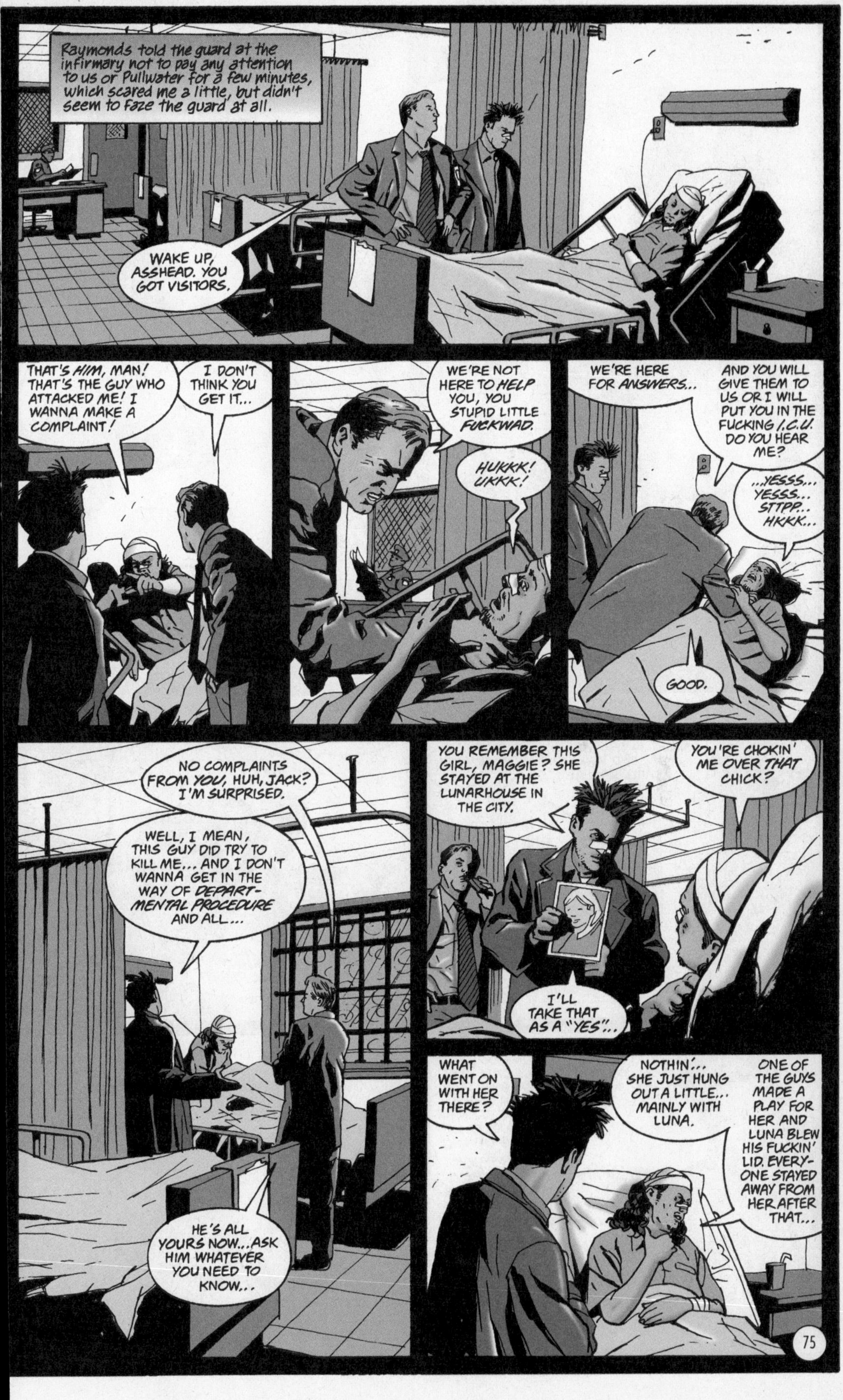

Raymonds told the guard at the infirmary not to pay any attention to us or Pullwater for a few minutes, which scared me a little, but didn't seem to faze the guard at all.
WAKE UP, ASSHEAD. YOU GOT VISITORS.
THAT'S *HIM*, MAN! THAT'S THE GUY WHO ATTACKED ME! I WANNA MAKE A COMPLAINT!
I DON'T THINK YOU GET IT...
WE'RE NOT HERE TO *HELP* YOU, YOU STUPID LITTLE *FUCKWAD*.
HUKKK! UKKK!
WE'RE HERE FOR *ANSWERS*...
AND YOU WILL GIVE THEM TO US OR I WILL PUT YOU IN THE FUCKING *I.C.U.* DO YOU HEAR ME?
...YESSS... YESSS... STTPP... HKKK...
GOOD.
NO COMPLAINTS FROM *YOU*, HUH, JACK? I'M SURPRISED.
WELL, I MEAN, THIS GUY DID TRY TO KILL ME... AND I DON'T WANNA GET IN THE WAY OF *DEPARTMENTAL PROCEDURE* AND ALL...
HE'S ALL YOURS NOW... ASK HIM WHATEVER YOU NEED TO KNOW...
YOU REMEMBER THIS GIRL, MAGGIE? SHE STAYED AT THE LUNARHOUSE IN THE CITY.
YOU'RE CHOKIN' ME OVER *THAT* CHICK?
I'LL TAKE THAT AS A *"YES"*...
WHAT WENT ON WITH HER THERE?
NOTHIN'... SHE JUST HUNG OUT A LITTLE... MAINLY WITH LUNA.
ONE OF THE GUYS MADE A PLAY FOR HER AND LUNA BLEW HIS FUCKIN' LID. EVERYONE STAYED AWAY FROM HER AFTER THAT...

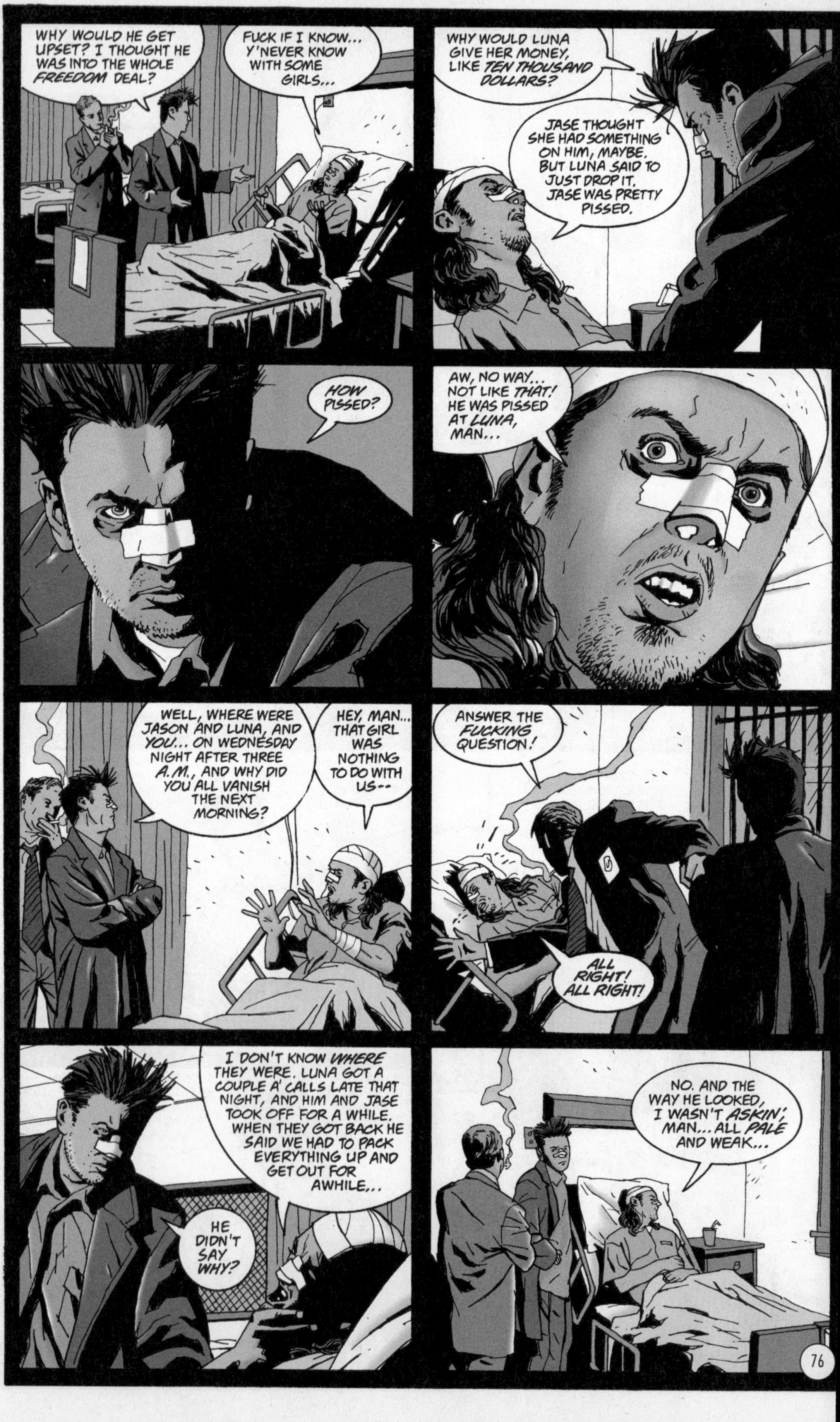
WHY WOULD HE GET UPSET? I THOUGHT HE WAS INTO THE WHOLE FREEDOM DEAL?
FUCK IF I KNOW... Y'NEVER KNOW WITH SOME GIRLS...
WHY WOULD LUNA GIVE HER MONEY, LIKE TEN THOUSAND DOLLARS?
JASE THOUGHT SHE HAD SOMETHING ON HIM, MAYBE. BUT LUNA SAID TO JUST DROP IT. JASE WAS PRETTY PISSED.
HOW PISSED?
AW, NO WAY... NOT LIKE THAT! HE WAS PISSED AT LUNA, MAN...
WELL, WHERE WERE JASON AND LUNA, AND YOU... ON WEDNESDAY NIGHT AFTER THREE A.M., AND WHY DID YOU ALL VANISH THE NEXT MORNING?
HEY, MAN... THAT GIRL WAS NOTHING TO DO WITH US--
ANSWER THE FUCKING QUESTION!
ALL RIGHT! ALL RIGHT!
I DON'T KNOW WHERE THEY WERE. LUNA GOT A COUPLE A' CALLS LATE THAT NIGHT, AND HIM AND JASE TOOK OFF FOR A WHILE. WHEN THEY GOT BACK HE SAID WE HAD TO PACK EVERYTHING UP AND GET OUT FOR AWHILE...
HE DIDN'T SAY WHY?
NO. AND THE WAY HE LOOKED, I WASN'T ASKIN', MAN... ALL PALE AND WEAK...

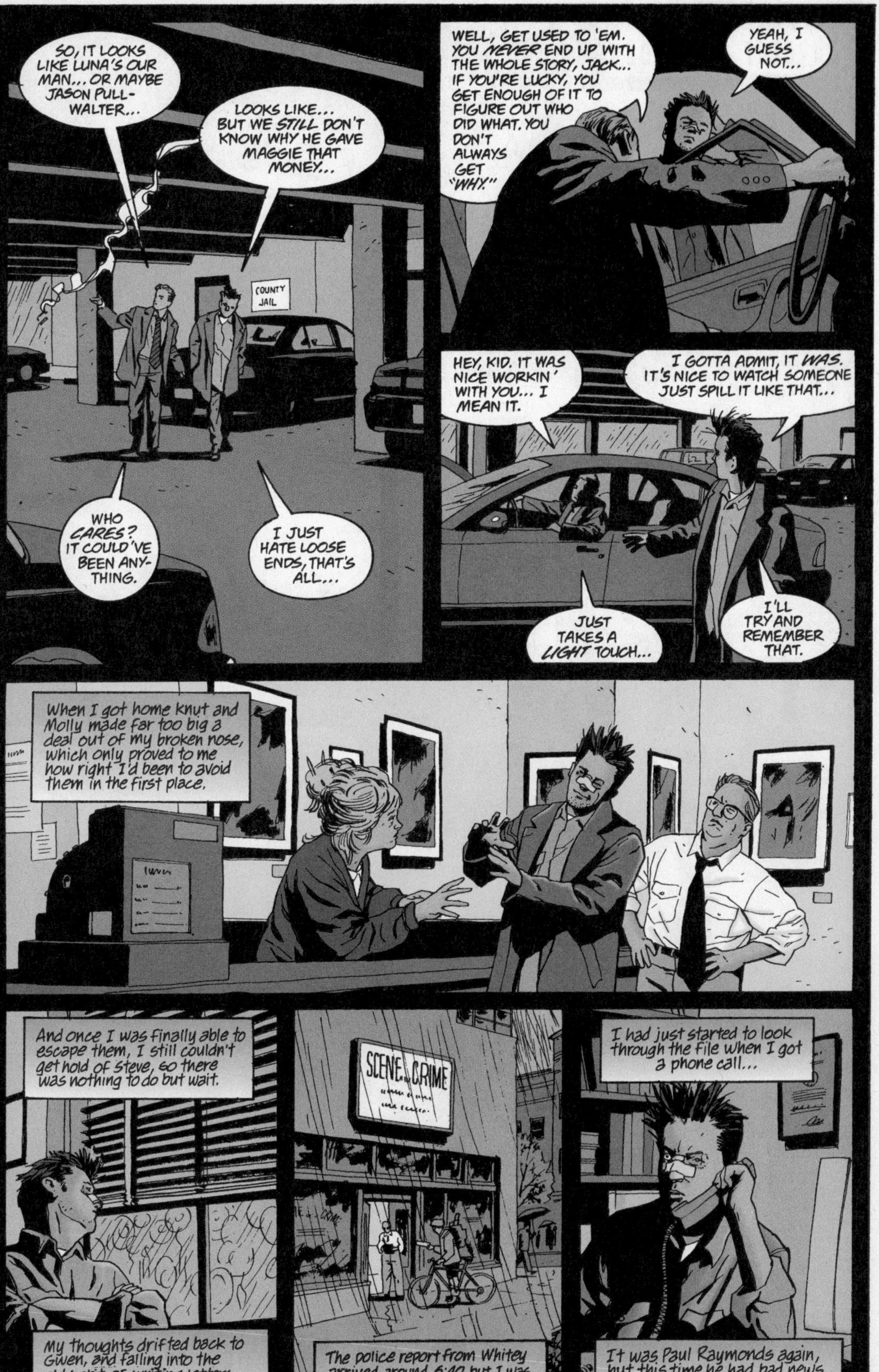
SO, IT LOOKS LIKE LUNA'S OUR MAN... OR MAYBE JASON PULL-WALTER...
LOOKS LIKE... BUT WE STILL DON'T KNOW WHY HE GAVE MAGGIE THAT MONEY...
COUNTY JAIL
WHO CARES? IT COULD'VE BEEN ANY-THING.
I JUST HATE LOOSE ENDS, THAT'S ALL...
WELL, GET USED TO 'EM. YOU NEVER END UP WITH THE WHOLE STORY, JACK... IF YOU'RE LUCKY, YOU GET ENOUGH OF IT TO FIGURE OUT WHO DID WHAT. YOU DON'T ALWAYS GET "WHY."
YEAH, I GUESS NOT...
HEY, KID. IT WAS NICE WORKIN' WITH YOU... I MEAN IT.
I GOTTA ADMIT, IT WAS. IT'S NICE TO WATCH SOMEONE JUST SPILL IT LIKE THAT...
JUST TAKES A LIGHT TOUCH...
I'LL TRY AND REMEMBER THAT.
When I got home Knut and Molly made far too big a deal out of my broken nose, which only proved to me how right I'd been to avoid them in the first place.
And once I was finally able to escape them, I still couldn't get hold of Steve, so there was nothing to do but wait.
My thoughts drifted back to Gwen, and falling into the old habit of writing letters in my head, I began to seren-ade her in my imagination.
SCENE of the CRIME
The police report from Whitey arrived around 6:40, but I was still lost in my daydream and didn't get around to it for a while.
I had just started to look through the file when I got a phone call...
It was Paul Raymonds again, but this time he had bad news... Alexandra Jordan had tried to kill herself.

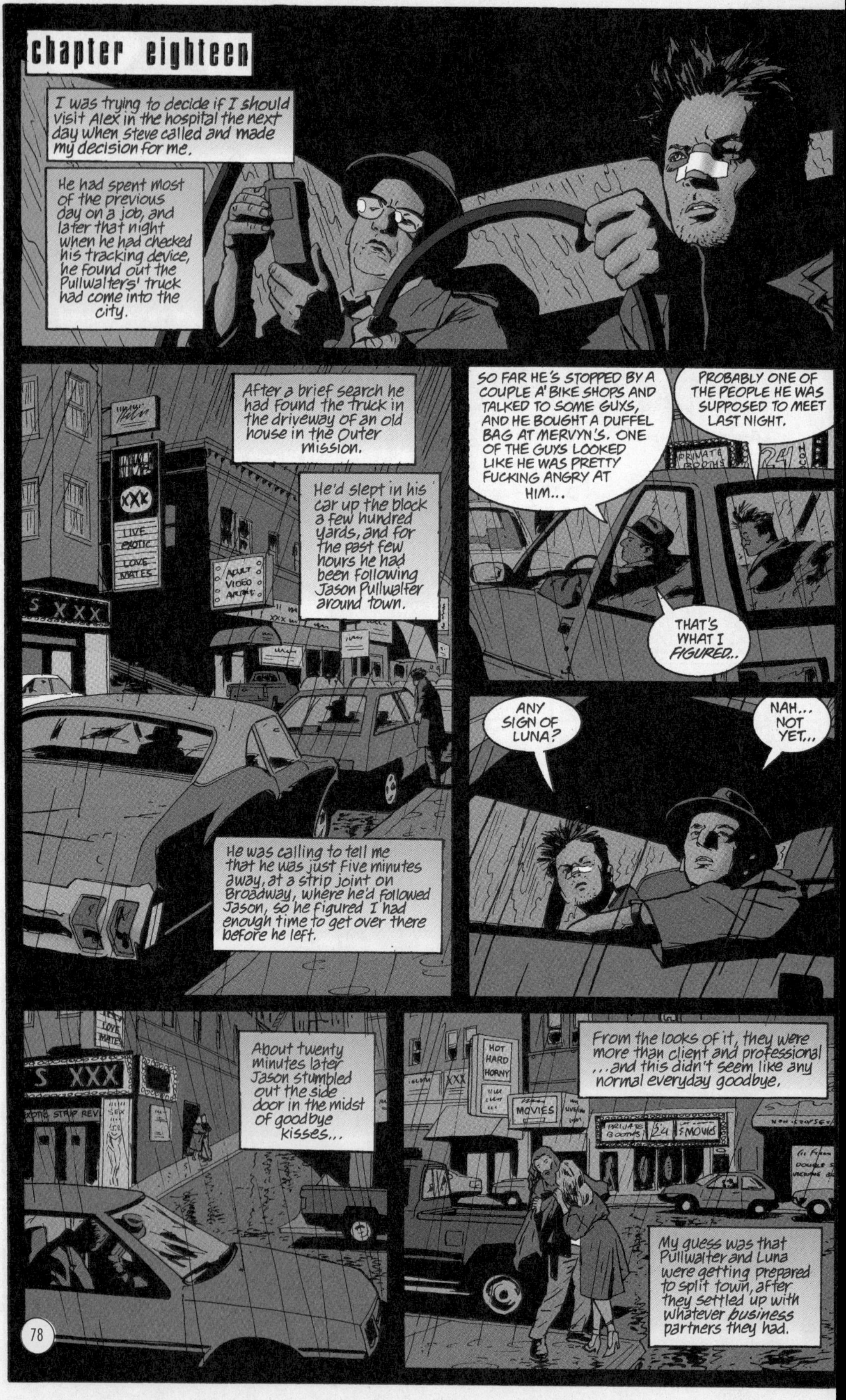
chapter eighteen
I was trying to decide if I should visit Alex in the hospital the next day when Steve called and made my decision for me.
He had spent most of the previous day on a job, and later that night when he had checked his tracking device, he found out the Pullwalters' truck had come into the city.
After a brief search he had found the truck in the driveway of an old house in the Outer Mission.
He'd slept in his car up the block a few hundred yards, and for the past few hours he had been following Jason Pullwalter around town.
He was calling to tell me that he was just five minutes away, at a strip joint on Broadway, where he'd followed Jason, so he figured I had enough time to get over there before he left.
XXX
LIVE EXOTIC LOVE MATES
ADULT VIDEO ARTS
S XXX
SO FAR HE'S STOPPED BY A COUPLE A' BIKE SHOPS AND TALKED TO SOME GUYS, AND HE BOUGHT A DUFFEL BAG AT MERVYN'S. ONE OF THE GUYS LOOKED LIKE HE WAS PRETTY FUCKING ANGRY AT HIM...
PROBABLY ONE OF THE PEOPLE HE WAS SUPPOSED TO MEET LAST NIGHT.
THAT'S WHAT I *FIGURED*...
ANY SIGN OF LUNA?
NAH... NOT YET...
About twenty minutes later Jason stumbled out the side door in the midst of goodbye kisses...
S XXX
SEX
From the looks of it, they were more than client and professional ...and this didn't seem like any normal everyday goodbye.
HOT HARD HORNY
MOVIES
PRIVATE BOOTHS
24
MOVIES
My guess was that Pullwalter and Luna were getting prepared to split town, after they settled up with whatever *business* partners they had.

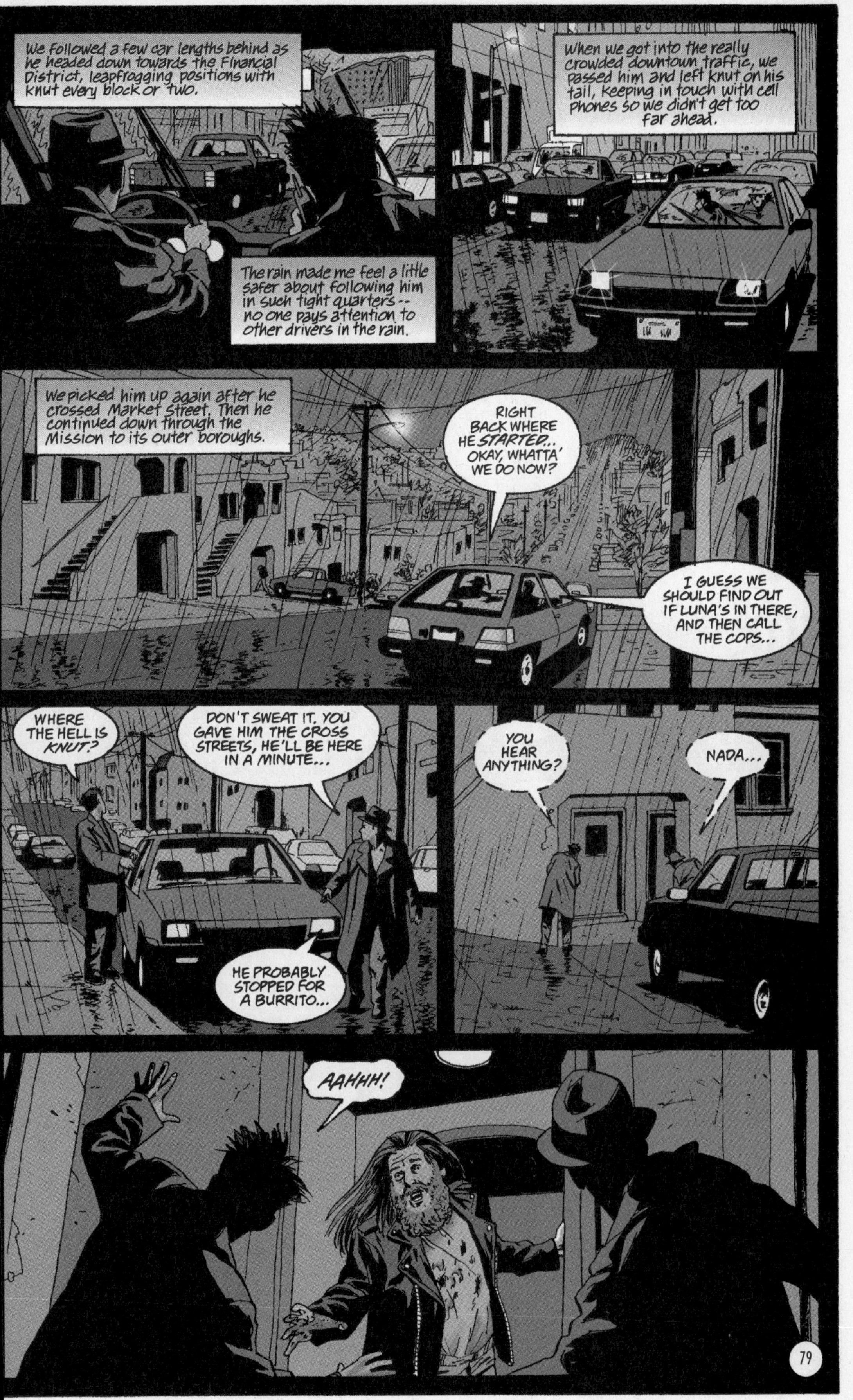
We followed a few car lengths behind as he headed down towards the Financial District, leapfrogging positions with knut every block or two.
The rain made me feel a little safer about following him in such tight quarters -- no one pays attention to other drivers in the rain.
When we got into the really crowded downtown traffic, we passed him and left knut on his tail, keeping in touch with cell phones so we didn't get too far ahead.
We picked him up again after he crossed Market Street. Then he continued down through the Mission to its outer boroughs.
RIGHT BACK WHERE HE STARTED... OKAY, WHATTA' WE DO NOW?
I GUESS WE SHOULD FIND OUT IF LUNA'S IN THERE, AND THEN CALL THE COPS...
WHERE THE HELL IS KNUT?
DON'T SWEAT IT. YOU GAVE HIM THE CROSS STREETS, HE'LL BE HERE IN A MINUTE...
HE PROBABLY STOPPED FOR A BURRITO...
YOU HEAR ANYTHING?
NADA...
AAHHH!

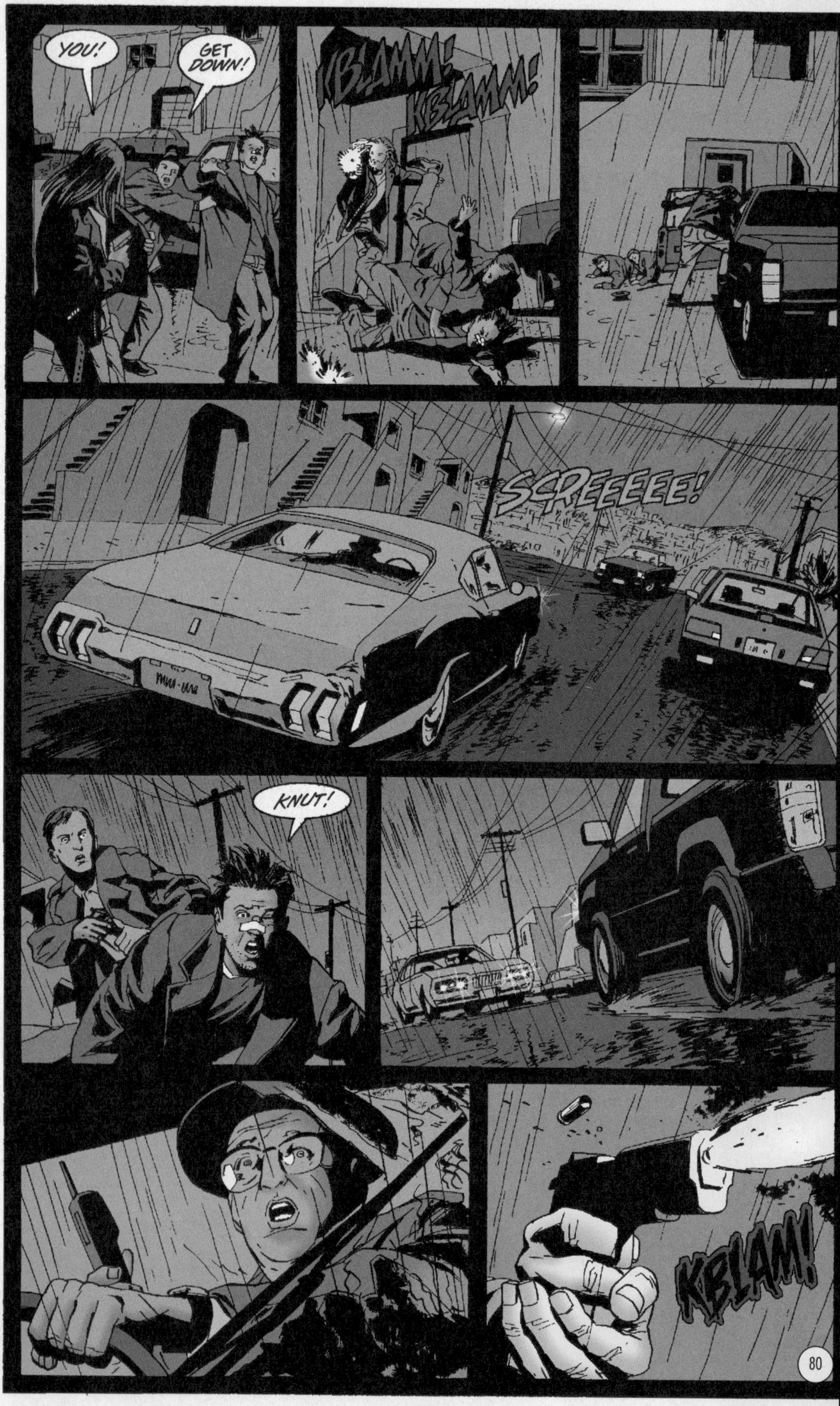
YOU!
GET DOWN!
KBLAMM! KBLAMM!
SCREEEEEE!
KNUT!
KBLAM!

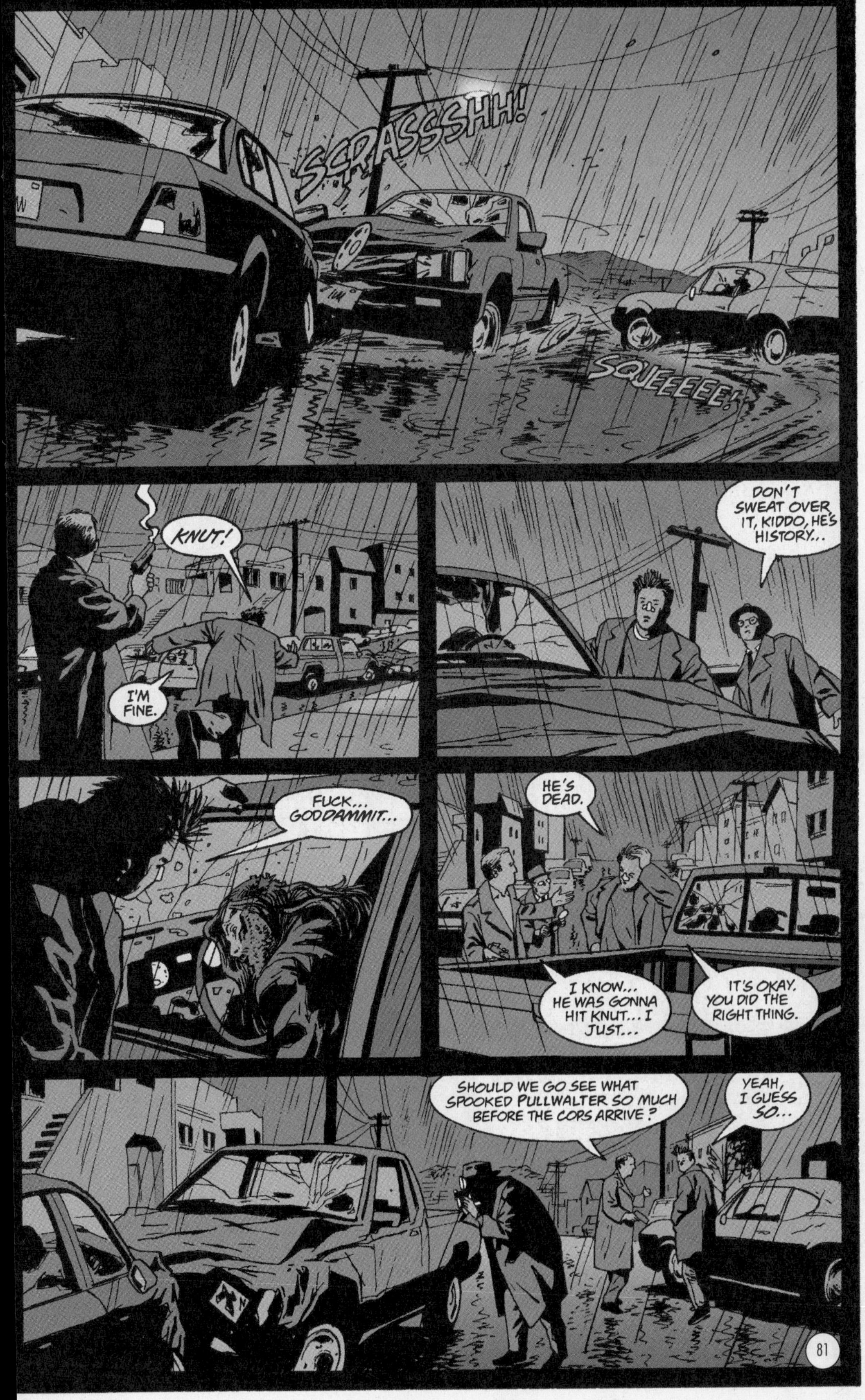
SCRASSSSHH!
SQUEEEEEE!
KNUT!
I'M FINE.
DON'T SWEAT OVER IT, KIDDO, HE'S HISTORY...
FUCK... GODDAMMIT...
HE'S DEAD.
I KNOW... HE WAS GONNA HIT KNUT... I JUST...
IT'S OKAY. YOU DID THE RIGHT THING.
SHOULD WE GO SEE WHAT SPOOKED PULLWALTER SO MUCH BEFORE THE COPS ARRIVE?
YEAH, I GUESS SO...

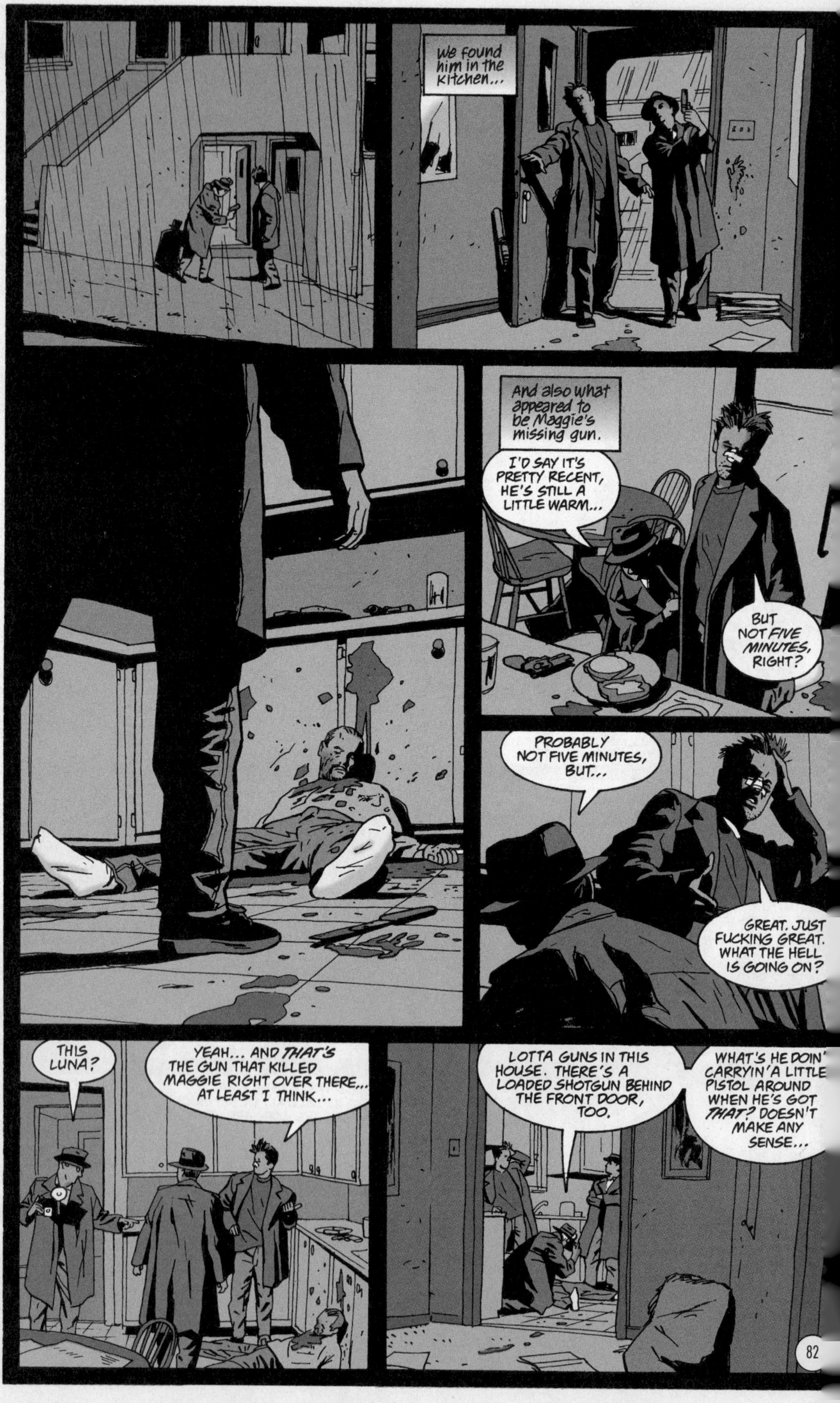

We found him in the kitchen...
And also what appeared to be Maggie's missing gun.
I'D SAY IT'S PRETTY RECENT, HE'S STILL A LITTLE WARM...
BUT NOT FIVE MINUTES, RIGHT?
PROBABLY NOT FIVE MINUTES, BUT...
GREAT. JUST FUCKING GREAT. WHAT THE HELL IS GOING ON?
THIS LUNA?
YEAH... AND THAT'S THE GUN THAT KILLED MAGGIE RIGHT OVER THERE... AT LEAST I THINK...
LOTTA GUNS IN THIS HOUSE. THERE'S A LOADED SHOTGUN BEHIND THE FRONT DOOR, TOO.
WHAT'S HE DOIN' CARRYIN' A LITTLE PISTOL AROUND WHEN HE'S GOT THAT? DOESN'T MAKE ANY SENSE...

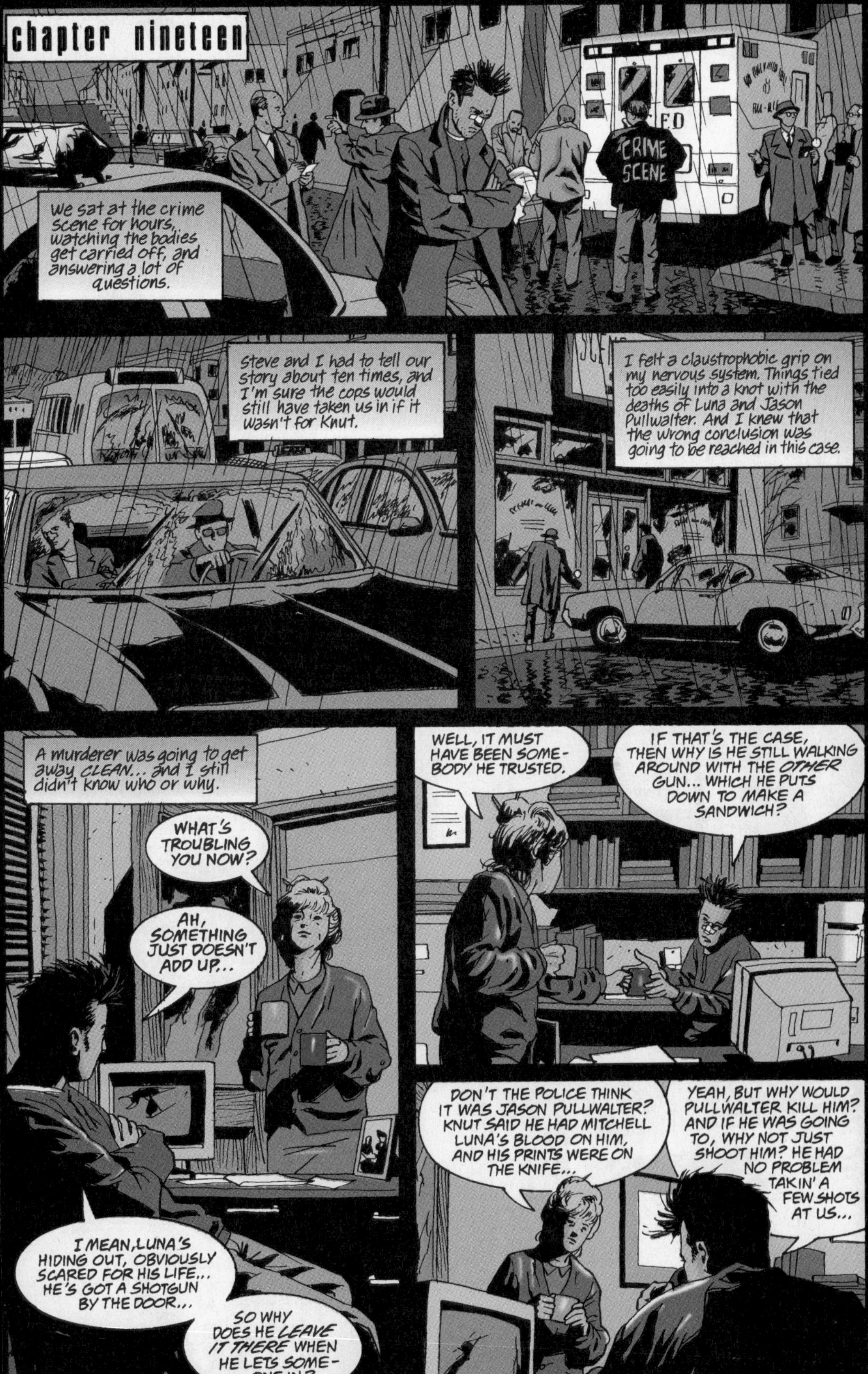
chapter nineteen
We sat at the crime scene for hours, watching the bodies get carried off, and answering a lot of questions.
CRIME SCENE
Steve and I had to tell our story about ten times, and I'm sure the cops would still have taken us in if it wasn't for Knut.
I felt a claustrophobic grip on my nervous system. Things tied too easily into a knot with the deaths of Luna and Jason Pullwalter. And I knew that the wrong conclusion was going to be reached in this case.
A murderer was going to get away CLEAN... and I still didn't know who or why.
WHAT'S TROUBLING YOU NOW?
AH, SOMETHING JUST DOESN'T ADD UP...
I MEAN, LUNA'S HIDING OUT, OBVIOUSLY SCARED FOR HIS LIFE... HE'S GOT A SHOTGUN BY THE DOOR...
SO WHY DOES HE LEAVE IT THERE WHEN HE LETS SOME-ONE IN?
WELL, IT MUST HAVE BEEN SOME-BODY HE TRUSTED.
IF THAT'S THE CASE, THEN WHY IS HE STILL WALKING AROUND WITH THE OTHER GUN... WHICH HE PUTS DOWN TO MAKE A SANDWICH?
DON'T THE POLICE THINK IT WAS JASON PULLWALTER? KNUT SAID HE HAD MITCHELL LUNA'S BLOOD ON HIM, AND HIS PRINTS WERE ON THE KNIFE...
YEAH, BUT WHY WOULD PULLWALTER KILL HIM? AND IF HE WAS GOING TO, WHY NOT JUST SHOOT HIM? HE HAD NO PROBLEM TAKIN' A FEW SHOTS AT US...

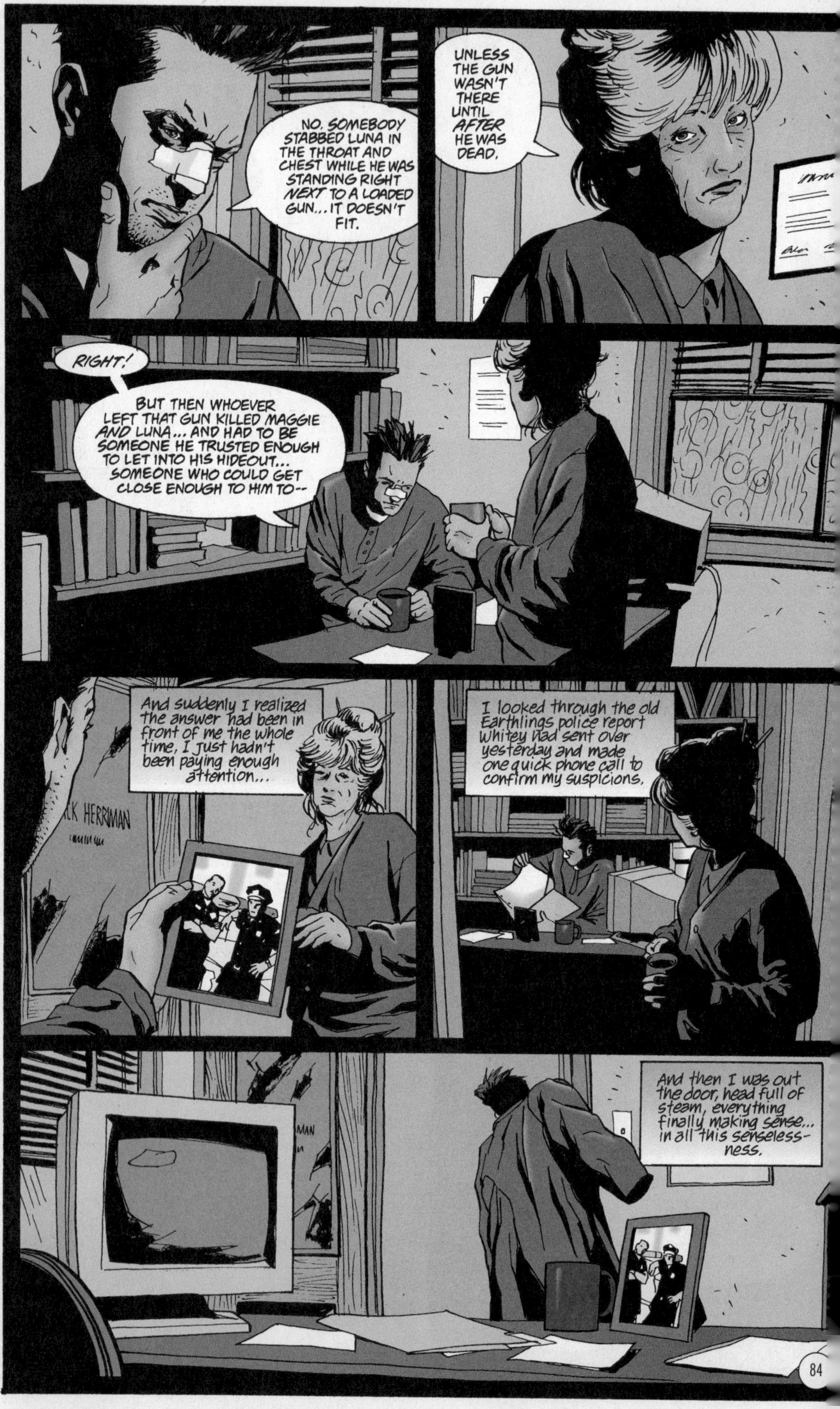
NO. SOMEBODY STABBED LUNA IN THE THROAT AND CHEST WHILE HE WAS STANDING RIGHT NEXT TO A LOADED GUN... IT DOESN'T FIT.
UNLESS THE GUN WASN'T THERE UNTIL AFTER HE WAS DEAD.
RIGHT!
BUT THEN WHOEVER LEFT THAT GUN KILLED MAGGIE AND LUNA... AND HAD TO BE SOMEONE HE TRUSTED ENOUGH TO LET INTO HIS HIDEOUT... SOMEONE WHO COULD GET CLOSE ENOUGH TO HIM TO--
And suddenly I realized the answer had been in front of me the whole time, I just hadn't been paying enough attention...
I looked through the old Earthlings police report Whitey had sent over yesterday and made one quick phone call to confirm my suspicions.
And then I was out the door, head full of steam, everything finally making sense... in all this senseless-ness.

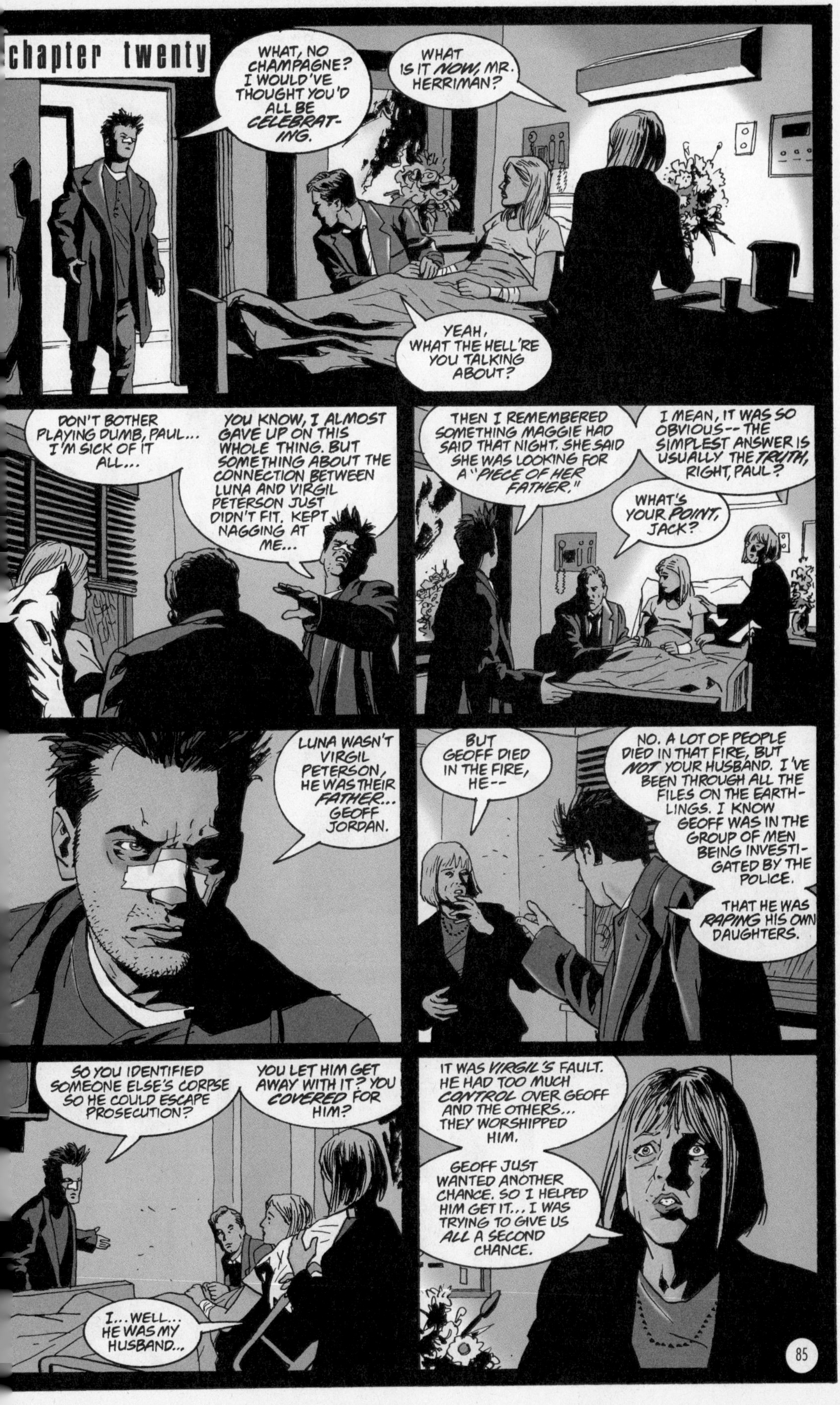
chapter twenty
WHAT, NO CHAMPAGNE? I WOULD'VE THOUGHT YOU'D ALL BE CELEBRATING.
WHAT IS IT NOW, MR. HERRIMAN?
YEAH, WHAT THE HELL'RE YOU TALKING ABOUT?
DON'T BOTHER PLAYING DUMB, PAUL... I'M SICK OF IT ALL...
YOU KNOW, I ALMOST GAVE UP ON THIS WHOLE THING. BUT SOMETHING ABOUT THE CONNECTION BETWEEN LUNA AND VIRGIL PETERSON JUST DIDN'T FIT. KEPT NAGGING AT ME...
THEN I REMEMBERED SOMETHING MAGGIE HAD SAID THAT NIGHT. SHE SAID SHE WAS LOOKING FOR A "PIECE OF HER FATHER."
I MEAN, IT WAS SO OBVIOUS-- THE SIMPLEST ANSWER IS USUALLY THE TRUTH, RIGHT, PAUL?
WHAT'S YOUR POINT, JACK?
LUNA WASN'T VIRGIL PETERSON, HE WAS THEIR FATHER... GEOFF JORDAN.
BUT GEOFF DIED IN THE FIRE, HE--
NO. A LOT OF PEOPLE DIED IN THAT FIRE, BUT NOT YOUR HUSBAND. I'VE BEEN THROUGH ALL THE FILES ON THE EARTHLINGS. I KNOW GEOFF WAS IN THE GROUP OF MEN BEING INVESTIGATED BY THE POLICE.
THAT HE WAS RAPING HIS OWN DAUGHTERS.
SO YOU IDENTIFIED SOMEONE ELSE'S CORPSE SO HE COULD ESCAPE PROSECUTION?
YOU LET HIM GET AWAY WITH IT? YOU COVERED FOR HIM?
I... WELL... HE WAS MY HUSBAND...
IT WAS VIRGIL'S FAULT. HE HAD TOO MUCH CONTROL OVER GEOFF AND THE OTHERS... THEY WORSHIPPED HIM.
GEOFF JUST WANTED ANOTHER CHANCE. SO I HELPED HIM GET IT... I WAS TRYING TO GIVE US ALL A SECOND CHANCE.

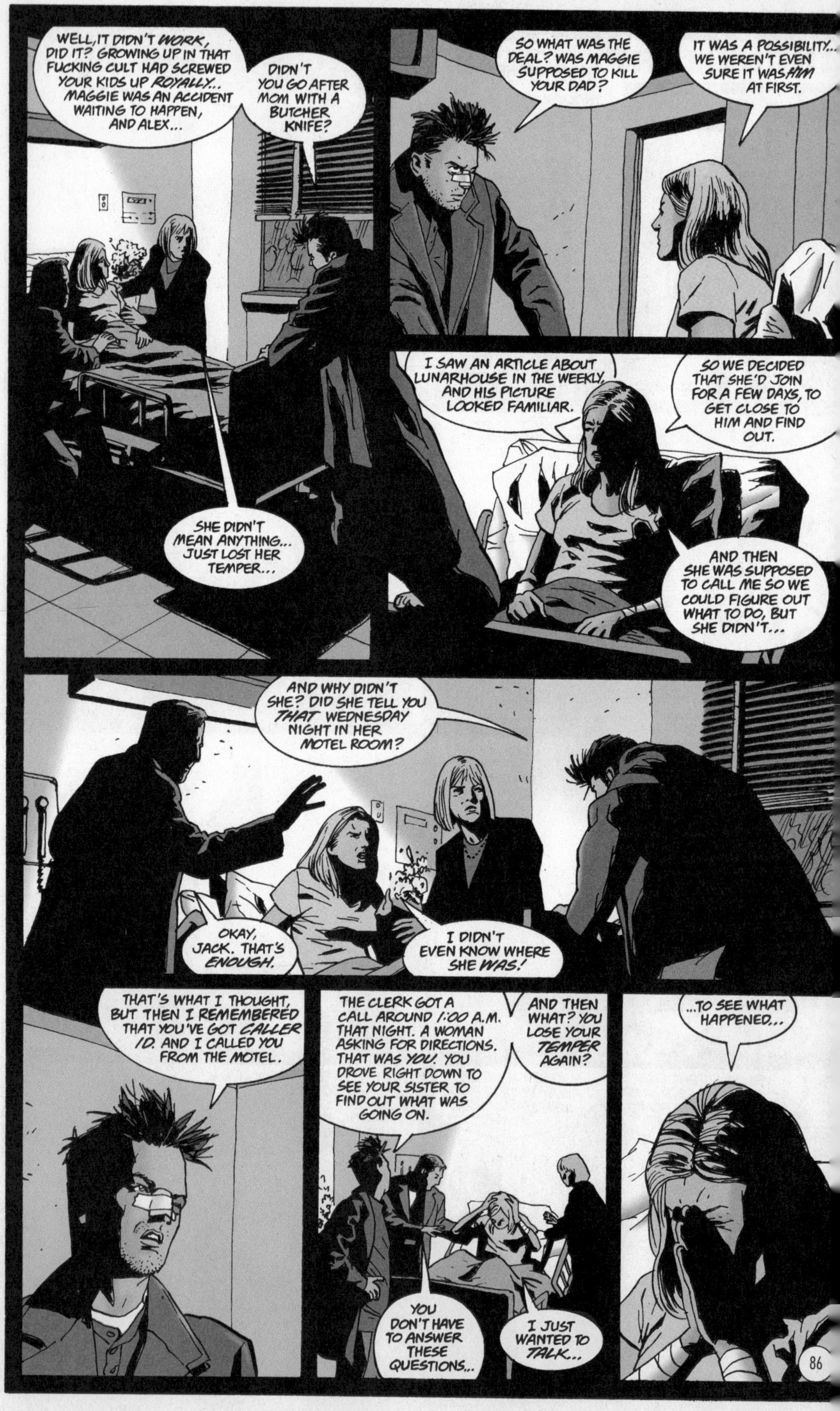
WELL, IT DIDN'T WORK, DID IT? GROWING UP IN THAT FUCKING CULT HAD SCREWED YOUR KIDS UP ROYALLY... MAGGIE WAS AN ACCIDENT WAITING TO HAPPEN, AND ALEX...
DIDN'T YOU GO AFTER MOM WITH A BUTCHER KNIFE?
SHE DIDN'T MEAN ANYTHING... JUST LOST HER TEMPER...
SO WHAT WAS THE DEAL? WAS MAGGIE SUPPOSED TO KILL YOUR DAD?
IT WAS A POSSIBILITY... WE WEREN'T EVEN SURE IT WAS HIM AT FIRST.
I SAW AN ARTICLE ABOUT LUNARHOUSE IN THE WEEKLY, AND HIS PICTURE LOOKED FAMILIAR.
SO WE DECIDED THAT SHE'D JOIN FOR A FEW DAYS, TO GET CLOSE TO HIM AND FIND OUT.
AND THEN SHE WAS SUPPOSED TO CALL ME SO WE COULD FIGURE OUT WHAT TO DO, BUT SHE DIDN'T...
AND WHY DIDN'T SHE? DID SHE TELL YOU THAT WEDNESDAY NIGHT IN HER MOTEL ROOM?
OKAY, JACK. THAT'S ENOUGH.
I DIDN'T EVEN KNOW WHERE SHE WAS!
THAT'S WHAT I THOUGHT, BUT THEN I REMEMBERED THAT YOU'VE GOT CALLER I.D. AND I CALLED YOU FROM THE MOTEL.
THE CLERK GOT A CALL AROUND 1:00 A.M. THAT NIGHT. A WOMAN ASKING FOR DIRECTIONS. THAT WAS YOU. YOU DROVE RIGHT DOWN TO SEE YOUR SISTER TO FIND OUT WHAT WAS GOING ON.
AND THEN WHAT? YOU LOSE YOUR TEMPER AGAIN?
YOU DON'T HAVE TO ANSWER THESE QUESTIONS...
I JUST WANTED TO TALK...
...TO SEE WHAT HAPPENED...

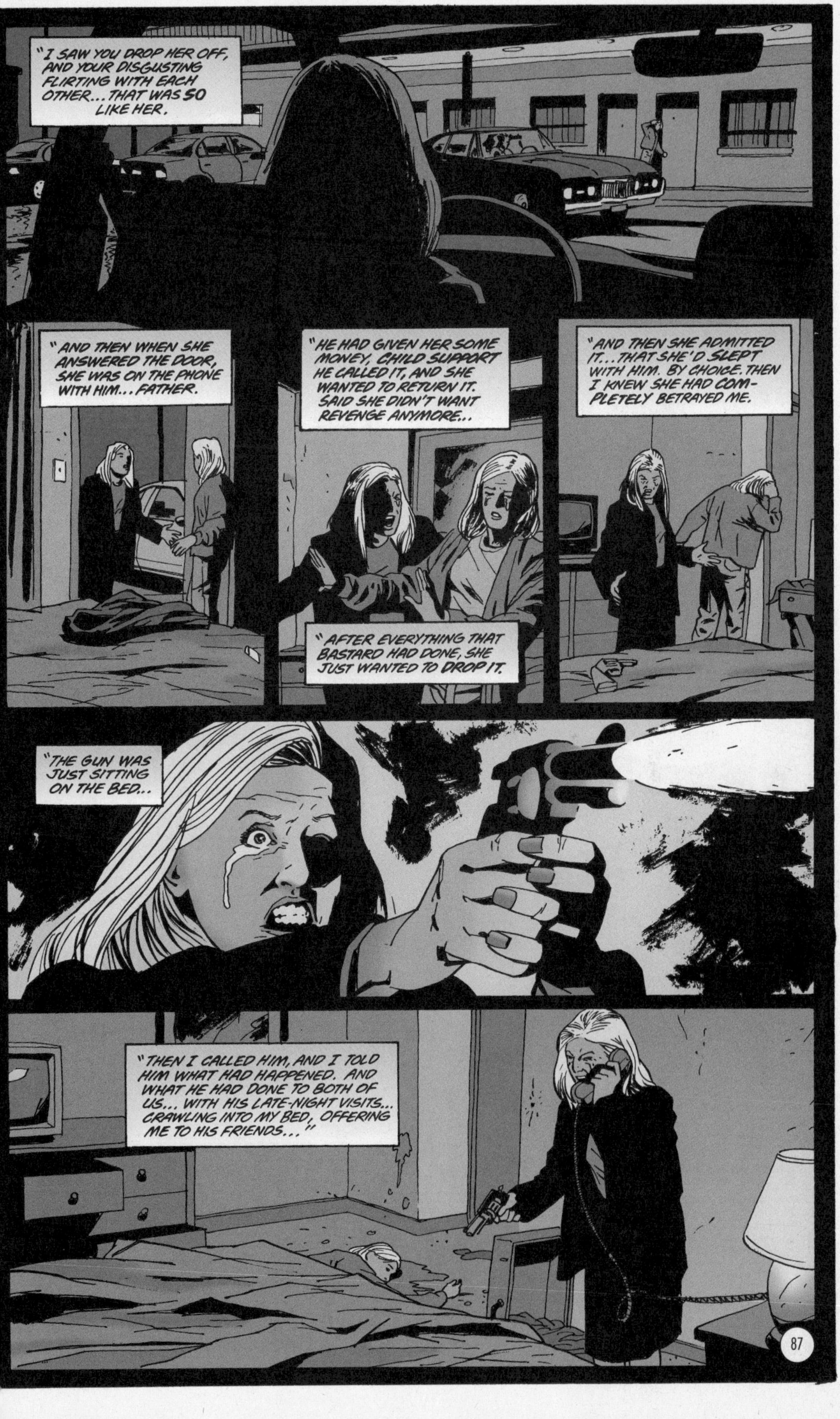
"I SAW YOU DROP HER OFF, AND YOUR DISGUSTING FLIRTING WITH EACH OTHER... THAT WAS SO LIKE HER.
"AND THEN WHEN SHE ANSWERED THE DOOR, SHE WAS ON THE PHONE WITH HIM... FATHER.
"HE HAD GIVEN HER SOME MONEY, CHILD SUPPORT HE CALLED IT, AND SHE WANTED TO RETURN IT. SAID SHE DIDN'T WANT REVENGE ANYMORE...
"AFTER EVERYTHING THAT BASTARD HAD DONE, SHE JUST WANTED TO DROP IT.
"AND THEN SHE ADMITTED IT... THAT SHE'D SLEPT WITH HIM. BY CHOICE. THEN I KNEW SHE HAD COMPLETELY BETRAYED ME.
"THE GUN WAS JUST SITTING ON THE BED...
"THEN I CALLED HIM, AND I TOLD HIM WHAT HAD HAPPENED. AND WHAT HE HAD DONE TO BOTH OF US... WITH HIS LATE-NIGHT VISITS... CRAWLING INTO MY BED, OFFERING ME TO HIS FRIENDS..."

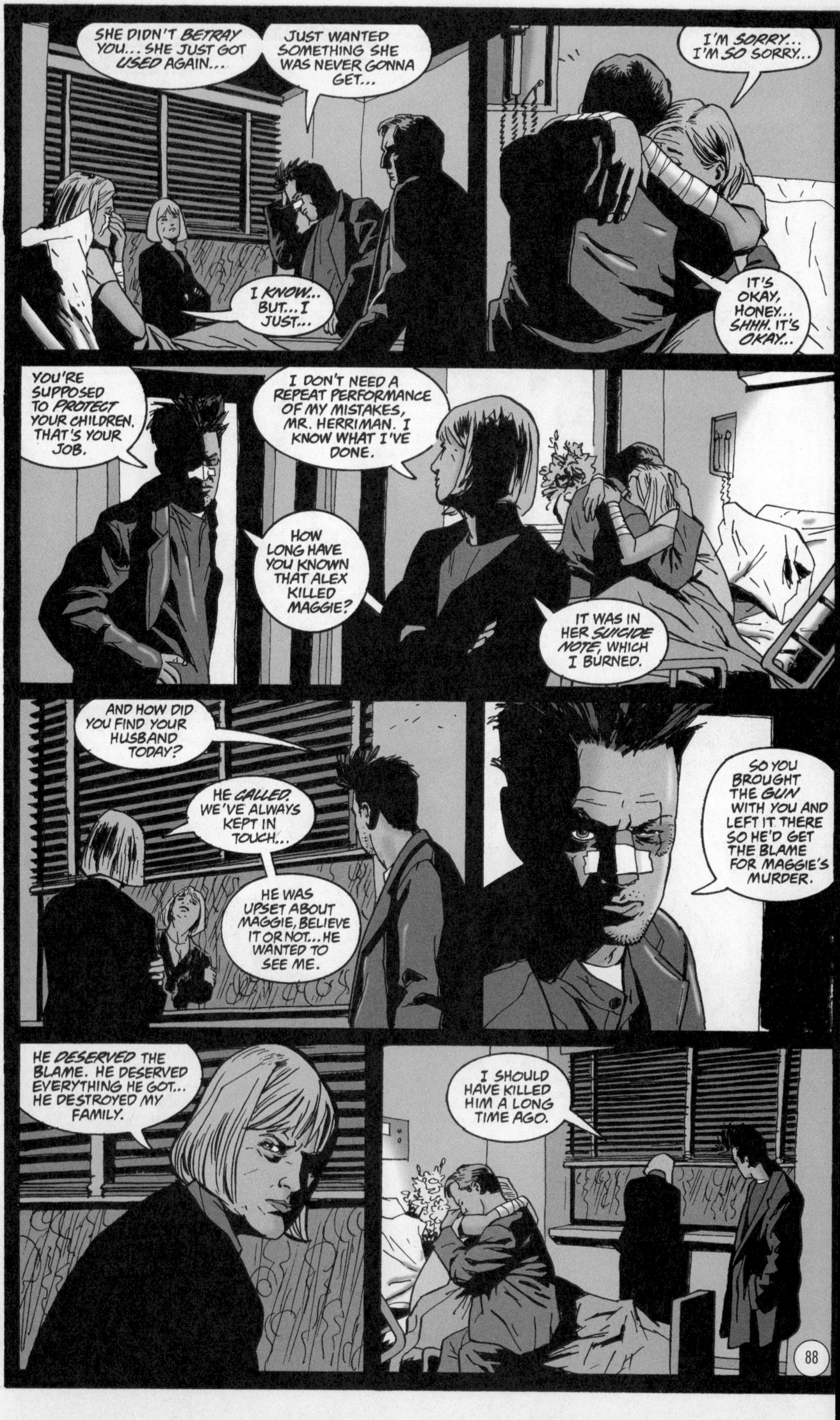

SHE DIDN'T BETRAY YOU... SHE JUST GOT USED AGAIN...
JUST WANTED SOMETHING SHE WAS NEVER GONNA GET...
I KNOW... BUT... I JUST...
I'M SORRY... I'M SO SORRY...
IT'S OKAY, HONEY... SHHH. IT'S OKAY...
YOU'RE SUPPOSED TO PROTECT YOUR CHILDREN. THAT'S YOUR JOB.
I DON'T NEED A REPEAT PERFORMANCE OF MY MISTAKES, MR. HERRIMAN. I KNOW WHAT I'VE DONE.
HOW LONG HAVE YOU KNOWN THAT ALEX KILLED MAGGIE?
IT WAS IN HER SUICIDE NOTE, WHICH I BURNED.
AND HOW DID YOU FIND YOUR HUSBAND TODAY?
HE CALLED. WE'VE ALWAYS KEPT IN TOUCH...
HE WAS UPSET ABOUT MAGGIE, BELIEVE IT OR NOT... HE WANTED TO SEE ME.
SO YOU BROUGHT THE GUN WITH YOU AND LEFT IT THERE SO HE'D GET THE BLAME FOR MAGGIE'S MURDER.
HE DESERVED THE BLAME. HE DESERVED EVERYTHING HE GOT... HE DESTROYED MY FAMILY.
I SHOULD HAVE KILLED HIM A LONG TIME AGO.

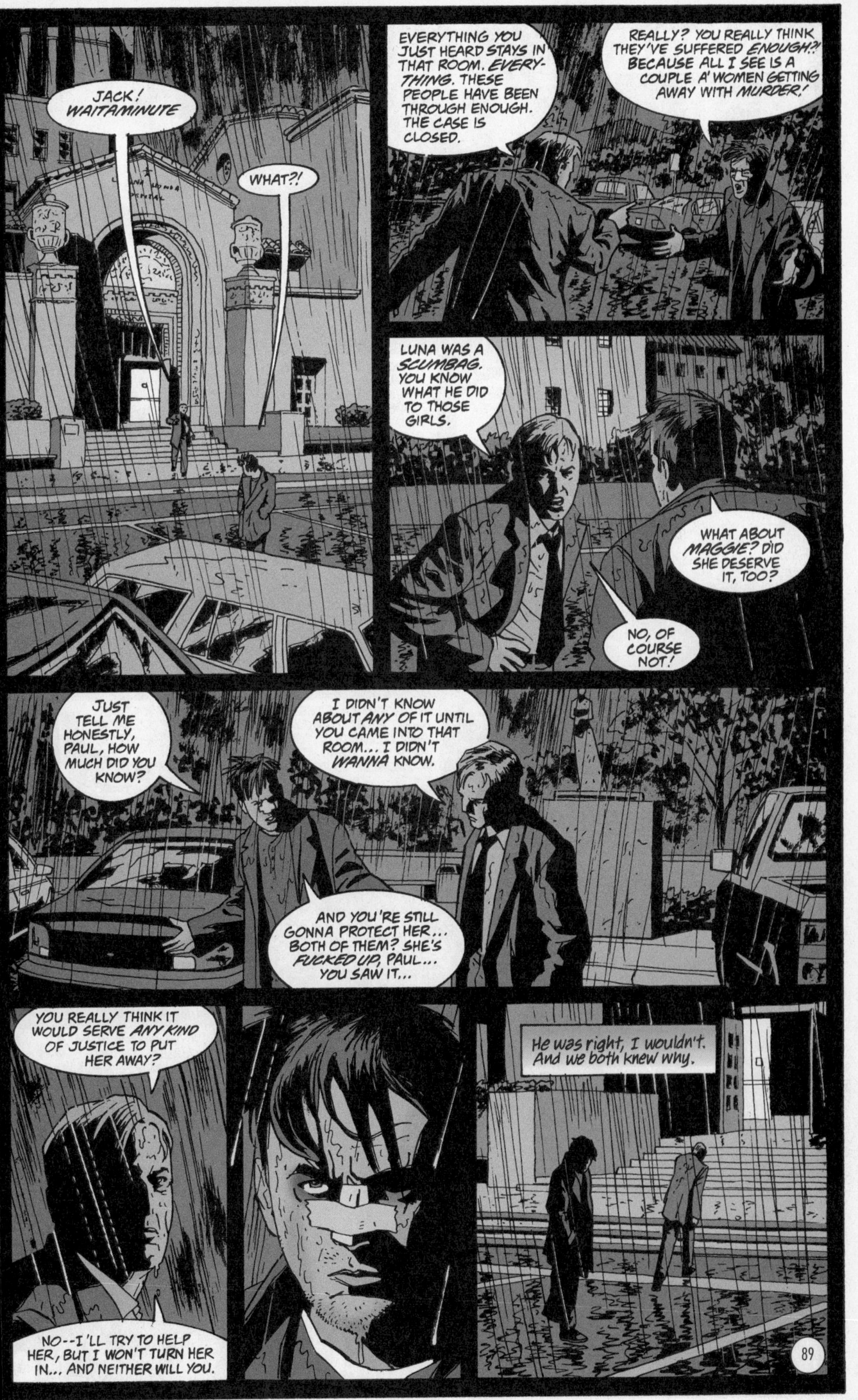
JACK! WAITAMINUTE
WHAT?!
EVERYTHING YOU JUST HEARD STAYS IN THAT ROOM. EVERYTHING. THESE PEOPLE HAVE BEEN THROUGH ENOUGH. THE CASE IS CLOSED.
REALLY? YOU REALLY THINK THEY'VE SUFFERED ENOUGH?! BECAUSE ALL I SEE IS A COUPLE A' WOMEN GETTING AWAY WITH MURDER!
LUNA WAS A SCUMBAG. YOU KNOW WHAT HE DID TO THOSE GIRLS.
WHAT ABOUT MAGGIE? DID SHE DESERVE IT, TOO?
NO, OF COURSE NOT!
JUST TELL ME HONESTLY, PAUL, HOW MUCH DID YOU KNOW?
I DIDN'T KNOW ABOUT ANY OF IT UNTIL YOU CAME INTO THAT ROOM... I DIDN'T WANNA KNOW.
AND YOU'RE STILL GONNA PROTECT HER... BOTH OF THEM? SHE'S FUCKED UP, PAUL... YOU SAW IT...
YOU REALLY THINK IT WOULD SERVE ANY KIND OF JUSTICE TO PUT HER AWAY?
NO--I'LL TRY TO HELP HER, BUT I WON'T TURN HER IN... AND NEITHER WILL YOU.
He was right, I wouldn't. And we both knew why.

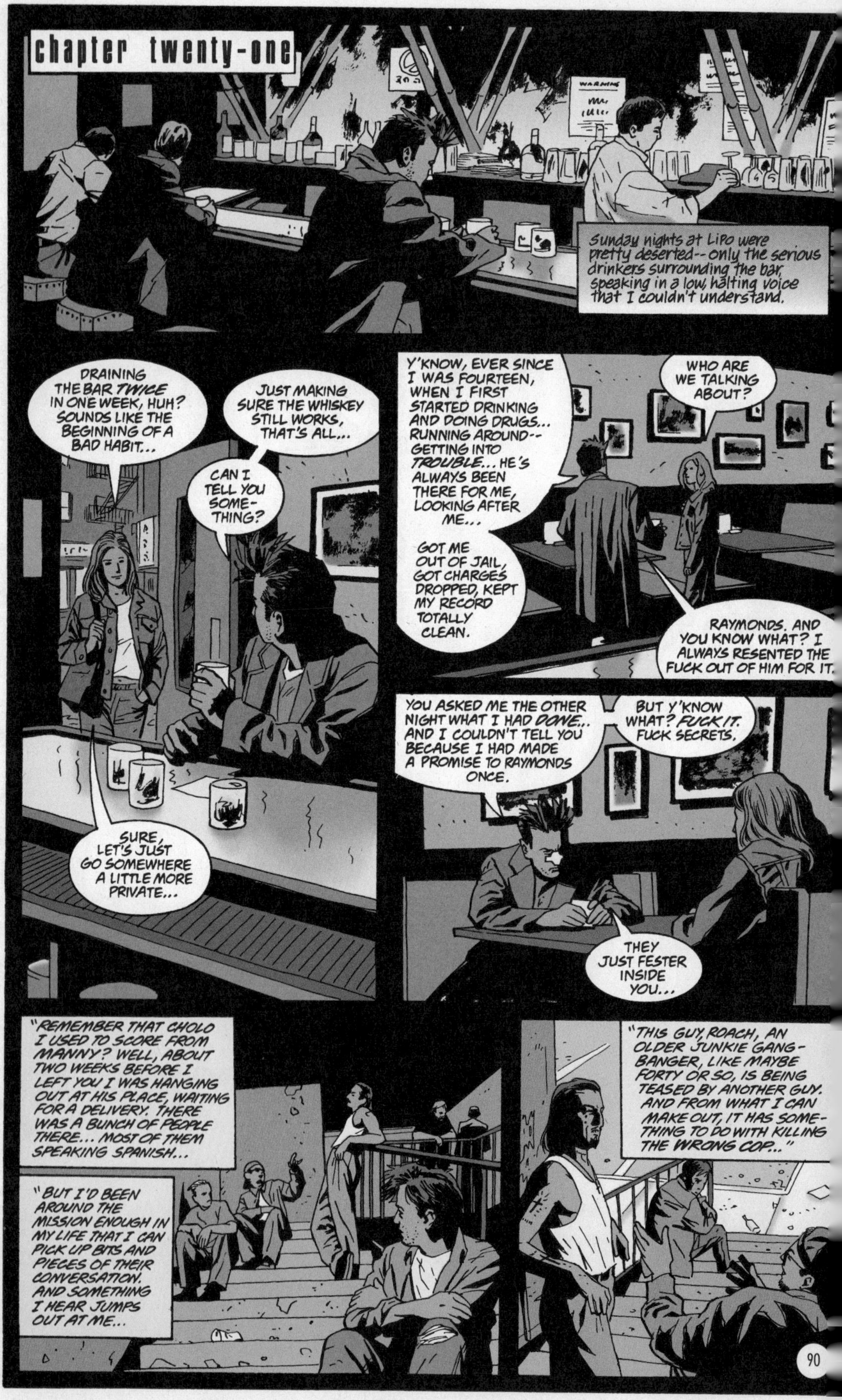

chapter twenty-one
Sunday nights at Lipo were pretty deserted-- only the serious drinkers surrounding the bar, speaking in a low, halting voice that I couldn't understand.
DRAINING THE BAR TWICE IN ONE WEEK, HUH? SOUNDS LIKE THE BEGINNING OF A BAD HABIT...
JUST MAKING SURE THE WHISKEY STILL WORKS, THAT'S ALL...
CAN I TELL YOU SOME-THING?
SURE, LET'S JUST GO SOMEWHERE A LITTLE MORE PRIVATE...
Y'KNOW, EVER SINCE I WAS FOURTEEN, WHEN I FIRST STARTED DRINKING AND DOING DRUGS... RUNNING AROUND-- GETTING INTO TROUBLE... HE'S ALWAYS BEEN THERE FOR ME, LOOKING AFTER ME...
GOT ME OUT OF JAIL, GOT CHARGES DROPPED, KEPT MY RECORD TOTALLY CLEAN.
WHO ARE WE TALKING ABOUT?
RAYMONDS. AND YOU KNOW WHAT? I ALWAYS RESENTED THE FUCK OUT OF HIM FOR IT.
YOU ASKED ME THE OTHER NIGHT WHAT I HAD DONE... AND I COULDN'T TELL YOU BECAUSE I HAD MADE A PROMISE TO RAYMONDS ONCE.
BUT Y'KNOW WHAT? FUCK IT. FUCK SECRETS.
THEY JUST FESTER INSIDE YOU...
"REMEMBER THAT CHOLO I USED TO SCORE FROM MANNY? WELL, ABOUT TWO WEEKS BEFORE I LEFT YOU I WAS HANGING OUT AT HIS PLACE, WAITING FOR A DELIVERY. THERE WAS A BUNCH OF PEOPLE THERE... MOST OF THEM SPEAKING SPANISH...
"BUT I'D BEEN AROUND THE MISSION ENOUGH IN MY LIFE THAT I CAN PICK UP BITS AND PIECES OF THEIR CONVERSATION. AND SOMETHING I HEAR JUMPS OUT AT ME...
"THIS GUY, ROACH, AN OLDER JUNKIE GANG-BANGER, LIKE MAYBE FORTY OR SO, IS BEING TEASED BY ANOTHER GUY. AND FROM WHAT I CAN MAKE OUT, IT HAS SOME-THING TO DO WITH KILLING THE WRONG COP..."

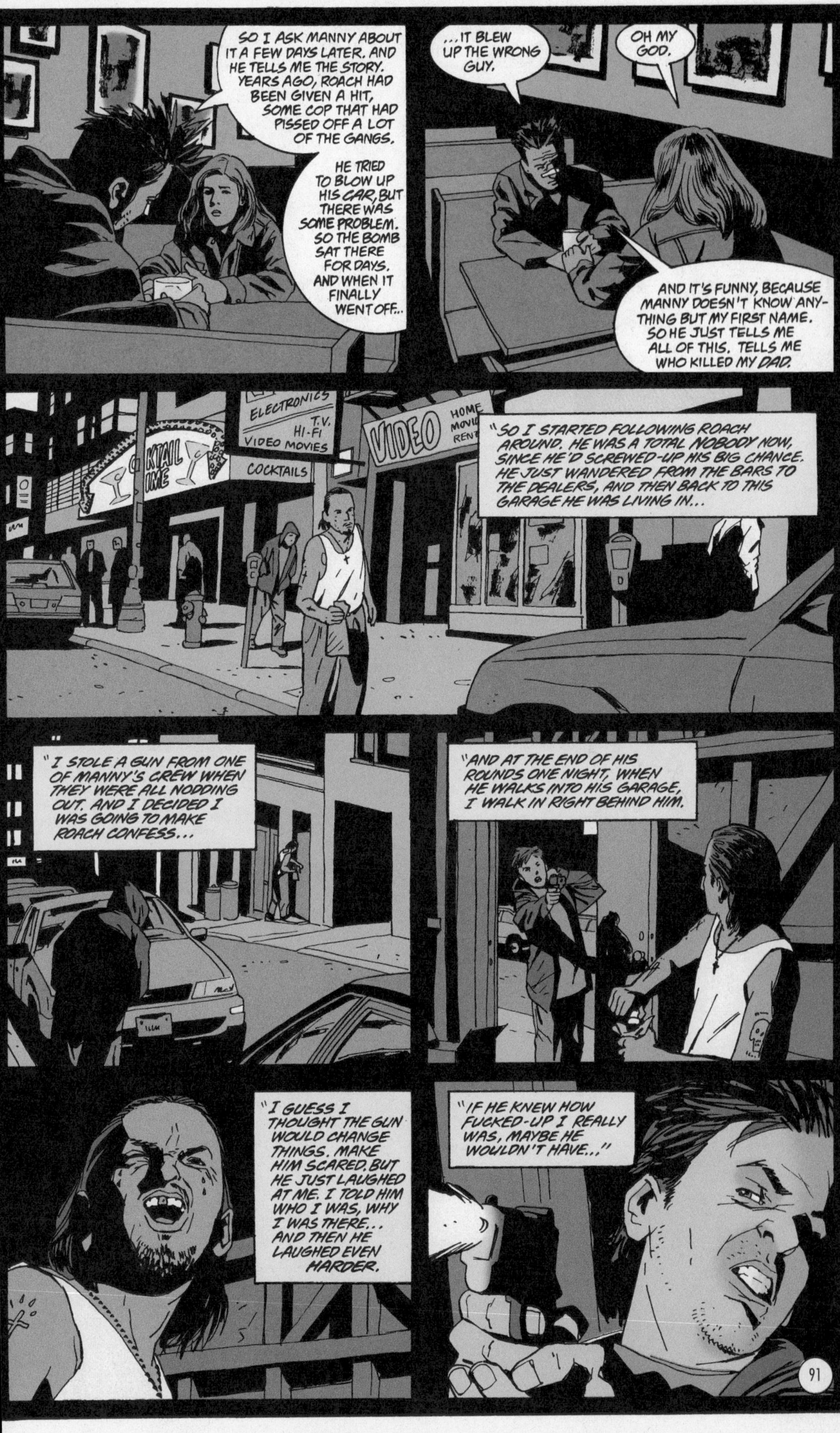
SO I ASK MANNY ABOUT IT A FEW DAYS LATER. AND HE TELLS ME THE STORY. YEARS AGO, ROACH HAD BEEN GIVEN A HIT, SOME COP THAT HAD PISSED OFF A LOT OF THE GANGS.
HE TRIED TO BLOW UP HIS CAR, BUT THERE WAS SOME PROBLEM. SO THE BOMB SAT THERE FOR DAYS. AND WHEN IT FINALLY WENT OFF...
...IT BLEW UP THE WRONG GUY.
OH MY GOD.
AND IT'S FUNNY, BECAUSE MANNY DOESN'T KNOW ANYTHING BUT MY FIRST NAME. SO HE JUST TELLS ME ALL OF THIS. TELLS ME WHO KILLED MY DAD.
ELECTRONICS
T.V.
HI-FI
VIDEO MOVIES
COCKTAILS
VIDEO
HOME MOVIE RENT
"SO I STARTED FOLLOWING ROACH AROUND. HE WAS A TOTAL NOBODY NOW, SINCE HE'D SCREWED-UP HIS BIG CHANCE. HE JUST WANDERED FROM THE BARS TO THE DEALERS, AND THEN BACK TO THIS GARAGE HE WAS LIVING IN...
"I STOLE A GUN FROM ONE OF MANNY'S CREW WHEN THEY WERE ALL NODDING OUT. AND I DECIDED I WAS GOING TO MAKE ROACH CONFESS...
"AND AT THE END OF HIS ROUNDS ONE NIGHT, WHEN HE WALKS INTO HIS GARAGE, I WALK IN RIGHT BEHIND HIM.
"I GUESS I THOUGHT THE GUN WOULD CHANGE THINGS. MAKE HIM SCARED. BUT HE JUST LAUGHED AT ME. I TOLD HIM WHO I WAS, WHY I WAS THERE... AND THEN HE LAUGHED EVEN HARDER.
"IF HE KNEW HOW FUCKED-UP I REALLY WAS, MAYBE HE WOULDN'T HAVE..."

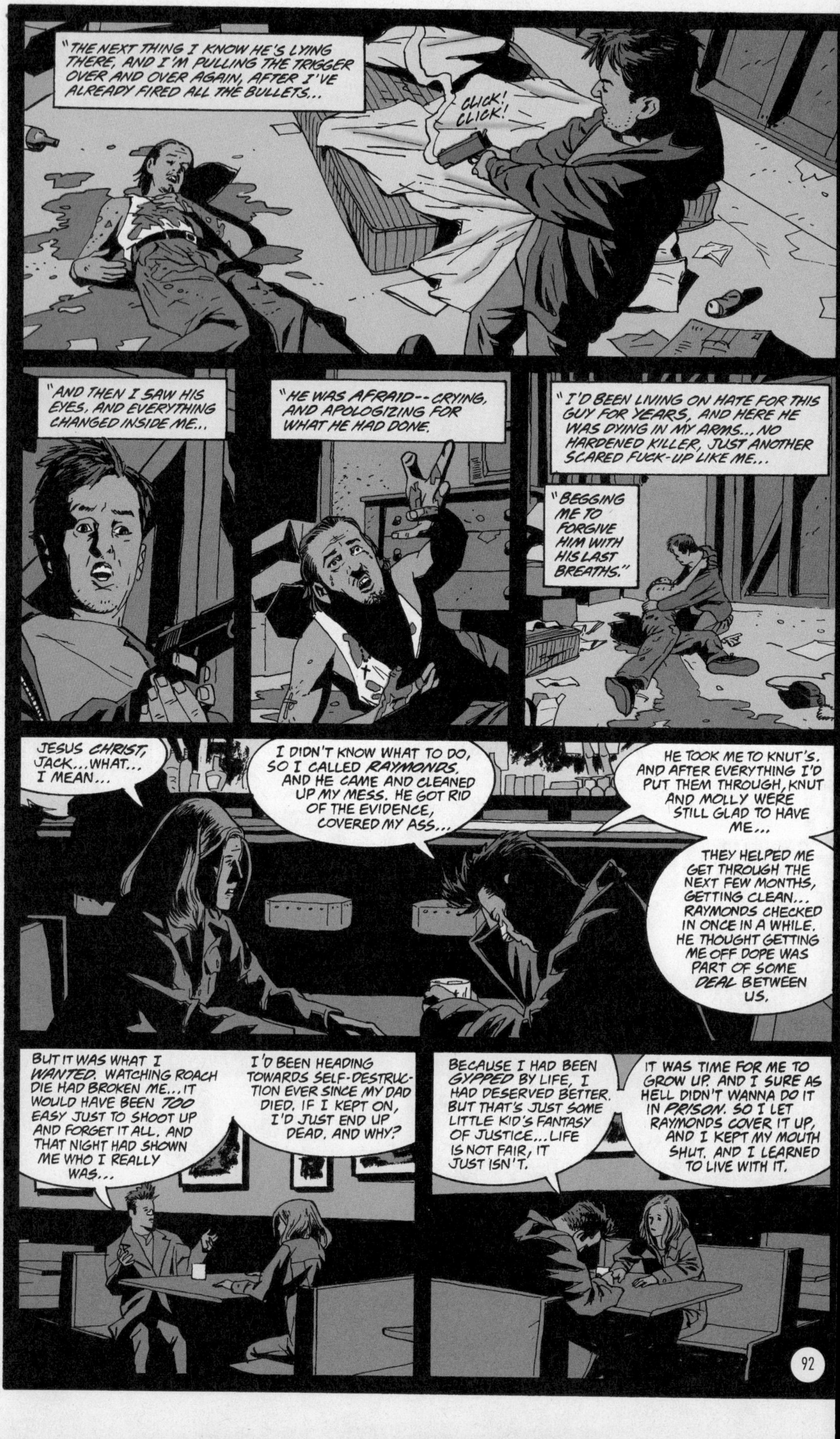
"THE NEXT THING I KNOW HE'S LYING THERE, AND I'M PULLING THE TRIGGER OVER AND OVER AGAIN, AFTER I'VE ALREADY FIRED ALL THE BULLETS...
CLICK! CLICK!
"AND THEN I SAW HIS EYES, AND EVERYTHING CHANGED INSIDE ME...
"HE WAS AFRAID-- CRYING, AND APOLOGIZING FOR WHAT HE HAD DONE.
"I'D BEEN LIVING ON HATE FOR THIS GUY FOR YEARS, AND HERE HE WAS DYING IN MY ARMS... NO HARDENED KILLER, JUST ANOTHER SCARED FUCK-UP LIKE ME...
"BEGGING ME TO FORGIVE HIM WITH HIS LAST BREATHS."
JESUS CHRIST, JACK... WHAT... I MEAN...
I DIDN'T KNOW WHAT TO DO, SO I CALLED RAYMONDS, AND HE CAME AND CLEANED UP MY MESS. HE GOT RID OF THE EVIDENCE, COVERED MY ASS...
HE TOOK ME TO KNUT'S. AND AFTER EVERYTHING I'D PUT THEM THROUGH, KNUT AND MOLLY WERE STILL GLAD TO HAVE ME...
THEY HELPED ME GET THROUGH THE NEXT FEW MONTHS, GETTING CLEAN... RAYMONDS CHECKED IN ONCE IN A WHILE. HE THOUGHT GETTING ME OFF DOPE WAS PART OF SOME DEAL BETWEEN US.
BUT IT WAS WHAT I WANTED. WATCHING ROACH DIE HAD BROKEN ME... IT WOULD HAVE BEEN TOO EASY JUST TO SHOOT UP AND FORGET IT ALL. AND THAT NIGHT HAD SHOWN ME WHO I REALLY WAS...
I'D BEEN HEADING TOWARDS SELF-DESTRUCTION EVER SINCE MY DAD DIED. IF I KEPT ON, I'D JUST END UP DEAD. AND WHY?
BECAUSE I HAD BEEN GYPPED BY LIFE, I HAD DESERVED BETTER. BUT THAT'S JUST SOME LITTLE KID'S FANTASY OF JUSTICE... LIFE IS NOT FAIR, IT JUST ISN'T.
IT WAS TIME FOR ME TO GROW UP. AND I SURE AS HELL DIDN'T WANNA DO IT IN PRISON. SO I LET RAYMONDS COVER IT UP, AND I KEPT MY MOUTH SHUT. AND I LEARNED TO LIVE WITH IT.

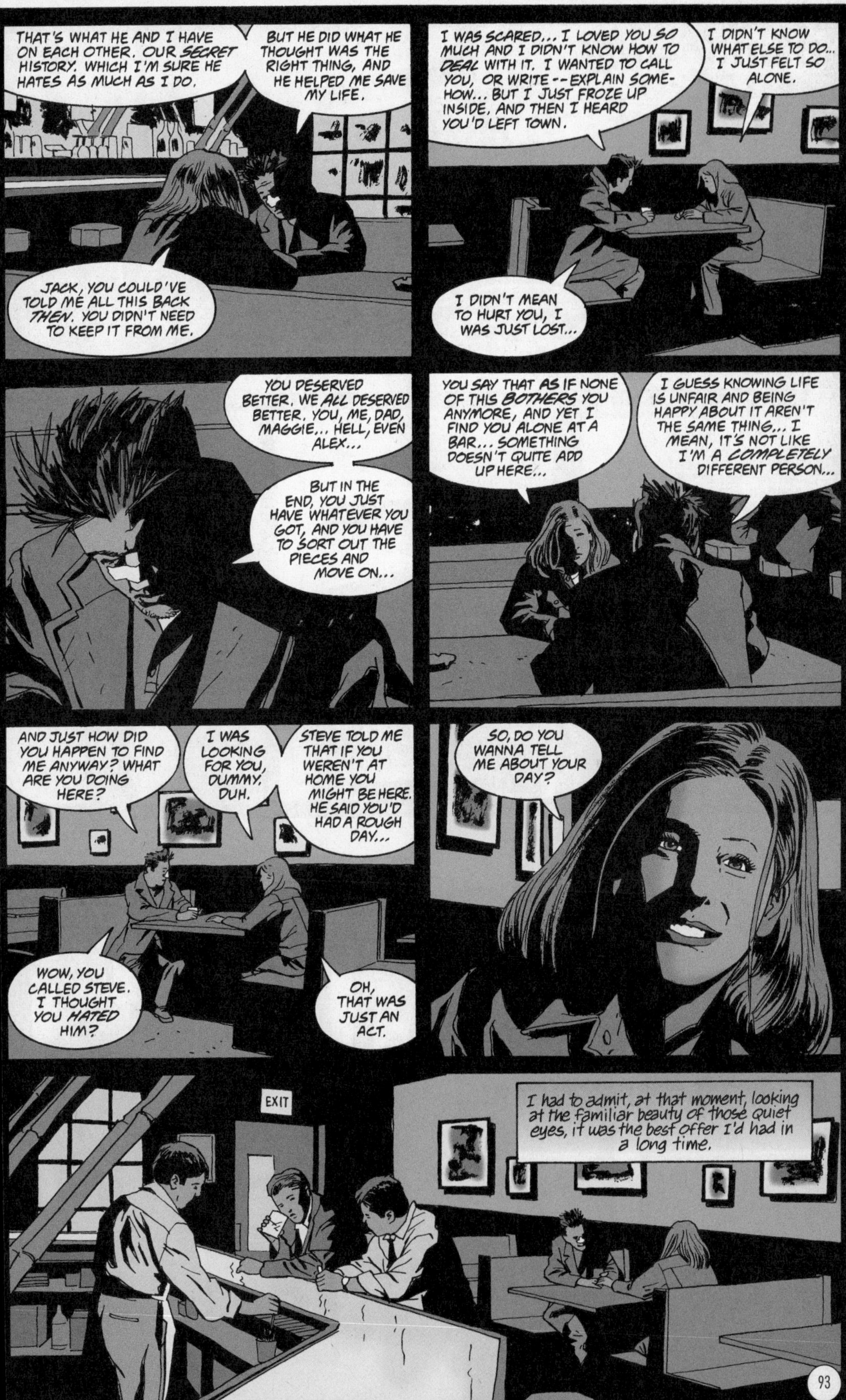
THAT'S WHAT HE AND I HAVE ON EACH OTHER. OUR SECRET HISTORY. WHICH I'M SURE HE HATES AS MUCH AS I DO.
BUT HE DID WHAT HE THOUGHT WAS THE RIGHT THING, AND HE HELPED ME SAVE MY LIFE.
JACK, YOU COULD'VE TOLD ME ALL THIS BACK THEN. YOU DIDN'T NEED TO KEEP IT FROM ME.
I WAS SCARED... I LOVED YOU SO MUCH AND I DIDN'T KNOW HOW TO DEAL WITH IT. I WANTED TO CALL YOU, OR WRITE--EXPLAIN SOMEHOW... BUT I JUST FROZE UP INSIDE, AND THEN I HEARD YOU'D LEFT TOWN.
I DIDN'T KNOW WHAT ELSE TO DO... I JUST FELT SO ALONE.
I DIDN'T MEAN TO HURT YOU, I WAS JUST LOST...
YOU DESERVED BETTER. WE ALL DESERVED BETTER. YOU, ME, DAD, MAGGIE... HELL, EVEN ALEX...
BUT IN THE END, YOU JUST HAVE WHATEVER YOU GOT, AND YOU HAVE TO SORT OUT THE PIECES AND MOVE ON...
YOU SAY THAT AS IF NONE OF THIS BOTHERS YOU ANYMORE, AND YET I FIND YOU ALONE AT A BAR... SOMETHING DOESN'T QUITE ADD UP HERE...
I GUESS KNOWING LIFE IS UNFAIR AND BEING HAPPY ABOUT IT AREN'T THE SAME THING... I MEAN, IT'S NOT LIKE I'M A COMPLETELY DIFFERENT PERSON...
AND JUST HOW DID YOU HAPPEN TO FIND ME ANYWAY? WHAT ARE YOU DOING HERE?
I WAS LOOKING FOR YOU, DUMMY. DUH.
STEVE TOLD ME THAT IF YOU WEREN'T AT HOME YOU MIGHT BE HERE. HE SAID YOU'D HAD A ROUGH DAY...
WOW, YOU CALLED STEVE. I THOUGHT YOU HATED HIM?
OH, THAT WAS JUST AN ACT.
SO, DO YOU WANNA TELL ME ABOUT YOUR DAY?
EXIT
I had to admit, at that moment, looking at the familiar beauty of those quiet eyes, it was the best offer I'd had in a long time.

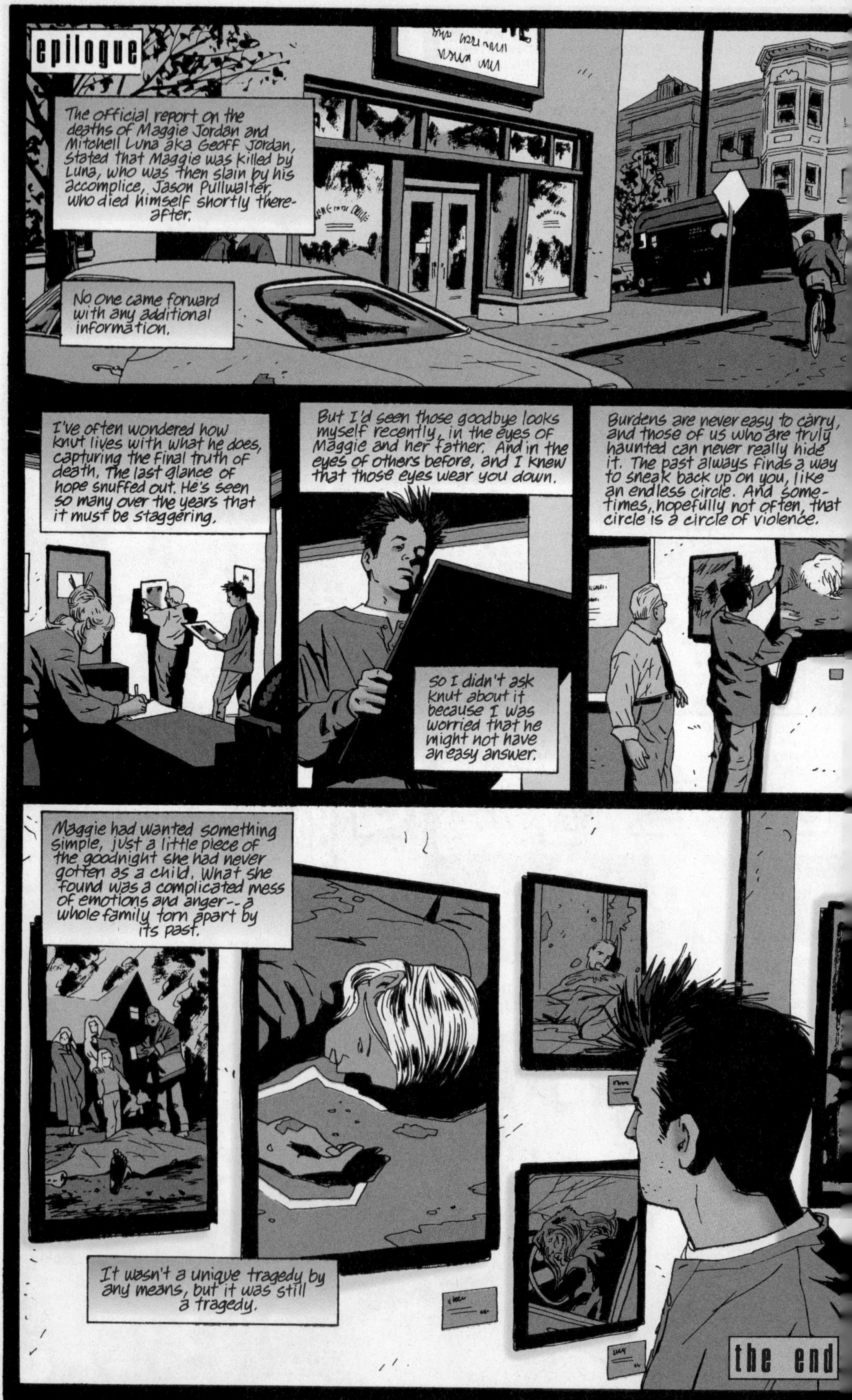
epilogue
The official report on the deaths of Maggie Jordan and Mitchell Luna aka Geoff Jordan, stated that Maggie was killed by Luna, who was then slain by his accomplice, Jason Pullwalter, who died himself shortly thereafter.
No one came forward with any additional information.
I've often wondered how Knut lives with what he does, capturing the final truth of death. The last glance of hope snuffed out. He's seen so many over the years that it must be staggering.
But I'd seen those goodbye looks myself recently, in the eyes of Maggie and her father. And in the eyes of others before, and I knew that those eyes wear you down.
So I didn't ask Knut about it because I was worried that he might not have an easy answer.
Burdens are never easy to carry, and those of us who are truly haunted can never really hide it. The past always finds a way to sneak back up on you, like an endless circle. And sometimes, hopefully not often, that circle is a circle of violence.
Maggie had wanted something simple, just a little piece of the goodnight she had never gotten as a child. What she found was a complicated mess of emotions and anger--a whole family torn apart by its past.
It wasn't a unique tragedy by any means, but it was still a tragedy.
the end

GOD & SINNERS

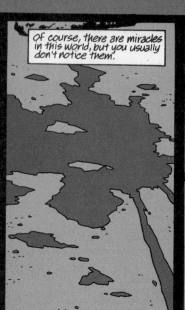

Of course, there are miracles in this world, but you usually don't notice them.

You get caught up by distractions and the grind of your day-to-day routine. So you fail to really see things--a perfect smile, two people embracing tearfully at an airport, a child's curiosity.

But then the smashing of one second into the next, the random injustice of the universe, brings everything to light.

And you realize that there are miracles in this world.

God and Sinners

a SCENE OF THE CRIME
Christmas Mystery

ED BRUBAKER writer
MICHAEL LARK artist
JOHN COSTANZA letters
JAMES SINCLAIR colors
JENNIFER LEE ass't editor
SHELLY ROEBERG editor

SCENE OF THE CRIME created by
BRUBAKER and LARK

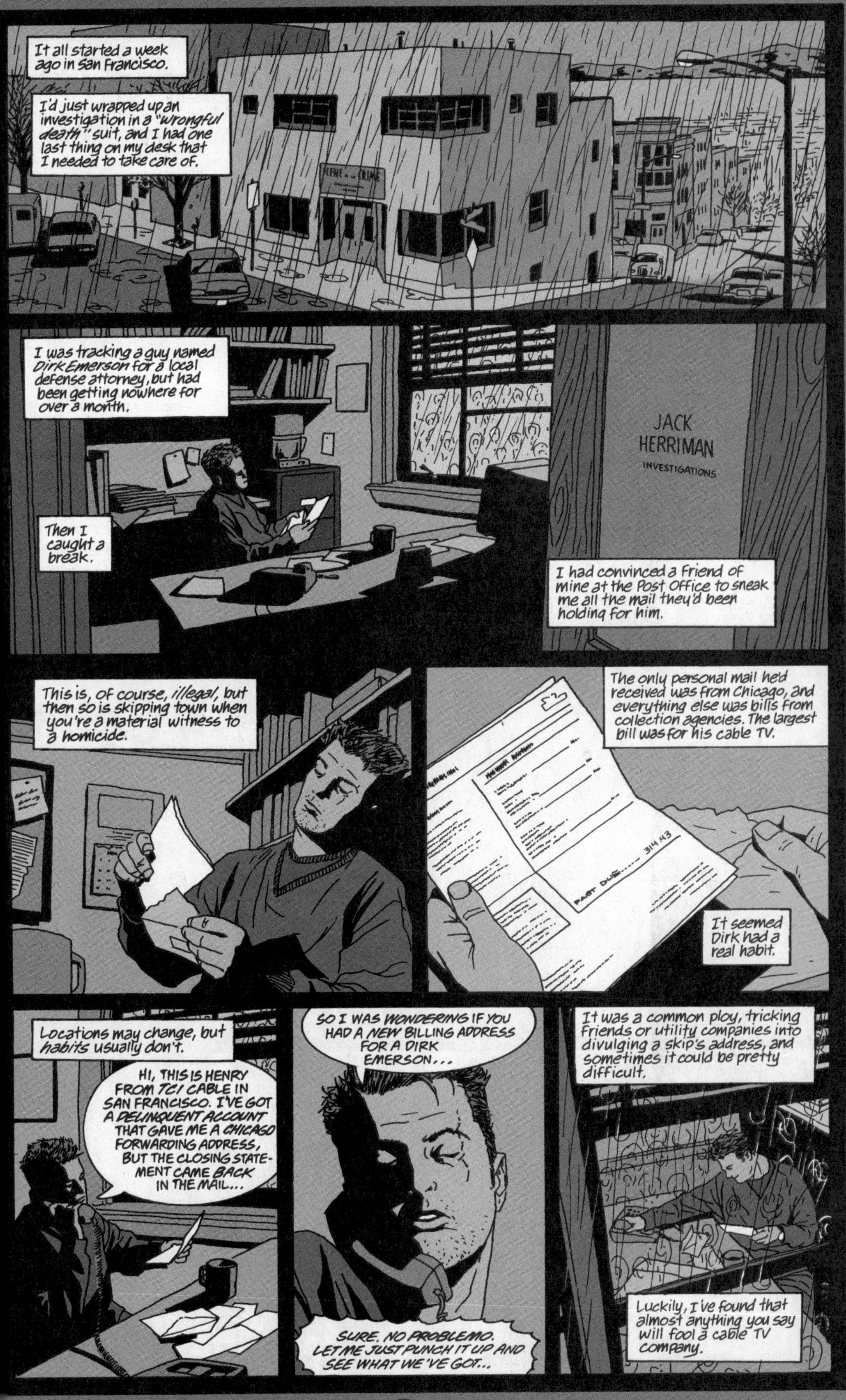
It all started a week ago in San Francisco.
I'd just wrapped up an investigation in a "wrongful death" suit, and I had one last thing on my desk that I needed to take care of.
I was tracking a guy named Dirk Emerson for a local defense attorney, but had been getting nowhere for over a month.
Then I caught a break.
JACK HERRIMAN INVESTIGATIONS
I had convinced a friend of mine at the Post Office to sneak me all the mail they'd been holding for him.
This is, of course, illegal, but then so is skipping town when you're a material witness to a homicide.
The only personal mail he'd received was from Chicago, and everything else was bills from collection agencies. The largest bill was for his cable TV.
PAST DUE......... 314.43
It seemed Dirk had a real habit.
Locations may change, but habits usually don't.
HI, THIS IS HENRY FROM TCI CABLE IN SAN FRANCISCO. I'VE GOT A DELINQUENT ACCOUNT THAT GAVE ME A CHICAGO FORWARDING ADDRESS, BUT THE CLOSING STATEMENT CAME BACK IN THE MAIL...
SO I WAS WONDERING IF YOU HAD A NEW BILLING ADDRESS FOR A DIRK EMERSON...
SURE. NO PROBLEMO. LET ME JUST PUNCH IT UP AND SEE WHAT WE'VE GOT...
It was a common ploy, tricking friends or utility companies into divulging a skip's address, and sometimes it could be pretty difficult.
Luckily, I've found that almost anything you say will fool a cable TV company.

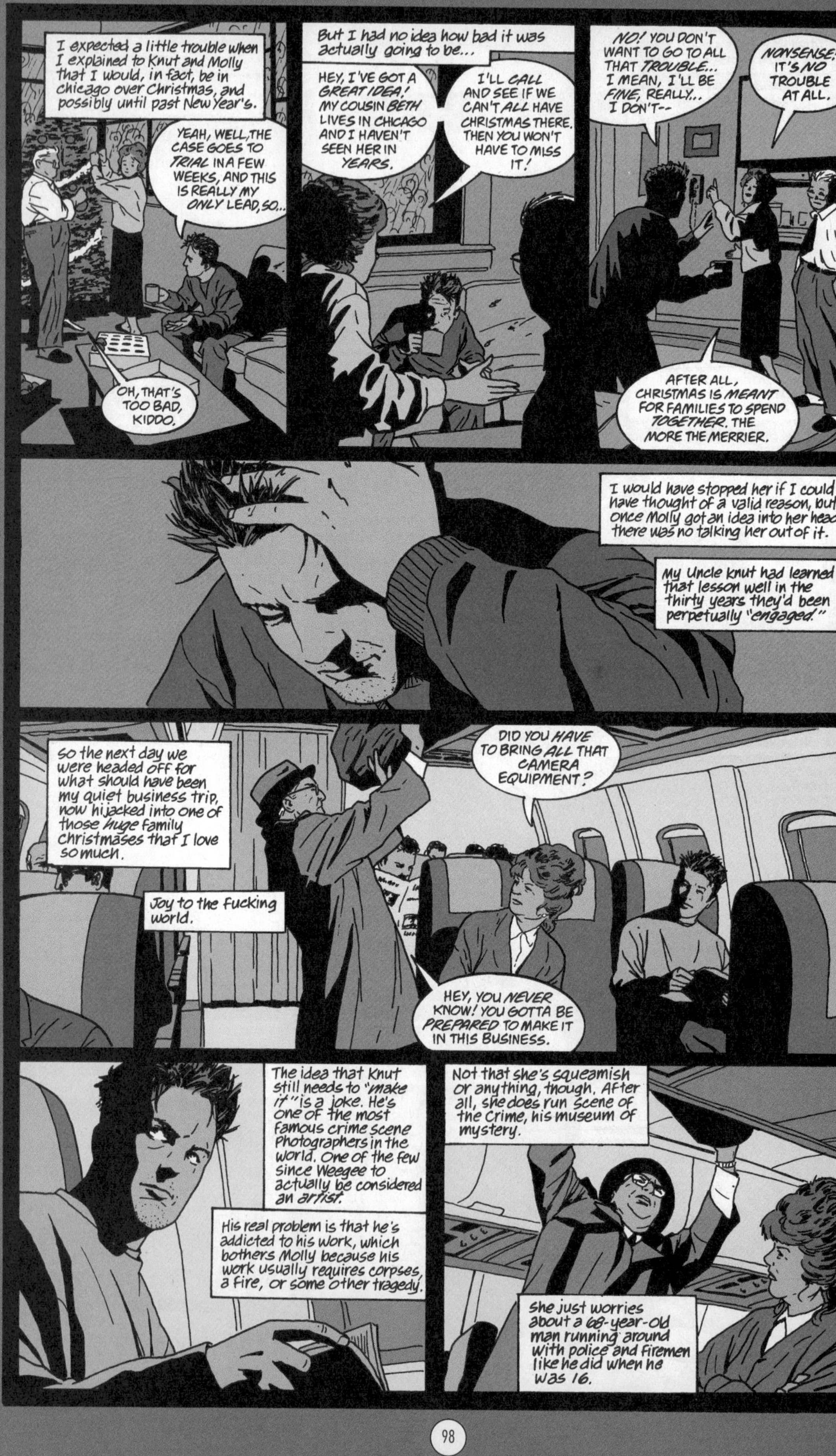
I expected a little trouble when I explained to Knut and Molly that I would, in fact, be in chicago over Christmas, and possibly until past New Year's.
YEAH, WELL, THE CASE GOES TO TRIAL IN A FEW WEEKS, AND THIS IS REALLY MY ONLY LEAD, SO...
OH, THAT'S TOO BAD, KIDDO.
But I had no idea how bad it was actually going to be...
HEY, I'VE GOT A GREAT IDEA! MY COUSIN BETH LIVES IN CHICAGO AND I HAVEN'T SEEN HER IN YEARS.
I'LL CALL AND SEE IF WE CAN'T ALL HAVE CHRISTMAS THERE. THEN YOU WON'T HAVE TO MISS IT!
NO! YOU DON'T WANT TO GO TO ALL THAT TROUBLE... I MEAN, I'LL BE FINE, REALLY... I DON'T--
NONSENSE! IT'S NO TROUBLE AT ALL.
AFTER ALL, CHRISTMAS IS MEANT FOR FAMILIES TO SPEND TOGETHER. THE MORE THE MERRIER.
I would have stopped her if I could have thought of a valid reason, but once Molly got an idea into her head, there was no talking her out of it.
My Uncle Knut had learned that lesson well in the thirty years they'd been perpetually "engaged."
So the next day we were headed off for what should have been my quiet business trip, now hijacked into one of those huge family christmases that I love so much.
Joy to the fucking world.
DID YOU HAVE TO BRING ALL THAT CAMERA EQUIPMENT?
HEY, YOU NEVER KNOW! YOU GOTTA BE PREPARED TO MAKE IT IN THIS BUSINESS.
The idea that Knut still needs to "make it" is a joke. He's one of the most famous crime scene photographers in the world. One of the few since Weegee to actually be considered an artist.
His real problem is that he's addicted to his work, which bothers Molly because his work usually requires corpses, a fire, or some other tragedy.
Not that she's squeamish or anything, though. After all, she does run Scene of the Crime, his museum of mystery.
She just worries about a 68-year-old man running around with police and firemen like he did when he was 16.

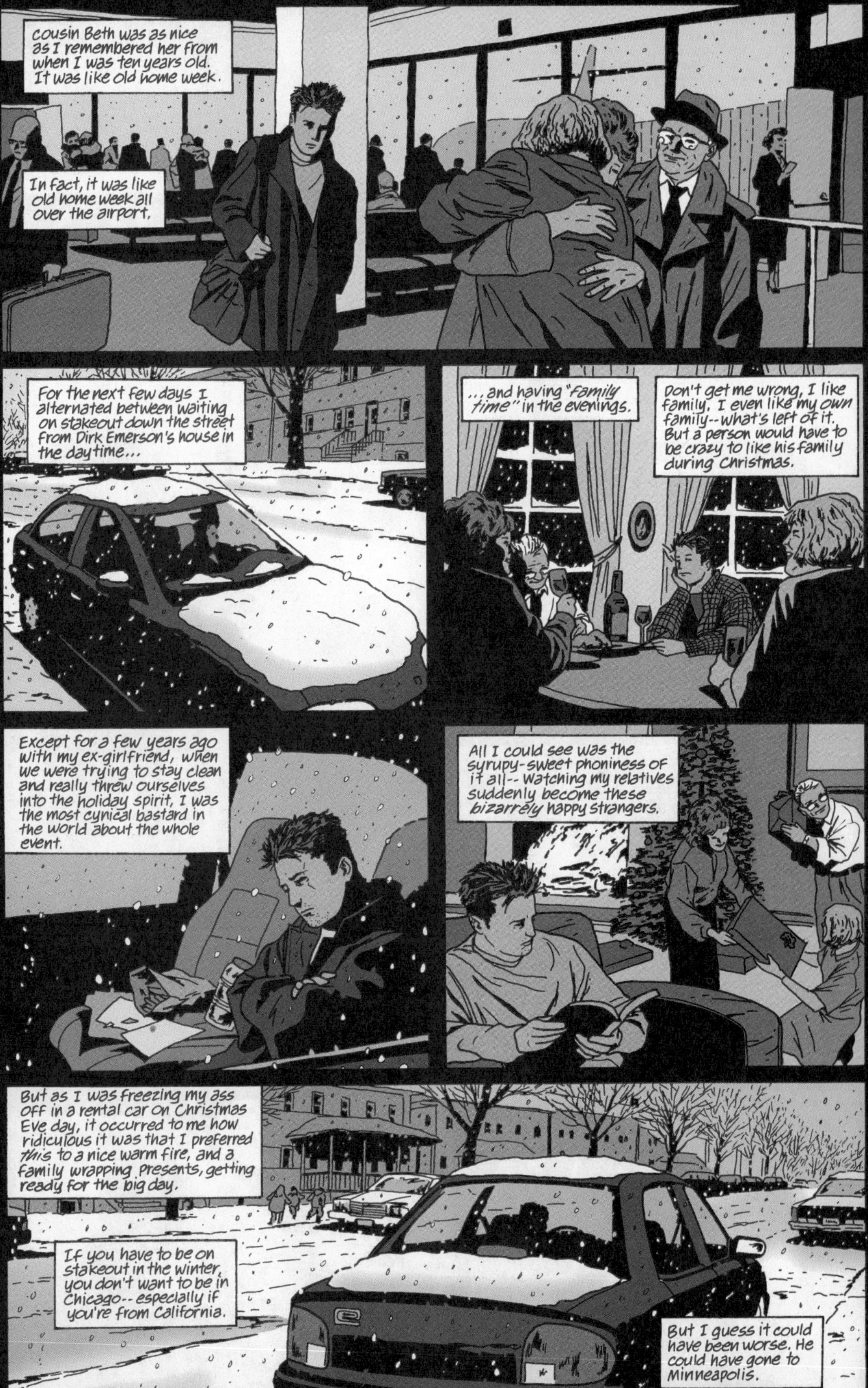
Cousin Beth was as nice as I remembered her from when I was ten years old. It was like old home week.
In fact, it was like old home week all over the airport.
For the next few days I alternated between waiting on stakeout down the street from Dirk Emerson's house in the daytime...
...and having "family time" in the evenings.
Don't get me wrong, I like family. I even like my own family--what's left of it. But a person would have to be crazy to like his family during Christmas.
Except for a few years ago with my ex-girlfriend, when we were trying to stay clean and really threw ourselves into the holiday spirit, I was the most cynical bastard in the world about the whole event.
All I could see was the syrupy-sweet phoniness of it all--watching my relatives suddenly become these bizarrely happy strangers.
But as I was freezing my ass off in a rental car on Christmas Eve day, it occurred to me how ridiculous it was that I preferred this to a nice warm fire, and a family wrapping presents, getting ready for the big day.
If you have to be on stakeout in the winter, you don't want to be in Chicago--especially if you're from California.
But I guess it could have been worse. He could have gone to Minneapolis.

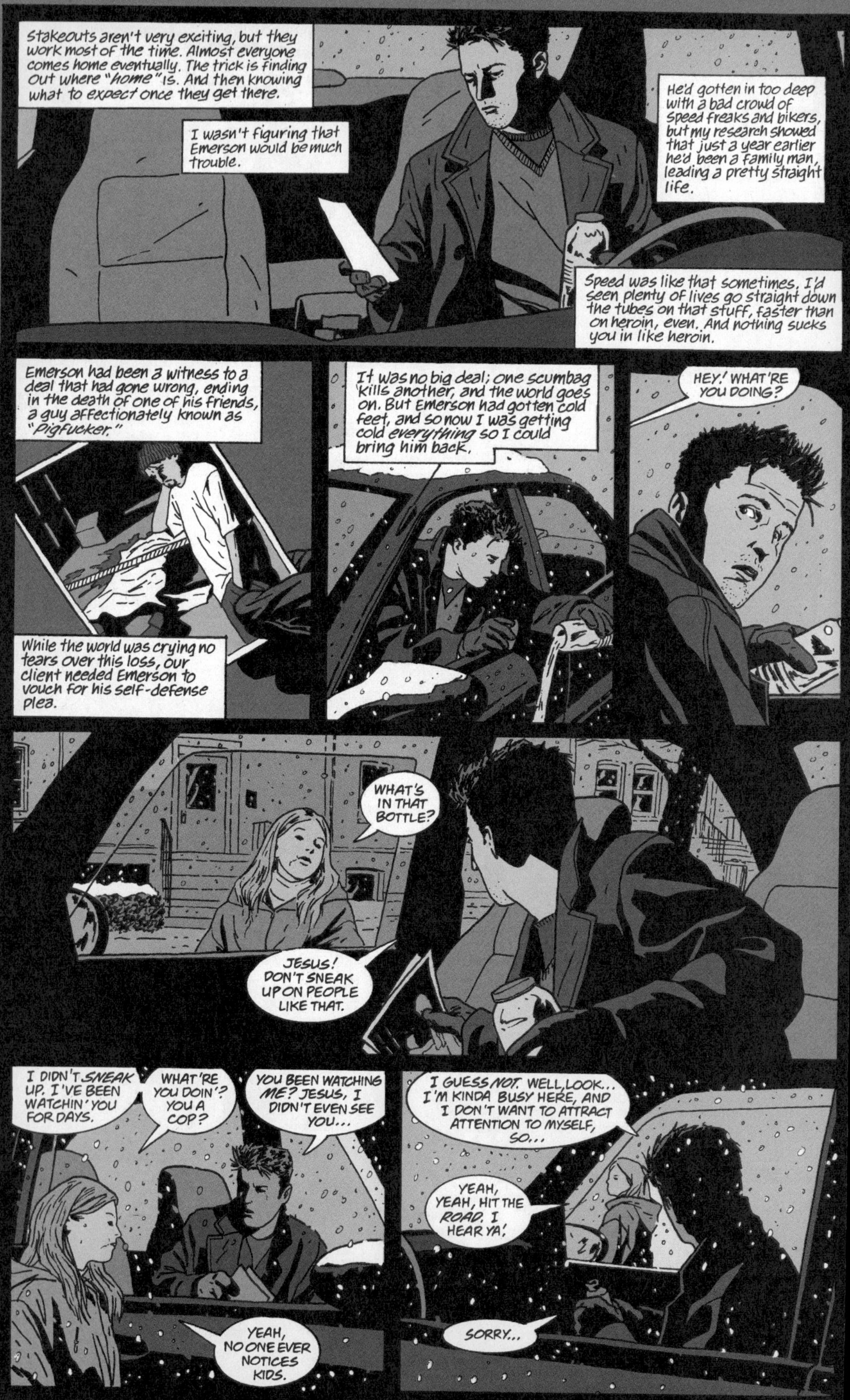
Stakeouts aren't very exciting, but they work most of the time. Almost everyone comes home eventually. The trick is finding out where "home" is. And then knowing what to expect once they get there.
I wasn't figuring that Emerson would be much trouble.
He'd gotten in too deep with a bad crowd of speed freaks and bikers, but my research showed that just a year earlier he'd been a family man, leading a pretty straight life.
Speed was like that sometimes. I'd seen plenty of lives go straight down the tubes on that stuff, faster than on heroin, even. And nothing sucks you in like heroin.
Emerson had been a witness to a deal that had gone wrong, ending in the death of one of his friends, a guy affectionately known as "Pigfucker."
While the world was crying no tears over this loss, our client needed Emerson to vouch for his self-defense plea.
It was no big deal; one scumbag kills another, and the world goes on. But Emerson had gotten cold feet, and so now I was getting cold everything so I could bring him back.
HEY! WHAT'RE YOU DOING?
WHAT'S IN THAT BOTTLE?
JESUS! DON'T SNEAK UP ON PEOPLE LIKE THAT.
I DIDN'T SNEAK UP. I'VE BEEN WATCHIN' YOU FOR DAYS.
WHAT'RE YOU DOIN'? YOU A COP?
YOU BEEN WATCHING ME? JESUS, I DIDN'T EVEN SEE YOU...
YEAH, NO ONE EVER NOTICES KIDS.
I GUESS NOT. WELL, LOOK... I'M KINDA BUSY HERE, AND I DON'T WANT TO ATTRACT ATTENTION TO MYSELF, SO...
YEAH, YEAH, HIT THE ROAD. I HEAR YA!
SORRY...

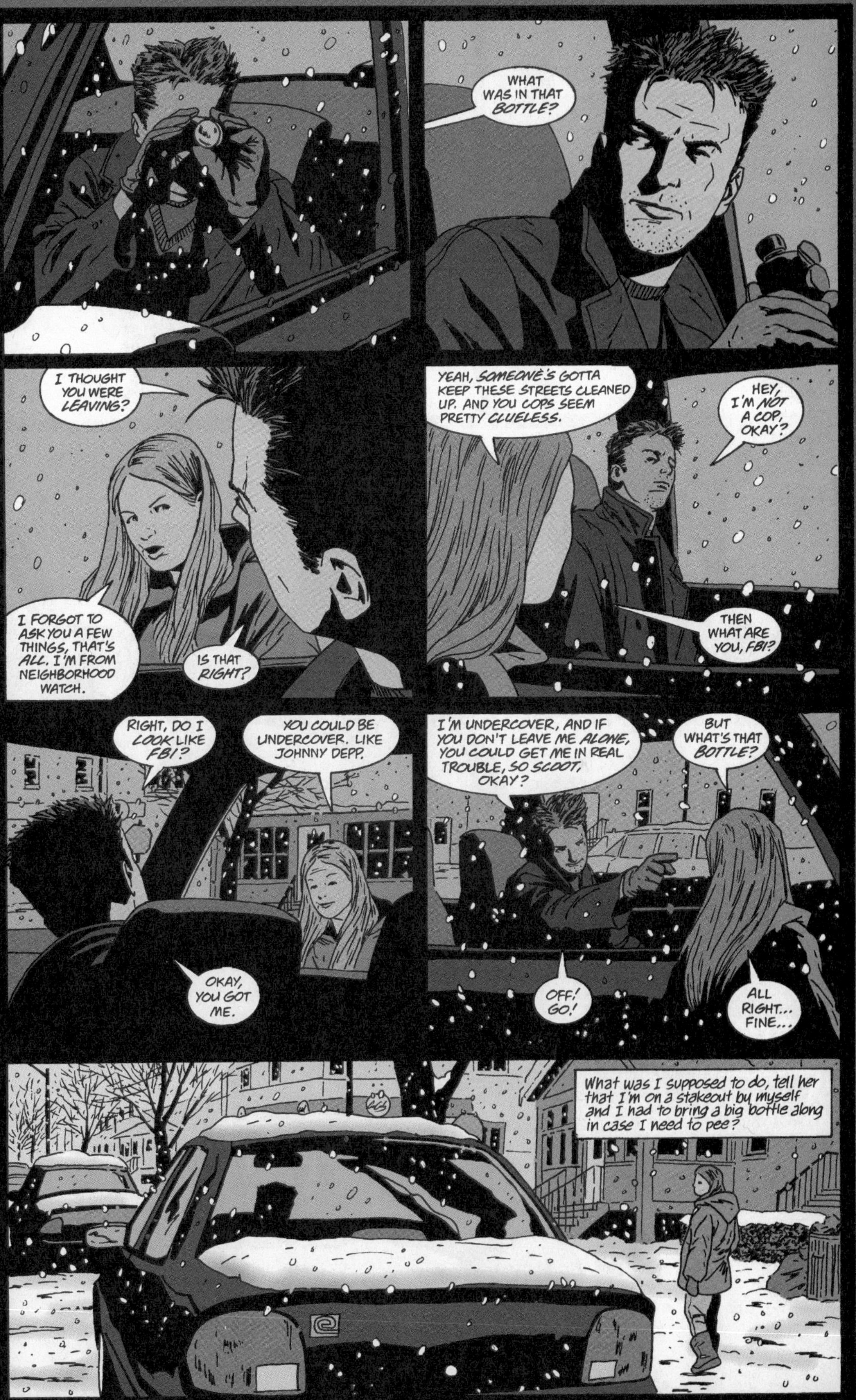
WHAT WAS IN THAT BOTTLE?
I THOUGHT YOU WERE LEAVING?
I FORGOT TO ASK YOU A FEW THINGS, THAT'S ALL. I'M FROM NEIGHBORHOOD WATCH.
IS THAT RIGHT?
YEAH, SOMEONE'S GOTTA KEEP THESE STREETS CLEANED UP. AND YOU COPS SEEM PRETTY CLUELESS.
HEY, I'M NOT A COP, OKAY?
THEN WHAT ARE YOU, FBI?
RIGHT, DO I LOOK LIKE FBI?
YOU COULD BE UNDERCOVER. LIKE JOHNNY DEPP.
OKAY, YOU GOT ME.
I'M UNDERCOVER, AND IF YOU DON'T LEAVE ME ALONE, YOU COULD GET ME IN REAL TROUBLE, SO SCOOT, OKAY?
BUT WHAT'S THAT BOTTLE?
OFF! GO!
ALL RIGHT... FINE...
What was I supposed to do, tell her that I'm on a stakeout by myself and I had to bring a big bottle along in case I need to pee?

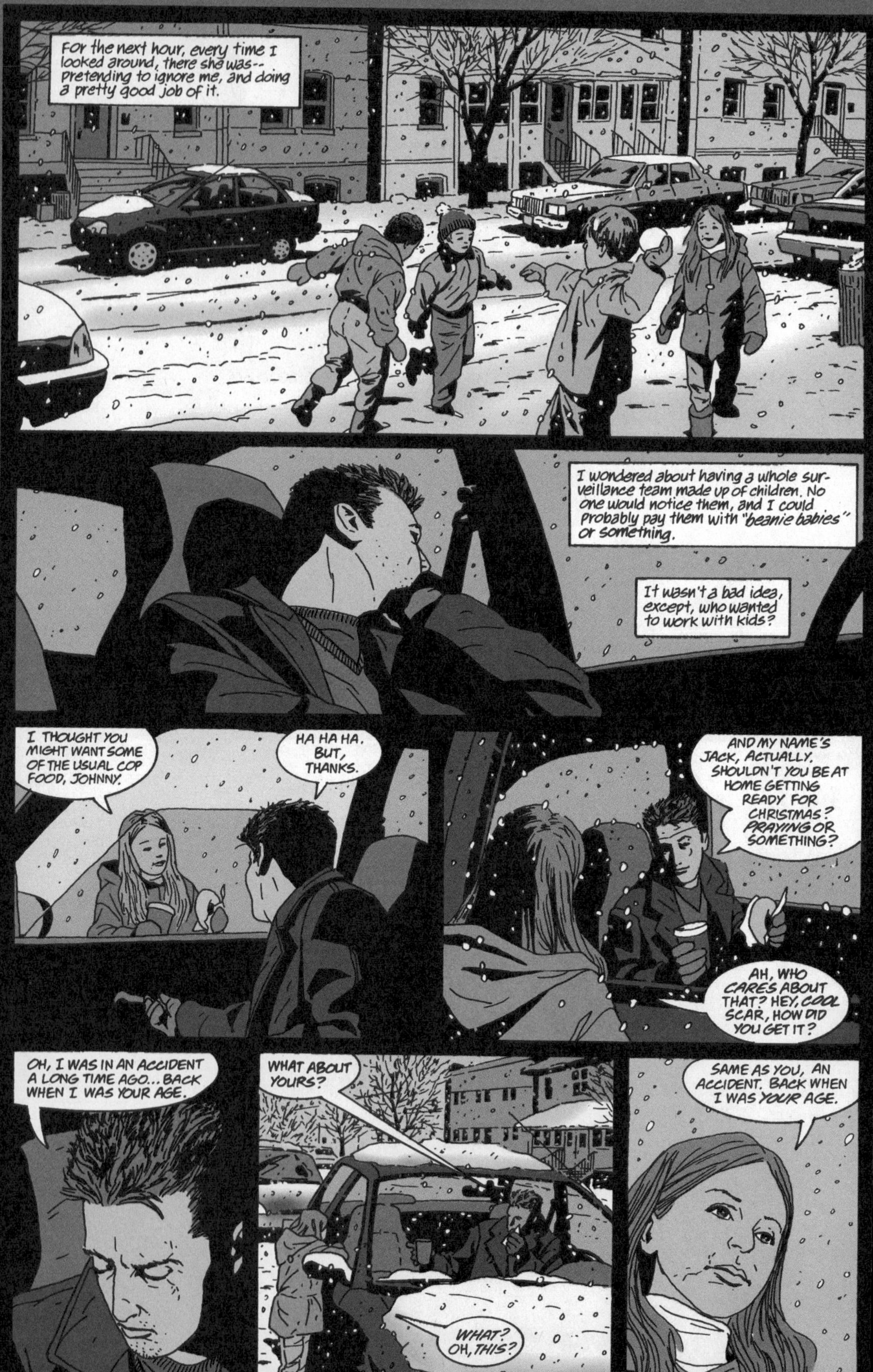

For the next hour, every time I looked around, there she was--pretending to ignore me, and doing a pretty good job of it.
I wondered about having a whole surveillance team made up of children. No one would notice them, and I could probably pay them with "beanie babies" or something.
It wasn't a bad idea, except, who wanted to work with kids?
I THOUGHT YOU MIGHT WANT SOME OF THE USUAL COP FOOD, JOHNNY.
HA HA HA. BUT, THANKS.
AND MY NAME'S JACK, ACTUALLY. SHOULDN'T YOU BE AT HOME GETTING READY FOR CHRISTMAS? PRAYING OR SOMETHING?
AH, WHO CARES ABOUT THAT? HEY, COOL SCAR, HOW DID YOU GET IT?
OH, I WAS IN AN ACCIDENT A LONG TIME AGO... BACK WHEN I WAS YOUR AGE.
WHAT ABOUT YOURS?
WHAT? OH, THIS?
SAME AS YOU, AN ACCIDENT. BACK WHEN I WAS YOUR AGE.

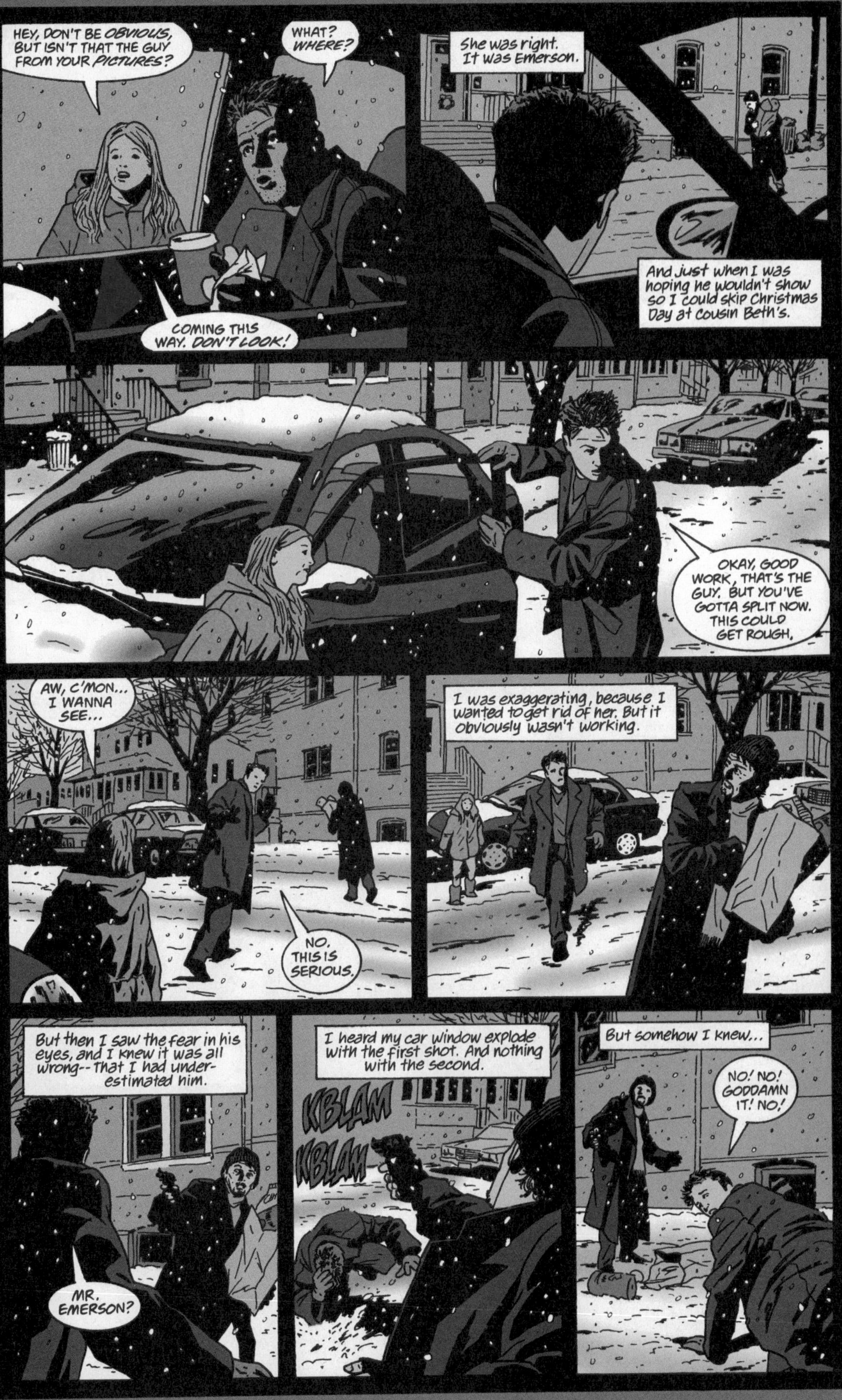
HEY, DON'T BE OBVIOUS, BUT ISN'T THAT THE GUY FROM YOUR PICTURES?
WHAT? WHERE?
COMING THIS WAY. DON'T LOOK!
She was right. It was Emerson.
And just when I was hoping he wouldn't show so I could skip Christmas Day at cousin Beth's.
OKAY, GOOD WORK, THAT'S THE GUY. BUT YOU'VE GOTTA SPLIT NOW. THIS COULD GET ROUGH.
AW, C'MON... I WANNA SEE...
NO. THIS IS SERIOUS.
I was exaggerating, because I wanted to get rid of her. But it obviously wasn't working.
But then I saw the fear in his eyes, and I knew it was all wrong--that I had underestimated him.
MR. EMERSON?
I heard my car window explode with the first shot. And nothing with the second.
KBLAM
KBLAM
But somehow I knew...
NO! NO! GODDAMN IT! NO!

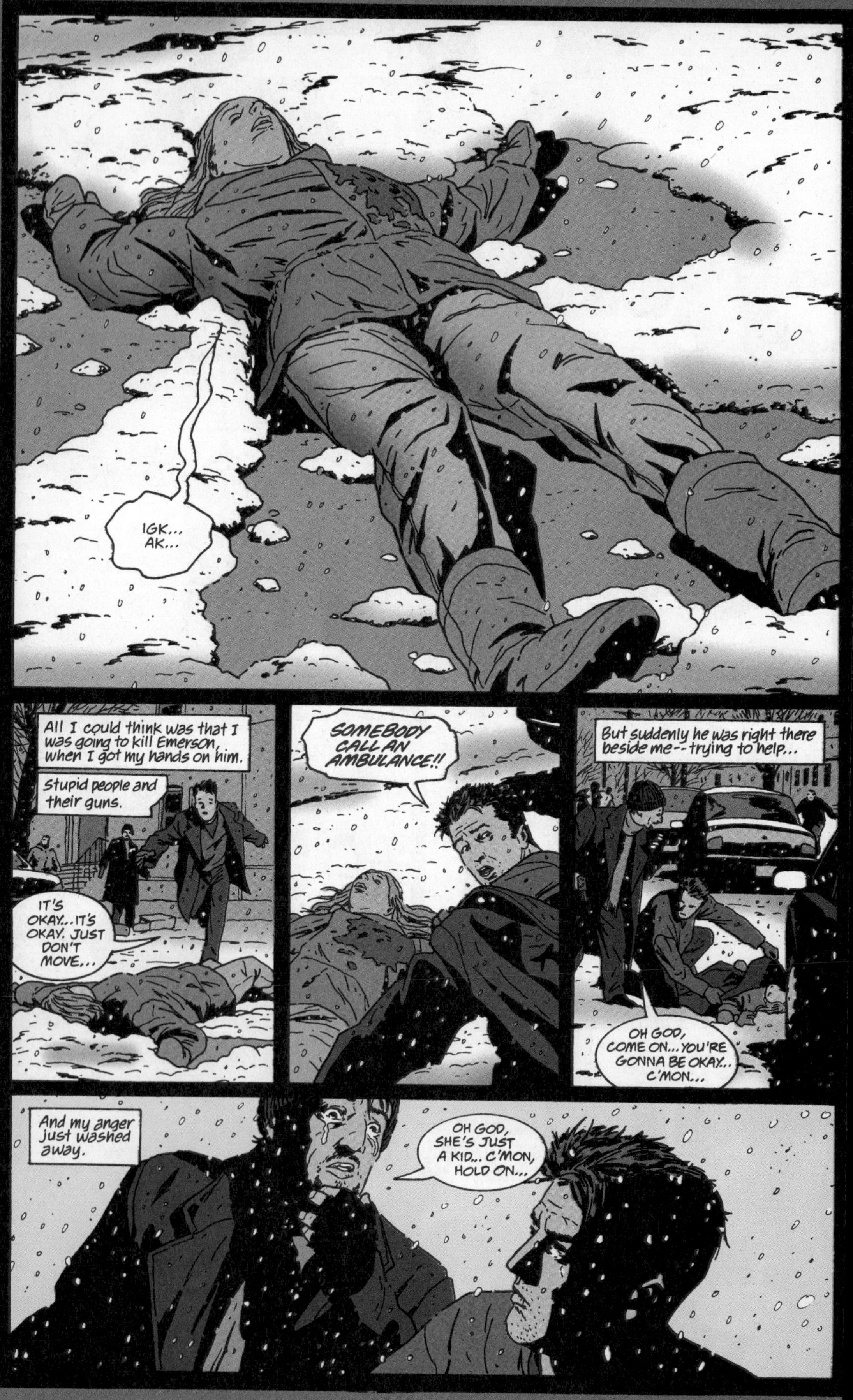
IGK... AK...
All I could think was that I was going to kill Emerson, when I got my hands on him.
Stupid people and their guns.
IT'S OKAY... IT'S OKAY. JUST DON'T MOVE...
SOMEBODY CALL AN AMBULANCE!!
But suddenly he was right there beside me-- trying to help...
OH GOD, COME ON... YOU'RE GONNA BE OKAY... C'MON...
And my anger just washed away.
OH GOD, SHE'S JUST A KID... C'MON, HOLD ON...

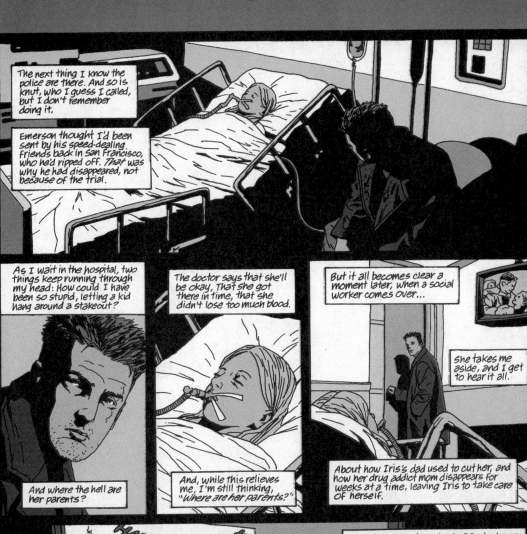

The next thing I know the police are there. And so is knut, who I guess I called, but I don't remember doing it.

Emerson thought I'd been sent by his speed-dealing friends back in San Francisco, who he'd ripped off. *That* was why he had disappeared, not because of the trial.

As I wait in the hospital, two things keep running through my head: How could I have been so stupid, letting a kid hang around a stakeout?

And where the hell are her parents?

The doctor says that she'll be okay, That she got there in time, that she didn't lose too much blood.

And, while this relieves me, I'm still thinking, *"Where are her parents?"*

But it all becomes clear a moment later, when a social worker comes over...

She takes me aside, and I get to hear it all.

About how Iris's dad used to cut her, and how her drug addict mom disappears for weeks at a time, leaving Iris to take care of herself.

How she's been in and out of foster homes most of her life, always ending up back with her mom. But never for too long.

That's where she'll go, when she gets out of here, back into foster care--thanks to me.

And those miracles I was talking about, the ones you don't notice? You're probably wondering right now what the hell I meant...

The miracle is that she's even made it this far.

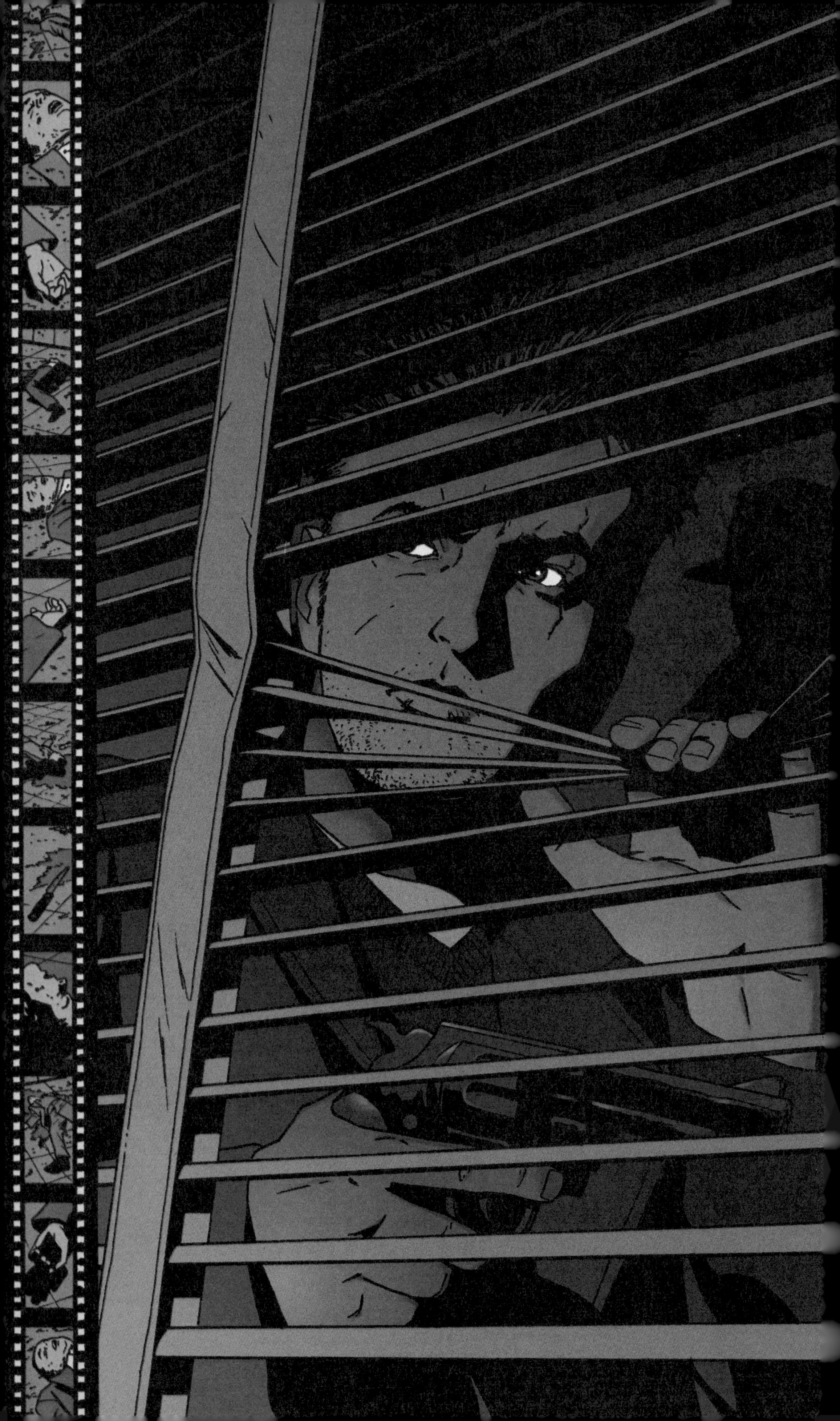

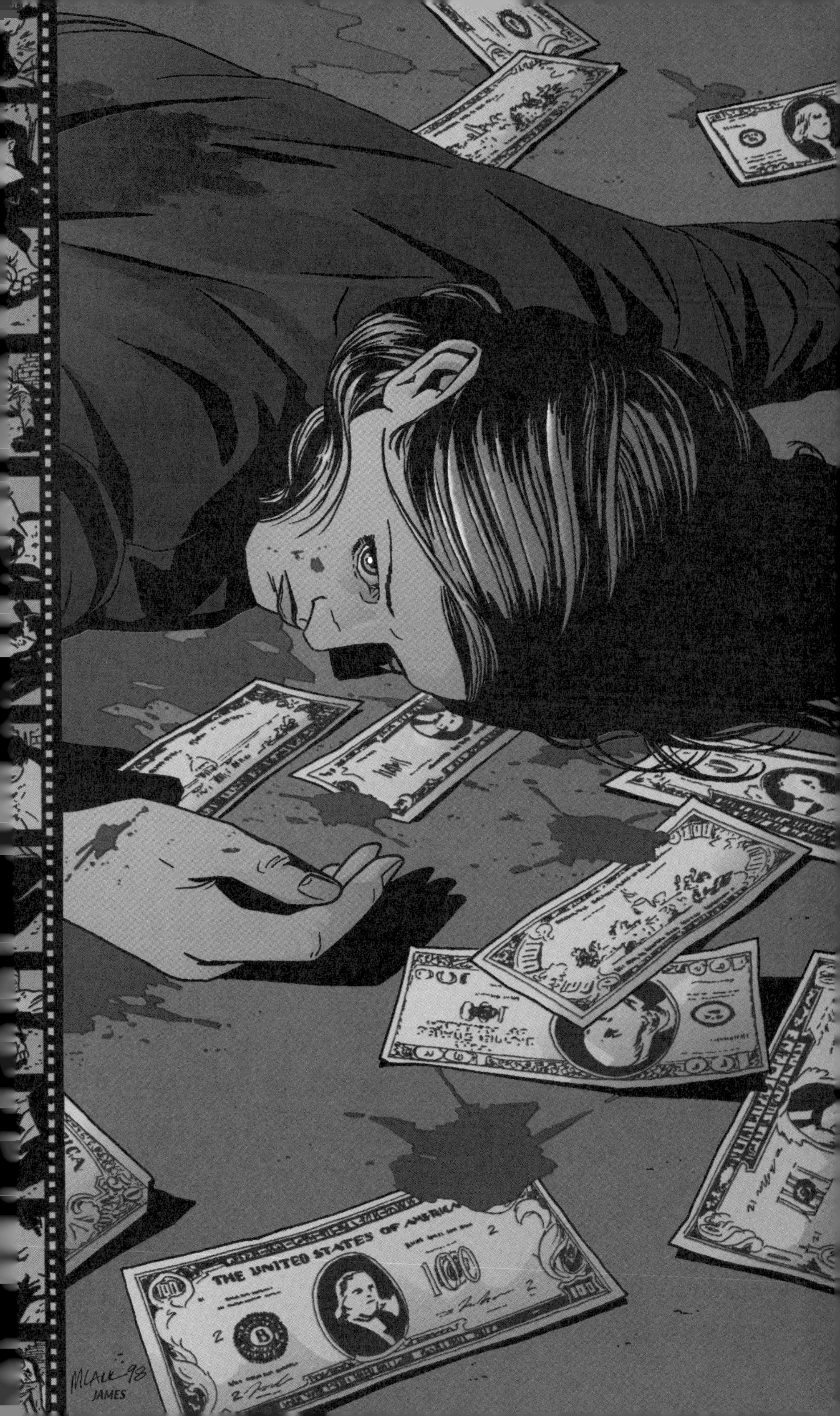
THE UNITED STATES OF AMERICA
JAMES

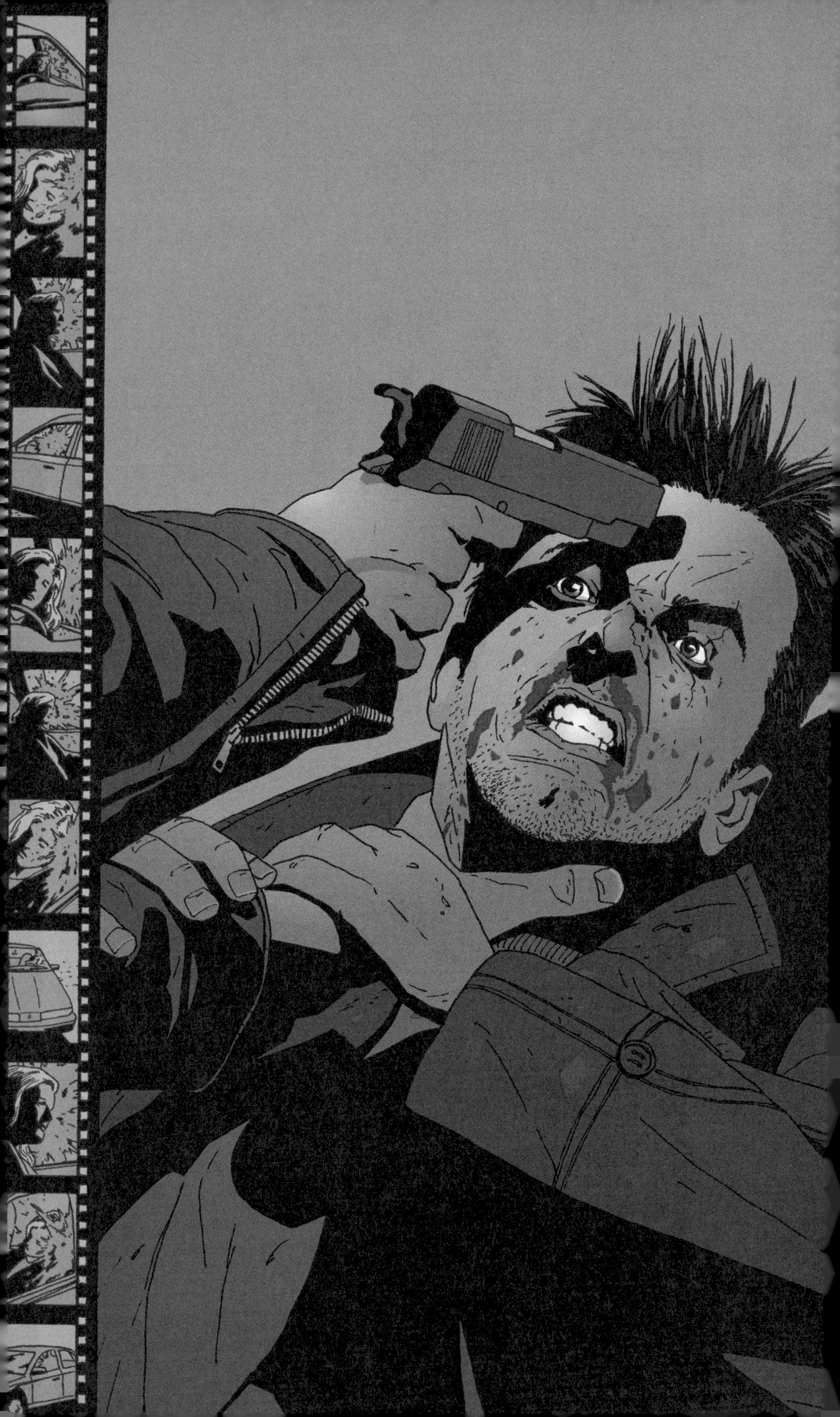

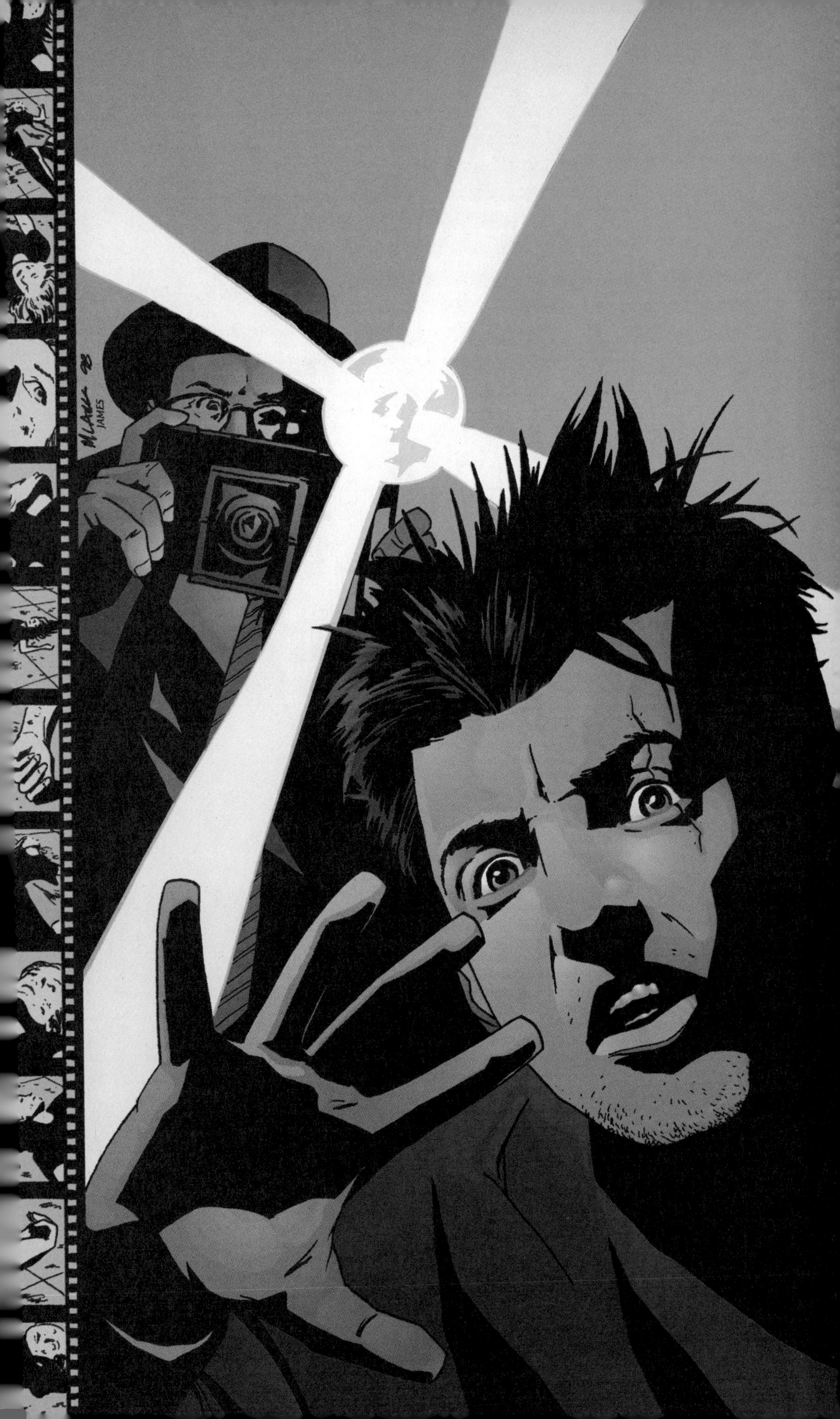

ED BRUBAKER

Ed Brubaker has lived in San Francisco on and off for the last ten years. As both a writer and a cartoonist, he has been nominated for Eisner, Harvey, and Ignatz awards, some of the highest honors in the U.S. comics industry. His previous works include *Lowlife, Detour, An Accidental Death*, PREZ, and *The Fall*. His work has been translated into seven languages around the world. In his life he has held many jobs and committed at least a few felonies, but he has never been a private eye and has only spent a few days in jail.

MICHAEL LARK

Michael Lark is an inveterate reader of mysteries, especially the works of Dashiel Hammett, Raymond Chandler, and Ross Macdonald. His previous comics work includes *Raymond Chandler's The Little Sister*, TERMINAL CITY, TERMINAL CITY: AERIAL GRAFFITI, and SUPERMAN: WAR OF THE WORLDS. He has also done short stints on a variety of DC and Vertigo titles, including SANDMAN MYSTERY THEATRE, SHADE THE CHANGING MAN, THE INVISIBLES, and ALL STAR COMICS. He lives, works, and sweats in Dallas, Texas, with his wife and a very plump cat.

SEAN PHILLIPS

For twenty years (he started young), Sean Phillips has drawn a wide variety of comics. These include HELLBLAZER, SHADE, HEART OF THE BEAST, HELL ETERNAL, THE MINX, SUPERGIRL, SUPERMAN, BATMAN and THE INVISIBLES for DC Comics; *Spider-Man* and *X-Men* for Marvel; *Judge Dredd* and *Devlin Waugh* for Fleetway; and *Star Wars* and *Aliens* for Dark Horse. He lives in Yorkshire, England with his wife Janette and their three sons Fred, Jake and Archie. He is currently drawing WILDCATS every month, for WildStorm; BATMAN: GOTHAM NOIR, for DC; and painting USER for Vertigo.

Look for these other Vertigo books:

All VERTIGO backlist books are suggested for mature readers

THE INVISIBLES:
BLOODY HELL IN AMERICA
Grant Morrison/Phil Jimenez/ John Stokes

THE INVISIBLES: COUNTING TO NONE
Grant Morrison/Phil Jimenez/ John Stokes

NEIL GAIMAN & CHARLES VESS' STARDUST
Neil Gaiman/Charles Vess

NEVADA
Steve Gerber/Phil Winslade/
Steve Leialoha/Dick Giordano

PREACHER: GONE TO TEXAS
Garth Ennis/Steve Dillon

PREACHER: UNTIL THE END OF THE WORLD
Garth Ennis/Steve Dillon

PREACHER: PROUD AMERICANS
Garth Ennis/Steve Dillon

PREACHER: ANCIENT HISTORY
Garth Ennis/Steve Pugh/
Carlos Ezquerra/Richard Case

PREACHER: DIXIE FRIED
Garth Ennis/Steve Dillon

PREACHER: WAR IN THE SUN
Garth Ennis/Steve Dillon/Peter Snejbjerg

THE SYSTEM
Peter Kuper

TERMINAL CITY
Dean Motter/Michael Lark

TRANSMETROPOLITAN: BACK ON THE STREET
Warren Ellis/Darick Robertson/ various

TRANSMETROPOLITAN: LUST FOR LIFE
Warren Ellis/Darick Robertson

TRUE FAITH
Garth Ennis/Warren Pleece

UNCLE SAM
Steve Darnall/Alex Ross

UNKNOWN SOLDIER
Garth Ennis/Kilian Plunkett

V FOR VENDETTA
Alan Moore/David Lloyd

VAMPS
Elaine Lee/William Simpson

WITCHCRAFT
James Robinson/Peter Snejbjerg/
Michael Zulli/SteveYeowell/Teddy Kristiansen

THE SANDMAN LIBRARY

THE SANDMAN: PRELUDES & NOCTURNES
Neil Gaiman/Sam Kieth/
Mike Dringenberg/Malcolm Jones III

THE SANDMAN: THE DOLL'S HOUSE
Neil Gaiman/Mike Dringenberg/ Malcolm Jones III/
Chris Bachalo/Michael Zulli/Steve Parkhouse

THE SANDMAN: DREAM COUNTRY
Neil Gaiman/Kelley Jones/Charles Vess/
Colleen Doran/ Malcolm Jones III

THE SANDMAN: SEASON OF MISTS
Neil Gaiman/Kelley Jones/Mike Dringenberg/
Malcolm Jones III/ various

THE SANDMAN: A GAME OF YOU
Neil Gaiman/Shawn McManus/ various

THE SANDMAN: FABLES AND REFLECTIONS
Neil Gaiman/various artists

THE SANDMAN: BRIEF LIVES
Neil Gaiman/Jill Thompson/Vince Locke

THE SANDMAN: WORLDS' END
Neil Gaiman/various artists

THE SANDMAN: THE KINDLY ONES
Neil Gaiman/Marc Hempel/ Richard Case/various

THE SANDMAN: THE WAKE
Neil Gaiman/Michael Zulli/
Jon J Muth/Charles Vess

DUST COVERS—THE COLLECTED SANDMAN COVERS
1989-1997
Dave McKean/Neil Gaiman

VER9811